Buttermilk Books Publishing

Myrtle Beach, S.C.

Copyright Winn-Greeson 2019

The right of T. Allen Winn and Benji Greeson to be identified as the authors of this work has been asserted by them in accordance with the Copyright, designs and Patents Act 1988.

All rights reserved.

Typecast in Times New Roman

Printed in the United States of America

ISBN 978-1-7331576-1-2

Good Ole Fashion Fictional, Factual, Football Fun

In our book, *All About the 'A', Faith, Family, Football and Forever to Thee*, Benji and I did our best to document traditional Abbeville Panthers football and its 100 years of amazing history. We researched everything available and interviewed as many people as possible to capture the essence of the game, the players, the coaches, cheerleaders and fans, the seasons, the ups and the downs of what makes Atown football what it is today. We apologize for any missed opportunities to include every single nugget and if we skewed any facts. We did the best we could in our nine months to bring the story to life. We learned plenty about our town and its rich history of football. Sure, we stumbled here and there but, in the end, we are proud as any parents in the baby we birthed.

This version of Panther football is a tad different than its predecessor. While it picks up where the last book ended, preparing for the 2017 football season and follows the Panthers through the 2018 season, it comes with a fictional twist. To make this a fun read, we've blended a bit of make belief with the facts and history that we hope will put a smile on your face, while not offending any diehard fans. The journey is real as documented by Benji. The characters and subplots along the way are straight out of the twisted mind of ole T. Allen. Think of this one as A Christmas Carol on steroids, loaded with hidden spiritual premonitions, my bud, Benji as the main character, dealing with something both confusing and confounding. Ultimately though, the fairytale ending is real, the Panthers doing what they do best, winning state championships.

Buckle up and prepare for a fun filled look at Abbeville Panther Football and the iconic figures that have left haunting impressions on us, the devout and loyal fans, the parents, grandparents, uncles and aunts, sisters and brothers who love those kids sporting the garnet and gold and have an undying respect for the coaches who mentor them.

It's All About the Angels in the Backfield

Dawn of a Dynasty

Chapters

Part 1 - All About the Angels in the Backfield

More Cowbell Please

Twas Once 1971

Iconic Three

Fishing for Answers

A Fine Line Betwixt and Between

Offensive Behavior

Game Zero, Ninety Six

Those Pesky Spoilers

Jiminy Crickets, A Caroling We Will Go

We're Not in Kansas, Toto

Don't Let the Green Grass Fool Ya

Magic Shoes

Beat to Smithereens Phase II Begins

The Spirited Panther Mascot

All Aboard the 'A' Train

Sharpen Those Sabers, Claws Out

Home is Where the Heart Belongs

The Playoffs, Are You Ready for Some Football?

The Basketball Game on Grass

Final Four Madness

Not by the Hair of My Chinny, Chin, Chin

Steaming is Not for Wussies

The Booth

Legends Never Die, A Wayne's World Moment

Reflections, Accolades and Honors

Part 2 – Dawn of a Dynasty

Spring Football Fever 2018

Fifty and Counting

Preseason Preview Vol. 1

Preseason Preview Vol. 2

Preseason Preview Vol. 3

August 8th This Week in Panther Football

Week Zero vs. Lincoln County Preview

August 18th - Posting Historical Dominance

August 23rd - Week One vs. Newberry

August 25th - Welcome to the Jungle

August 29th - Week Two vs. Emerald Preview

The A-train Rolls Through Emerald

Week Three vs. Southside Christian Preview

Southside Christian Sabres Review and Bye Week Thoughts

September 26th - Week Six Preview vs. Batesburg-Leesville

Week Seven Review @ Fox Creek

The Donut Gang

Week Eight Preview vs. Silver Bluff

Panthers Remain Undefeated

Week Nine Preview vs. Saluda

Road Warriors of October

Region Championship Preview

The Untouchables

November 7th - Round One Preview vs. Andrew Jackson

November 12th - Back in Black

November 14th - Second Round Preview vs. North Central

November 19th - The Pilgrims

November 21st - Quarter Finals Playoff Preview vs. Central

November 26th - Hello Upper State Championship Preview

Benedict Bound

December 6, 2018 AA State Championship Game Preview

Four-ever to Thee

2018 Post Season Accolades, Awards and New Beginnings

View from the Booth 2019

All About the Angels in the Backfield

Clunk-clunk…clunk-clunk…clunk-clunk…

Benji Greeson sat straight up in bed. Grasping the sheet, he began wiping perspiration from his brow. His wife, Tara, slept peacefully and undisturbed by his abrupt wakeup call. He vaguely remembered dreaming but dreaming what? That noise. Where had that noise originated? He had heard it before…somewhere. He was sure of it. Shaking free of the cobwebs, he convinced himself it had been nothing more than a crazy dream. Retrieving his cellphone from the nightstand, Benji checked the time. Eight minutes before his regular wakeup time. He decided to get up. No need to try and catch that last power nap. It was Friday and he had a busy day ahead at the radio station. He was hyped anyway. The 2017 WCTEL Kickoff Classic would be next week and then in a few more weeks the Panthers would have their first game of the season. Hite Stadium, Botts Field, Fridays just didn't get any better than that. Yes sir, Fridays were all about the 'A'. The mighty Panthers would begin the quest for their ninth state championship, potentially their third consecutive. Atown was abuzz with the possibility. Benji would fan those flames on his morning radio broadcast. *Clunk-clunk*, why couldn't he shake that echo in his brain?

More Cowbell Please

Sitting at the control panel inside the Golden Palaces, Benji laid the groundwork for his upcoming morning program. Research and preparation usually paid off. Improvising would come later. WZLA's Southern Fried Morning Show would be starting promptly at 6 AM, a four-hour segment Monday through Friday each week on Abbeville, South Carolina's FM radio station.

As advertised, *WZLA-FM plays your favorite Country Classics from the 80s, 70s and 60s plus, Carolina Beach and Gospel Music, Abbeville High School football and baseball, USC Gamecocks football, NASCAR Racing and much more! We love our listeners! See what all the fuss is about. 6-10 AM Monday-Friday on WZLA 92.9fm, wzlaradio.com, Streema Radio app or WCTEL channel 20.*

Clunk-Clunk...Benji spun around in his chair expecting to see someone standing in the doorway. Exhaling and then remembering to breathe, he realized he was just as alone as he had been the past twenty minutes. Anyone entering the station would have to pass by him manning the broadcast booth. Nobody had arrived, so that settled that. He wasn't sure why he was so edgy this morning. Maybe just a case of football season jitters. Pre-season jitters were common and a welcome change.

He returned to his prep work for the morning's show. Perfectionist by curse. A chill suddenly ran down his spine, goose bumps tingling his forearms. Odd, he rarely experienced chills. Whatever. He dismissed it and returned to his regimented work practices. After he was satisfied that he was as prepared as he could be, he stepped outside for a quick smoke. Well if you called using one of those electronic vapor cigarette gadgets taking a real smoke break. Technology had its perks. Five minutes to show time. Very little hustle and bustle appeared on North Main at nearly 6 AM. Benji stepped around to the side of the building and propped up on the tailgate of his truck. Something flashed through his mind, something obviously significant about those empty boxes in his truck bed. The empty boxes were the first empties of fourteen boxes drop shipped to the radio station by coauthor T. Allen Winn. He was proud yet nervous about the newly published book that currently was selling like hotcakes. This too was almost like pre-season jitters. The official rollout of his and T. Allen's book had been scheduled for the Kickoff Classic, but word had spread quickly. People had been pouring into the station seeking their preordered copies. Benji recalled that day when all those books arrived via UPS, three hundred books to be more specific. And, just how proud he had been to hold a copy in his hand.

Nearly two thirds of the three hundred had already been picked up at the station by those who had reserved copies. He had captured emptying that first box and his first book sold via a series of selfies. He could now check off 'published author' from his informal bucket list.

Not to be outdone, T. Allen Winn had texted him a photo of his first $20., a book sold at the beach.

Benji shrugged off his morning uneasiness. The Atown Panthers and his Clemson Tigers would soon be in full season throttle. That had to be it. His giddiness was a sign of football fever, like what hunters experienced, buck fever that first morning perched in their tree stand. That's all, nothing more. First time published author probably played just as much a part of it. This had been the experience of a lifetime, researching and writing about the Abbeville Panther football team, 100 years of tradition. This had indeed been a phenomenal find discovering that 2017 marked 100 years of Panther football, the first game being played in 1917, uneventful but a beginning just the same. The defending division AA state champions would be sporting a helmet this year signifying the 100th season with 1917-2017 appearing underneath the Block A. Coach Preston Cox from the 1971 championship team had laid claim to coming up with the original Block A design.

Clunk-Clunk. There is was again. Benji surveyed the parking lot for the sound he was sure he had heard. His truck was the only vehicle here. Not a person stirred, not even a mouse. He grinned thinking of the Christmas story words. *Clunk-clunk*. This time he replayed the sound in his head attempting to identify its origin. Nothing but blanks, no cigar this time either, just the vape's artificial version. One minute until 6, time to go inside and greet the wide eyed and bushy tailed folks preparing to listen in on his broadcast. His cohost, Amy Botts, would be arriving in a couple of hours. Until then he would be lord and master of the Golden Palaces. He stared at his reflection in the studio lobby window. The bearded man wearing a Clemson baseball cap and Abbeville Panther shirt smiled back at him. The face looked as familiar as always, the same guy who had been in his bathroom mirror back home. Benji made a scary face. The other guy mimicked it.

Showtime. He welcomed his listening audience and mentioned a few of his dedicated sponsors as he navigated through the morning agenda, the weather and then the sports. After a brief live engagement, he switched back to autopilot allowing a series of commercials and songs to run their course. A car passed by on North Main. The driver honked her horn and waved. A dog walker appeared across the street. Hustle and bustle in Atown had begun. Well, hustle and bustle were possibly overstated. That sound continued to dog him though. No. He hadn't heard it again, but he had replayed it inside his head. He was no closer to solving the mystery though. Henry Green from the town's newspaper, the Press and Banner, strolled up North Main on the opposite side of the street, a ritual the newsman repeated every morning. Benji smiled, not expecting Henry to look in his direction. Always predictable, Henry forged onward, seemingly unaware of the world around him.

Benji did a double take, catching a glimpse of a reflection in the business front window, a second figure walking just behind Henry. A chill ran down his spine, realizing that there was nobody walking directly behind the news hound. Just as quickly as he thought he had seen the mysterious figure, it was now gone. For the briefest of moments, he thought he had recognized the man in the reflection holding up three fingers. It was impossible and couldn't have possibly been who he thought it had been. Fletcher Ferguson long deceased had been a legend in sports writing for the local paper and former announcer of home football games. This had been just the product of too much research for the book. Benji managed to convince himself. Nothing more. Still, it haunted him just the same. Haunted, he thought, Atown spirits walking the streets.

The studio lights flickered. This wasn't uncommon. Luckily it hadn't tripped anything requiring a reboot. The phone ringing jolted him from his deepening thoughts. Too early to take a caller so he allowed it to go to the answering machine after not recognizing the number on the caller ID. Odd. Static prevailed. The automated greeting had not picked up prompting the caller to leave a message. *Clunk-clunk*. Not possible. How had the caller circumvented the system? Furthermore, was this some sort of sick joke, the clunking sound. Was someone trying to prank him, he wondered. If so, what was the significance of the sound? Apparently, he wasn't getting the joke, but he was getting extremely aggravated with the premise. The phone went dead. In eight minutes he would be going back live. Eight? Eight minutes before his normal wake uptime and now eight minutes before going back on the air, mere coincidence? Benji decided to call out the prankster on the air. He had previously gotten burned by a scam caller and didn't intend to fall victim a second time. Burn me once, shame on you. Burn me twice, shame on me.

"Good morning again from the Golden Palaces. I must confess I have suspicions that someone out there has been messing with me. I get it. I'm an easy target but I'm on to you now. That clunking clanking sound was a good one for a while, but the fun is over. Confess your sins and we can get this laugh behind us."

The phone blew up. Folks were calling in and jumping on the bandwagon, most requesting a further explanation concerning this inside joke. Nobody claimed responsibility and Benji really provided no additional information. Unsure what to say he said nothing and as quickly as possible moved on to other topics. Nothing odd transpired over the next couple of hours. Amy arrived around 8 AM. Birthday announcements were made followed by the drawing for a cake for one lucky winner. Autopilot engaged, Benji and Amy stepped out front to slip in a quick smoke. A truck passed. The driver yelled a morning greeting to the radio personality duo. Benji reluctantly decided to share the happenings with Amy. After all they would close the morning's broadcast with a Freaky Friday segment. This sure ranked as freaky.

Amy listened to his tale but offered no input that might explain the noise he had thought he had heard. She was a little skeptical, thinking that he might be attempting to spook her with a prank. She didn't call him on it though, unwilling to fall further into his little trap, if indeed he was pulling a fast one on her. Break over, the duo returned inside, Benji favoring a slight limp, the result of leg injury incurred during a baseball game. He feared he had possibly torn something but tried to nurse it as best he could. He and Amy assumed their designated spots in the radio station, Benji behind the control board and his laptop facing the street and Amy with her back to the window. In less than a minute they would be back on the air. Benji rubbed his sore and aching leg, headset in place, readying to go live. *'What do you want me to do, pee on it?'* Benji flinched at the sound of the voice in his headset. He gave Amy a panicked look, but she paid him no attention, lost in her morning ritual of applying makeup.

"Did you hear that?"

"Hear what?"

"The voice on the headset."

"Did we have a caller? I didn't hear the phone ring."

"Wasn't a caller. Never mind. Ten seconds to airtime."

What do you want me to do, pee on it? There had been no mistaking it. Time to get back in the game, or back on the radio, thought Benji. Too much book hype and research, rest in peace Coach Tommy Hite. Benji recalled how this had come up several times during interviews for the book, players and even Coach Hite's son, recanting how the coach would examine injuries of his players, dismissing them as not serious, lastly saying, *'What do you want me to do, pee on it?'* before sending them back in the game. Some injuries were serious, but players did as he asked. Benji smiled, thinking how the intense research, writing, promoting and now release of the book had probably taken its toll on his psyche. He wondered if ole T. Allen went through stuff like this when he released other books. This would be his coauthor's lucky #13 to be published. He was probably an old pro at it by now. The next couple of hours passed uneventfully.

The WCTEL Kickoff Classic would be on the agenda next Friday. He and T. Allen would hopefully sell the remaining fifty books there. *All About the A, Faith, Family, Football and Forever to Thee* had been an instant success. Atown embraced their hometown team and ate up the historical journey, most showing their appreciation for the research and dedication it had taken to write the book and document the Panthers rich heritage.

Twas Once 1971

Benji had landed the perfect gig, a dream job, working the Panther games with Wayne Stevenson, WZLA radio personality and the 'voice of Panther Football.' The 2017 season would place him in the booth as co-commentator with the long-time veteran. The Kickoff Classic loomed near but instead of the broadcast booth, Benji would be anchoring the book signing booth with ole T. Allen. Football was football in Abbeville and the diehards would be attending at Hite Stadium, Dennis Boots Field for the series of four scrimmage games, eight teams. As it would have it, Abbeville would be playing 3A Newberry in one of the late quarters.

Empty boxes from the books continued to accumulate in the back of Benji's truck, a testimonial that the 'All About the A' book continued to be a red-hot item for those followers of Atown football. At times Benji found it quite challenging to peddle books and keep a foothold on his day job at the radio station. Oscar Reid at WZLA took it in stride, saying it was good for Abbeville and the radio station. He had even grown accustomed to making transactions in Benji's absence. T. Allen Winn had the easy part at the beach and on the sidelines leading up to the WCTEL Classic. Well, as Benji insisted, 'T' had brought the book together on the front end, arranging the chapter flow and publishing the book via his Buttermilk Books Publishing. Each of the coauthors had pulled their share of the load and had embraced every second of the experience.

Benji, troubled by the uneasiness lately, decided to take a little break after the morning's Southern Fried show, some Benji quiet time. For no specific reason he navigated his truck to the walking park sanctuary where the old Chestnut Street School once stood and where many of those early football games were played. This was something he had never done before; he had been compelled to do it just the same. Parking there, window down, he rested his head against the back of the seat. Just what the doctor had prescribed, thought Benji. He reflected, remembering Horace Beauford and the Tolbert sisters and their many shared memories and stories about the tradition of football on this hallowed ground.

James, the Tolbert sisters' father, had played heroically here, as had a young 'Horse' Beauford before he heeded the call of patriotism and joined the armed forces. The younger Beauford had eventually become a tank driver, crashing onto Omaha Beach in WWII. Benji also thought about that donnybrook back in the fifties that broke out during a mud fest, that time when Bill Ashcraft had mistakenly slammed his fist into an official's mouth causing him to lose his dentures. The poor ref had been unable to locate his false teeth in the field's muck. Benji stared at the embankment at the far-left end of where the football field had once existed. He envisioned players digging the white dirt from that very bank to be used to mark the gridiron lines. Abbeville surely oozed football from every pore, no matter when the game was played.

Eyes closed, the radio personality sponged in the solitude the tranquil environment offered. That is, until, he got a whiff of something odd yet familiar. Eyes still closed, he breathed in deeply and shock waves invaded his thoughts, his senses jolting him to his very core. Locker room. The smell was that of a locker room, an offensive stench to most but almost calming to athletes accustomed to the smell. Flashes, memories flickered, those of Nick Lomax, a Panther from the fifties, remarking how he had loved the smell of a locker room, especially the one down on Chestnut Street. A smile broke across Benji's face as he recalled Horace Beauford's tale of finding that jockstrap on the locker room floor, taking it home and his mom washing it over and over until it was clean enough for her son to wear. Horace had laughed, saying his family hadn't been able to afford him one and now, by luck, he wore it proudly.

Benji drifted somewhere between awake and almost asleep, skimming the surface of his memories. The locker room smell barely lingered. Next, he heard a sound, one that made him jerk to attention and peruse his surroundings. Still alone, he shook off a chill running down his spine. Had he heard what he thought he had heard or was it just a mere dream? He focused, thinking about it and he then came to an awe-inspiring realization that he had indeed heard it or had at least thought it vividly enough to have made him think he had. Benji whispered, 'Cleats, cleats on the sidewalk.' Linda Tolbert Nickles, Coach Nick's mom, had described that sound during an interview, football shoe cleats echoing off the sidewalk's pavement. Nick Lomax had remembered that sound as well. Now, Benji thought he had heard it, had experienced the ambiance from long ago. Smells and sounds, enough to drive a normal guy over the edge but Benji was a football fanatic and this phenomenon, real or not, had been a wonderful experience. Taking an overdue breath, he fired up the truck and headed back to the Golden Palaces, the WZLA station, still confused about why he had driven there in the first place. For now, he kept the experience close to the vest, unwilling to portray himself as a looney, one card shy of a full deck.

The week had passed quickly and Friday's WCTEL Classic would be tomorrow. Benji focused his attention and energy in preparing for the book's official rollout and looked forward to seeing ole T. Allen, scheduled to stop by Friday morning for a little airtime and visit on the broadcast. It had been nine months since the two had begun researching Abbeville Panther football. Benji felt as proud as a new papa that they had birthed a real gem. As in any pregnancy, carrying and preparing for the delivery of the 'A' book had been a long tedious process, filled with rewards and surprises. Benji had logged in many hours in Abbeville's public library researching every year of microfilm, often being run out at closing time. His bloodhound efforts had paid off, tracing the conception of Abbeville football back to 1917. A nugget indeed, marking the rollout of the 'A' book as the 100th year anniversary of Atown football. The Panthers had won their 8th championship December of 2016 to further justify writing the book. Could 2017 toss another championship run their way?

Benji's morning had again been disturbed by that *clunk-clunk* sound after he first arrived at the radio station. It had sounded as if it had originated from everywhere and nowhere in particular. He had tried as best he could to convince himself that the sounds had come from inside his head. Amy Botts hadn't arrived yet so that left him with nobody to validate that the odd noises were for real. If they were indeed a figment of his imagination, should he interpret that his sanity was at stake? Piss on it, he caught himself thinking. He grinned, thinking again about Coach Hite's approach to player injuries. Coach Hite had been a unique individual for sure. Everyone, so it seemed, had a Coach Tommy Hite story to tell. Capturing them in the 'A' book had been a God wink for the readers.

Thursday came and went with no further distractions or oddities for Benji. He spent a routine afternoon and night with his family. With his kids and wife Tara now in beddy-bye time, he mentally prepared for tomorrow, his day at the station and then the Kickoff Classic at Hite Stadium, Botts Field where he and his coauthor pal would have their first official book signing. Less than a third of the 300 books originally ordered remained. They had been literally jumping off the shelf at WZLA since he had announced their arrival. He hoped they had enough available for those attending the game. Exhausted from overthinking the events to come, Benji finally gave in and headed to bed. He was down for the count instantly, sleeping like a baby.

Sometime later, in the wee hours of the morning, that smell infiltrated his space among the snoring. He blinked and then blinked again, attempting to roust from deep slumber. His surroundings were out of sync. He wasn't in his familiar cozy bed in his bedroom. Instead he sat on a bench, slumped over, hands resting on the laces of his cleated shoes. Out of habit, he finished tying his shoes and then straightened himself. He rubbed his eyes and then took a second gander. No mistaking it, he was in the locker room of the athletic building at Abbeville High School. Odder still, he was dressed out in his old #64 Panther uniform. It kind of felt like a dream and yet it didn't. Nothing was very dreamlike. All was too vivid, bright, filled with garnet and gold, a gratifying gameday feel to it.

Benji stood, adjusted his shoulder pads and repositioned his jockstrap. His block A helmet rested on the bench. Without thinking he slipped on the helmet and fastened the chin strap. After completing a 360 assessment of his surroundings, he strolled from the locker room into the weight room. Everything was as he had remembered it; except, he was the only one here. Noises, rumbling and tumbling, drew his attention to another room. The sounds were familiar, the washer and dryer in full operation, cleaning the soiled uniforms. The antiques were still in full functional status, having been donated to the team in 1971, forty-six years ago, the very year the Panthers had won their first state championship. Lured by the sounds as surely as a bass snagged on Dennis Bott's line, Benji made his way to the laundry room.

There they were, churning and tumbling, full throttle. The smell of detergent and heated material permeated his nostrils. They weren't as he last remembered them. Both were as shinny as a new penny, bronze colored at that. Benji partially placed one hand over his eyes, the glimmer almost too much to behold. He wavered on rubbery legs and back peddled a step. The ancient machinery abruptly came to a stop. The dryer door flew open and a shimmering light shone from the cavity. Mesmerized, Benji removed his hand from his face and wobbled off balance until finally taking one baby step in the direction of the appliances. He wasn't sure why, but his gut told him to look inside. Waded inside were the familiar Panther jerseys. He reached inside and plucked one of the jerseys from its crumpled resting places.

At first glance the front of the jersey with its gold number emblazed on garnet looked like any normal jersey. Benji held it up beaming with delight, Atown pride through and through. He rotated it to look at the front and the back. It sported the number '3'. He smiled. This belonged to quarterback Brice Jackson. He removed the second jersey, same number '3'. He emptied the dryer, nine jerseys in various sizes, all sporting the number '3'. Something was terribly wrong. Brice would not have nine jerseys. The washer lid flew open. Benji, unable to stop, removed the contents from the washer; nine more jerseys, all with the number '3'. Had the coaches received a bad delivery of new jerseys, each misprinted with the same number? This was a bit too crazy. Number 3 and in groups of nine, what did this really mean?

He checked the sizes and they indeed varied from mediums to extra, extra-large. The washer door began opening and closing, spewing suds onto the walls and floor, demon possessed so it appeared. The dryer door followed suit, spitting forth socks, jockstraps and pants, clothing that had not been previously there. The lights began flickering, the weight room next door came to life with the clanking sounds of equipment being used. The sound of an approaching army of cleat wearing warriors deafened the other noises. Benji had broken into a cold sweat, overwhelmed by the spiritual experience, a ghostly haunting in progress, a scene from one of those poltergeist sequels unfolding before his very eyes.

He sat straight up, gasping for breath, a fish out of water with Dennis Botts in hot pursuit. The grip on his arm tightened. He had been caught red handed, red handed doing what? Voices, no, a singular voice penetrated his awareness. He recognized that voice. It was Tara. Tara, his wife was saying something. Blinking, he turned to see her sitting beside him in bed, now rubbing the back of his neck and speaking something reassuring to him. The words were becoming clearer, drowning out those noises from the athletic building. Tara explained how she had been awakened by him having spasms and mumbling incoherently. Benji's breathing slowly but surely returned to normal as he attempted to deal with his dream state encounter.

"Tara, I was in the athletic building."

"Was some sort of monster chasing you?"

"Everything was crazy, alive and I saw it. I know I saw it."

"Saw what? What has shaken you so, Benji?"

"The football jerseys; what I saw on those jerseys and no, it didn't scare me. It just took me by surprise is all."

"You sure acted scared, shaking and mumbling like that."

"The jerseys were all number '3' and there were nine of them in the dryer and another nine in the washer."

"Why did that have such an impact on you, Benji?"

"Don't you get it? Can't you see it. Everyone was the same, all number '3'. Why were all of the same and why Brice Jackson's number?"

"You really need to try to get back to sleep. You must be up in less than two hours, one work day left and a big day ahead with the book signing and all. You're just excited about being an author. Think about it. That book will be around forever, even after you are gone."

A tear rolled now Benji's cheek when reality slammed him up close and personal. The book would indeed live on after he was long gone. Still, there was more to this than just the book.

"That washer and dryer has seen every state championship, beginning with the first, 1971. Just maybe there is more to this, some sort of weird omen. It just dawned on me; I think my #64 jersey was sporting the number '3' too after I went in the laundry room."

"Just maybe you need to go back to sleep and stop fretting over silly dreams."

Benji nodded but after Tara switched off the light he stared at the ceiling, replaying his encounter, one that seemed just a tad too significant, not your normal dream. Something special was happening, of that he had no doubt. The puzzle pieces were out there and gathering steam. Or, maybe, Tara was dead on. It might just be the excitement of his first published book getting the best of him. The number '3', could it be a sign of Back to Back to Back, he wondered. The ninth championship maybe. Dreams, just a silly ass dream and wishful thinking, he finally tried to convince himself.

Iconic Three

'A' day had arrived; not to be confused with Horace Beauford's D day on the beach, the Normandy Invasion. Benji and T. Allen did their best to lay the ground work for the book signing at tonight's WCTEL Classic for the radio's listening audience. Manning the booth, in addition to Benji Greeson and T. Allen Winn, would be their wives, Tara and Judy, and Judy's sister, Norma. T. Allen also had shirts available with the book cover depicted on the front, the coauthors names emblazed underneath the title's caption. T's friend and artist in Conway, Ron Walker had assisted with the shirt's design and the shirts were printed by Greenwood's Emerald Ink and Stitching Company.

Things got off to a bad start at Hite Stadium, Botts Field. Benji's tent was usable, a broken leg preventing its use. Still, there was plenty of time before the first kickoff. T. Allen's brother-in-law, Jerry Solomon, an employee of the City of Abbeville, solved the problem. He made a call to city officials and they granted the use of one of the city's portable tents. While the crew were setting up the tent and tables, Coach Tad Debose drove up on his golf cart with two iconic Panther artifacts in his possession. He had brought the Abbeville Panther bronze football helmet to be displayed along with his mom Miss Pidgey's original cowbell. A million-dollar policy with Lords of London had to be taken out to ensure the two items. Well, it should have been.

Norma picked up the bell and rang it, not knowing its significance. 'Clunk-clunk'.

"I'll be danged," said Benji. "That's it. That's what I've been hearing."

The others looked at him oddly. Benji just smiled and decided against trying to explain it. Who in their right mind would believe him anyway? Who in their right mind would admit it? More cowbell. He had been hearing 'more cowbell' for over a week. Specifically, he had been hearing Mrs. Pidgy Dubose's cowbell, a one of a kind according to Tad. His mom didn't take lightly ringing that bell. The Panthers had to do something special to earn the ringing. Benji wondered, was there something special in store for this season or again was it just the product of an overactive imagination and wishful heart?

The stage was set for 'It's All About the A' official book debut. The crowd had begun lining up at the gates. The 2017 preview to the high school football season was less than an hour away for the first scrimmage kickoff. The Tolbert sisters had dropped by, appreciative of the books already in their possession. With the bronze helmet and the cowbell in place, what could possibly make this night even more special? Simple, the arrival of the perfect guest and third iconic Abbeville football symbol; the oldest known living Panther player now graced the booth's presence. Horace Beauford was in Hite Stadium, ready to meet and greet. This man is the most lovable man, a true people person and real WWII hero, an encyclopedia of knowledge, Panther football and war time tragedies. The helmet, the cowbell and Mr. Beauford, it just didn't get any better than this. And to top this, there were multiple generations of the Beauford family represented at the game.

Generations of Beaufords

Horace recalled how his daddy had deeded the land for Hite Stadium in exchange for a cattle tunnel underneath the roadway for his pasture. Julian McWilliams, a writer for Greenwood's Index Journal dropped by the booth. He had previously interviewed Benji for an article about the book. He was encouraged to interview 93-year-old Horace, which he did. Prior though, Julian had asked if Mr. Beauford could carry on a normal conversation. To that everyone just laughed. Later Julian would be asked did he get what he needed, and he said, more than enough. The interview would be featured in the coming Sunday's issue - priceless.

Julian McWilliams Article from the Index

In the article, Horace Beauford was quoted saying,

> "It's great to come to your hometown and have people come up to you and shake your hand and everything like that. It's just great."

McWilliams interview stated that a lot had changed since Horace suited up for the Panthers. He remembered his team just having enough players to compete in an actual football game. They only had 11 or 12 players, had to play both ways, offense and defense. His playing days had been spent at Fulp Field on Chestnut Street. They played Friday afternoons because they had no lights at Fulp Field. Horace explained how he remembered what is now Hite Stadium, Dennis Botts Field,

> "Last time I was here this was a dirt hill. And I had to sit on a dirt bank. All of this is new to me. It's been years since I've been back. One of the main memories I have during my playing time is that I tackled one of my own men after he intercepted a pass and was running toward the wrong goal."

McWilliams recapped Horace Beauford's time in the military, driving a tank onto Omaha Beach during the Normandy invasion in 1944 during WWII. Horace received a Purple Heart and Bronze Star, but he is just as proud of his hometown though.

> "It makes me feel great that Abbeville has come along with football the way and size it was back then. And, the people still back them. And the coaches like Jamie Nickles are doing a great job bringing them along."

Finally, it was game time for the Panthers and Newberry. Wow thought Benji. That really summed up how many people felt as they filed out of Hite. The Panthers had looked to be in mid-season form. Tonight, would be their third WCTEL Kickoff Classic.

Abbeville had taken the opening kickoff and marched 70 yards right down the field and then scored with ease. Senior quarterback Brice Jackson scored the first touchdown of the night. Jackson rushed 9 times for 61 yards with a touchdown in the contest. He was also 2-5 for 40 yards in the air. Jackson hadn't played the whole scrimmage as the Panthers looked to be well in control of the outcome from the onset. Junior Rapley carried the ball 3 times for 39 yards (13 yards per carry). Dominick Washington had 8 carries for 37 yards. Cruz Temple had 2 carries for 6 yards and the last touchdown of the night. As a team the Panthers had totaled 31 carries for 172 yards (5.5 yards per carry) in the 24-minute contest.

The offense, while collecting a few too many penalties, which is expected in the first Jamboree of the season, looked fast and physical versus their 3A Newberry counterparts.

Defensively the Panthers were a suffocating force. The Panther defense had only allowed two Bulldog first downs and recorded a safety in the contest. The Panther front 7 controlled the line of scrimmage and applied serious pressure on the Bulldog quarterback. They clogged the running lanes and dominated the bigger Newberry offense for the entire scrimmage. A 16-0 Panther victory left the Garnet and Gold clad faithful with a big smile on their faces Friday night.

So, what's next, thought Benji. Practice Monday and then a scrimmage versus Lexington High on Tuesday. Lexington was coached by Perry Woolbright, who was the head coach at Batesburg last season. The Panthers would play in the Greenwood Jamboree this coming Thursday night. Coach Nick would settle for nothing less than spreading the mustard when on his field of play. One could only wonder if Tad had recorded any new Nick'isms recently.

The book signing had been a success as anticipated. Afterwards, Benji and T. Allen signed one of the book's posters used as display advertisement and presented it to Coach Tad Debose for the athletic building. The two were eager to return the cowbell and bronze helmet and to relinquish possession back to the rightful owners, extremely honored and appreciative for having been allowed to use them. Benji breathed in the scent from the locker room while there, thinking back on that dream from last night. He even took time for one quick glance in the laundry room. The washer and dryer looked nothing like what he had encountered, thankfully. He even snuck a peek inside both. There were no uniforms inside, no number '3's.

Benji had invited T. Allen and wife Judy to drop by the house after the Classic to settle up on book sales. The two coauthors beamed with delight. The 'A' continued to be a successful collaboration. Ole T gave Benji all the credit for coming up with the idea to write the book, jokingly blaming Benji for getting him in this nine-month adventure of a lifetime. Both had learned more about their hometown team than they could have ever imagined. Not to be denied, this had been a rigorous and time-consuming process, logging in countless hours of interviews and research, all for the greater good and forever preserved for the town.

Benji hoped for a more restful and uneventful peaceful night's sleep. He needed no more encounters with forty-six-year-old washers and dryers. Still, how ironic, the 1971 donated washer and dryer had cleaned the uniforms of every championship team since the first in that very same year. This made them iconic symbols too. One could only wonder what might happen when either of them ceased to function. Would it bring an end to the championship run? Superstitious folks might freak out over the possibility. Keeping these babies functional should probably be high on the priority list just in case. As Coach Nick might say, 'Playing football is not brain science.' Maybe maintaining this equipment shouldn't be either. They sure didn't want them to 'drop like hot flies', as Nick once referred to kids falling out on the practice field.

Fishing for Answers

Sleep didn't come easy for Benji, still caught in the grip of being a first-time author and the excitement of Panther football now in the air. Knowing he would be sharing the radio booth with Wayne Stevenson this season further hyped his emotions. Unlike Wayne, Benji came in a bit more prepared for his inaugural debut, having done color commentary for the McCormick football games. Wayne had reluctantly accepted Shelley Reid's offer in 1992 to be the radio voice for the Atown Panthers. It being a paying gig had weighed heavily into his decision to give it a try. 2017 would signify his 25th anniversary at the helm. Slowly the night time invader lulled Benji into nocturnal slumber. With it came more disturbing dreams.

Benji found himself slap dab in the middle of a bass boat bookended by two individuals he immediately recognized. Coach Dennis Botts sat at the bow and Coach Tommy Hite anchored the stern. The two coaches were debating fishing techniques.

"Hotalmighty, Coach Hite, we're not drowning worms here. This is bass fishing, an artful adventure, not a cork bobbing fiasco."

"Son, I keep telling you it's not the size of dog in the fight, it's the fight in the dog. You troll your waters and I'll do just fine trolling mine."

Benji was awe stricken. "You're Coach Dennis Botts and you're Coach Tommy Hite."

"And you better get that line in the water, boy, if you want to continue resting your ass on my boat. We're bass fishing in case you haven't noticed."

Benji quickly snatched up a rod, pricked his finger in the process and then made an awkward cast into the water. He was still nervous and giddy being in the presence of the two winningest coaches to date in Panther football history. Only Coach Nick seemed geared to break both their records and become the winningest coach ever, this upcoming season possibly. Both men in the boat looked to be in their prime.

Botts, agitated said, "Boy, don't be bleeding all over my seat, how about it?"

Hite wasn't cutting him any slack either. "Get in the game, son. What do you want me to do, pee on that finger for you?"

Benji felt whiplash coming on as he turned this way and that, caught in the rubber necking volley from the two coaches. He quickly stuck his bleeding finger in his mouth hoping to stop the bloodletting.

"Don't let your line go slack, Coach Hite."

"Don't be so cocky, son. Sure, you won a state championship going undefeated but only after you didn't win a game your opening season. That's a record you hold too, winless. 0-10. Records go both ways."

"And you, Coach Hite, you never won a state championship and you had so many winning seasons and chances, didn't you? What's the matter? Did you piss on too may wounds along the way?"

"Fine, I concede. You accomplished what I never did. You even edged me out on total wins. I salute you for that. Records are made to fall and that youngster, Nickles, is going to break mine and yours, just wait and see."

"I expect he will. He had a fine mentor, he did. I would be disappointed if he didn't shatter them all. Wind in that slack line, coach. Bass fishing is all technique, not a wet your hook waiting game."

"You're the fisherman. I'll concede that too. You did rub off on young Coach Nick. He has gone on to fill your shoes quite nicely. Mentor yes, but his demeanor and style are nothing like yours. May as well admit it, we are both old school. You may be a bit more abrasive than me though."

"Coach Hite, you have to butt kick them to get those boys herded in the right direction. I assure you it was done with the utmost love and affection; like beating your kids to let them know you care about what they do and how they act. It makes them turn out right, be respectful and all."

"I suppose we are cut from the same cloth somewhat, Coach Botts. We always had the interest of the kids in mind. We wanted them to make something of themselves after football."

Benji just sat there, mouth unhinged, unbelieving what he was witnessing and experiencing. Normally he would have had a flurry of questions but found himself speechless instead.

"Boy, you best pay closer attention to your line. Something is taking a nibble. Don't disappoint me. Snag that son of a…"

"Now, now, no need for that sort of talk here, must I remind you, Coach Botts."

"Sorry Coach Hite, old habits die hard."

Benji yanked the line, almost falling from the boat in the process. He reeled and fought his prey with reckless abandon. Finally, he had it close enough for Coach Botts to net it.

"I'll be damned. You caught yourself a barracuda."

Benji smiled, thinking of a Nick'ism, 'Yawl enjoy these first few days of summer, because when we come back, I'm going to be running you like a bunch of barracudas.'

"Coaches, do either of you have any inkling why I'm here? I mean right here with both of you in this boat. Surely there is some hidden agenda."

"Hidden, what the hell do you think you do on a boat? You fish. This isn't the football field. It's R&R, a time to bond and reflect, men's day on the water, us getting closer with the Lord I expect. What part of this has your sorry butt confused and conflicted?"

"Lighten up on him, Coach. Can't you see he's not one of us. He's a mere baby and in his prime."

"Coach Hite, this ole boy has long ago been weaned off the hind tit. Tell us. Just what landed you in my boat in the first place? You're damn well not here for the fishing."

"Sure, he is Coach Botts. He's here fishing for answers. A new football season is upon us. He's going to be that new fellow in the radio booth with Stevenson. I paddled Stevenson good that last day he attended Greenville Street School. No boy leaves grammar school under my watch without receiving a proper paddling from Principal Hite. For the life of me I don't know why Stevenson never crossed my path until that last day."

"You, old fart, you're rambling off topic again. Stevenson has nothing to do with why he's in my boat. You got questions, Greeson, then spit them out."

"I'm not sure what I should be asking. There is so much I could learn from both of you."

"Hotalmighty, stop wasting our time then. There's fish to be caught on this perfect day that the Lord created."

"Well, we're about to fire up the 2017 football season. I guess if I had anything to ask, I would want to know what sort of season we could expect. We've won back to back state titles. Could we win a third this year?"

"Boy, do we resemble a couple of Gypsy fortune tellers to you? Wars are won on the field, not by debating outcomes off the field."

"Coach Botts is right, son. If it is meant to be then it will happen. Records are meant to be set and to be broken. This season could be the one or maybe not," winked Hite.

"Just as sure as the grass grows and the wind blows, you can take that to the bank, son," added Botts.

"Coach Hite, Coach Botts, this could be it then, couldn't it? Your winning records could fall under the reign of Coach Jamie Nickles if he has an undefeated season and wins the State to boot. This could indeed be a ninth championship, third in a row?"

Botts rolled his eyes. "You snagged another one. Reel in that fish, Greeson. Fish don't bite for the mere hell of it. Don't you know anything about bass fishing?"

Hite added, "I should have brought my paddle and tanned his hide good. Nobody leaves Coach Bott's boat without a good paddling by me. I suppose this boat paddle will have to do. Over here, son, across my lap. It's time for yours before you leave."

Benji woke to the nudging of Tara. She said he had been squirming like a red wiggler on a hook or something to that fact; or had he just imagined she had said it. Now wide awake, he replayed his little fishing outing over and over in his head, attempting to yet make sense of more revelations. Maybe the 'A' book had prompted all these wild occurrences and thoughts after all, a product of a vivid imagination because of the book writing process. But, no denying it, there had been three of them in Bott's bass boat. Three. In two weeks the official football season would begin. Atown would be in full throttle supporting their Panthers. He, as they, could hardly wait.

A Fine Line Betwixt and Between

These unexplainable dreams and weird occurrences should be explainable thought Benji, being bombarded by premonitions or hauntings or whatever one might call them, one wishing to reclaim his sanity. Breathe in. Breathe out. Think about something other than these 'whatever the heck they were happenings' he feverishly attempted to convince himself. Think about something more calming he encouraged himself. What better way to relieve stressful events than to concentrate on A-Town football, this year's football team to be specific? Benji closed his eyes and did just that, recalling earlier weeks, the Panthers preparation for the upcoming season.

He was there. A few hundred Panther faithfuls had grabbed a seat to watch the defending AA State Champs buckle their chin straps for their annual "Garnet and White Spring Game" that Thursday evening at Hite Stadium, Dennis Botts Field. The sun-splashed afternoon saw big plays, turnovers, touchdowns, big hits and gave fans just enough of a football fix to hold them over until August.

Brice Jackson had led the white team at quarterback for most of the scrimmage. Sophomore JD Moore, who seems to be touted to be the back-up to Jackson this season, had shown some flashes of brilliance. JD Moore has been blessed with uncommon speed. In other words, he's really fast. He'll definitely play a factor in the success of the Panthers this season. The play of the game had been when Jackson dropped back to pass, scanned the field, checked his first, second and third options and finally decided to sling the ball down the left sideline. LeBron "Dooley" Sanders appeared to be covered as the ball was in the air, but he kicked his speed into another gear, separated from the defender, made the catch, and then strolled into the end zone.

That hadn't been the only big play of the game. Junior Rapley flashed his speed and juke-ability with a 40-yard touchdown scamper. A-Bone backfield teammate Courtney Jackson had not played in the Spring Game because of an injury he suffered while running track. He should be 100% by summer camp. Dominick Washington had raised some eyebrows while toting the rock Thursday evening as well. Washington runs with a bruising toughness that was absent on last year's championship team. He's going to be tough to tackle this fall and will add another element to an already potent offense.

The defense had been led by Charles Holback and Tyrese Paul. The two senior linebackers play fast and instinctive. They are physical tacklers and will direct a defense that was downright nasty last season. The defensive line is anchored by Don Jackson who regularly plays in the opposing backfield. He's a load to block and will eat up a lot of space and draw a lot of attention from opposing offenses this coming season. The kickers put on a show as well. Dylan Beauford was steady as usual. He nailed his PAT's and connected on 30+ yard field goals in the kicking portion of the scrimmage. Newcomer, Ross Cobb showed off a booming leg as well. His kickoffs were regularly teasing the end zone stripe.

All in all, it had been a successful Spring Game for the Panthers. There are areas to improve on, but that's what spring is all about. This team is fast and talented. There are some All-Region, even All-State caliber players that will be wearing the "A" this season. It should be a fun ride.

Benji was immediately feeling much better thinking back to that Thursday afternoon. Football, especially A-Town or Clemson, always leveled the mental playing field and had Benji slobbering for more. Panther Garnet and Gold, Tiger Orange and Purple, commingled in Benji veins and kept his heart pumping. He breathed easier strolling down memory lane, the football fanatic now recalling Abbeville's FCA 7 on 7 scrimmage.

Sunshine and blue skies had certainly been the perfect backdrop for the Abbeville High School FCA 7 on 7 scrimmage that Tuesday morning. Eight teams had made the trip to A-Town to work on their passing, route running, catching and defensive pass coverage skills. The day had started at 9 AM with all the teams participating in a devotion at Grace United Methodist Church. After the devotion the teams made their way to the practice field, which four teams used, and onto the hallowed grounds of Hite Stadium-Dennis Botts Field, which the other four teams played on. Crescent, McCormick, Ninety Six, Lincoln Co., Strom Thurmond, Seneca, Newberry and Abbeville had participated.

Things had started off fast for Abbeville. Senior quarterback Brice Jackson connected with Coach Temple directing the Abbeville offense vs Seneca. Malik Washington on the very first play had caught a 50-yard touchdown pass. The sidelines had erupted as Washington beat his defender and Jackson dropped a beautifully thrown tight spiral into the hands of Washington. Former Panther great and current Dallas Cowboy, Keenan Gilchrist was on hand and jumped up with excitement. "He's droppin' dimes. Man, that was so pretty," Gilchrist gloated about the Jackson touchdown pass. Abbeville went on to defeat McCormick 21-0 in the first quick session.

Abbeville next scrimmaged Seneca. A couple dropped passes had stalled the first two drives. Dooley Sanders caught the only touchdown in the second session versus the Bobcats. Seneca has a Clemson target, a strapping 6'5" 210lb tight end Braden

Galloway that caught the game tying touchdown on a fade route. Abbeville defensive coordinator and athletic director Tad Dubose was quick to point out to the Panther defender how and why he got beat. He demonstrated how to defend that route, and that ended the scrimmage tied at 7.

The Panthers then faced longtime foe, Lincoln County Red Devils. The Red Devils would be making a trip back to Abbeville for a regular season game on September 8th. Benji reflected, you might want to go ahead and set out your chairs for that one, thinking, the one glaring thing I noticed about Lincolnton was that last year's team, looked a good bit bigger. They are big and fast and talented but then again, they always are. They just didn't look as big, at the skill positions as they did a season ago. The Panthers dropped two touchdown passes and gave up a long touchdown to the Red Devils and that scrimmage ended with LC taking a 7-0 win.

Abbeville head coach Jamie Nickles had been playing the part of coordinator. Not offensive or defensive coordinator, he had been more of an event coordinator on that Tuesday. He kept up with the time, directed which team to go where and of course he kept track of the all-important lunch break which was catered by Chick-Fil-A.

Benji smiled, thinking back to how Coach Nick had described his role.

> "Days like today are just great. What else can you ask for? The guys are out there competing, flying around. We've got some football, food and fellowship, all in the name of Jesus. So I mean, you can't ask for much more. I've been all over the place out here today, but from what I've seen, Brice Jackson is really throwing the ball well. We need to catch it a little better. Rapley is catching it well out of the backfield. So that's promising. We've got to do a better job of not giving up the long ball. We gave up one or two in the spring and one or two here today. So that's got to be corrected and it will be. Our coaches do a great job with those kinds of things. I'm just ready to get out here on July 28th and have everybody together and start getting ready for the season."

The Panthers were scheduled to participate in summer workouts on Wednesday before hitting the practice field again on Thursday. They will take the week of July 4th off before reconvening on July 10 for the last two weeks of summer workouts and practices. The Panthers will host the WCTEL Kickoff Classic on August 4th at Hite Stadium. The regular season will start on August 18th with the first game being at Ninety Six. That August 4th date had loomed large for sure and not just because of the Kickoff Classic but because it had been slated at the official rollout of THE book. He was certainly thankful both events had been successful.

Benji recalled how about sixty Abbeville High School student athletes gathered on the practice fields behind Hite Stadium, Dennis Botts Field at 10 AM for the first official practice of the 2017 season. The Panthers, as mandated by state law, had only practiced in helmets and shorts for about two hours under mostly sunny skies. The temperature had inched past 90 degrees while the back to back state champion Panthers were going through their drills. Oblivious to any historical ramifications, these high schoolers would be embarking on a season that very well could rewrite the record books at Abbeville High. But why think about that? Why not just go play ball, which is exactly what they had done that afternoon?

The special teams' units had been the first to grab some time on the plush green turf.

Punting, punt coverage and long snapping was the focus early on. The teams split into position groups while the extra point team practiced the snap, hold and kick. The team then had rallied around Head Coach Jamie Nickles for a quick team meeting and prayer.

Benji recalled how Coach Nickles had told his team,

> "Guys, this is day one. The season starts today. There are games from here on out. Do not be late. Do not miss a practice. If you miss a practice you will not play that week. It's time to get focused and get after it. Now, a family that prays together stays together.'

The team had chanted that mantra proudly and loudly. Coach Nick had then led the team in a quick prayer and off they had gone, the team breaking into offensive and defensive groups on separate ends of the field and starting to run through scripted plays.

Benji ran through his thoughts and observations of that day.

> "A few things jumped off the page to me while watching practice today. The offensive line could have three sophomore starters. That is very young for a

Panther O-Line. An official depth chart will be released in the next week or so. There could be as many as eight offensive linemen seeing significant action this fall as well. Depth is the name of the game and other than one or two guys, there is not a ton of separation in that group.

Another observation is the usual run heavy Panther offense will be very capable of stretching the field through the air this year. Bryce Jackson has a 'cannon' of an arm, and he's got some weapons to choose from. You'll hear the names Dooley Sanders and Malik Washington mentioned many times this year. If speed kills, these guys are snipers. They have good body control and they attack the ball when it's in the air."

Benji felt much better after this calming mental stroll. Those clunk-clunk sounds had not disrupted his thoughts nor had any weird locker room smells or appliance scenes invaded his privacy. Just maybe, thought Benji, the best medicine to fight off insanity is good old fashion Panther football influence. But, then, wasn't that what all these invasions had been, deeply rooted Panther football visions and dreams. Spiritual intervention might be at work here. Nah, overworked and preseason giddiness, that's all. Still, positive premonitions should be welcomed when it came to Abbeville Football. What could it hurt, a possible state championship three-peat on the horizon. The coaches had said records are meant to be broken. That was just a dream, Benji boy, me, Coach Boots and Coach Hite in that bass boat catching barracudas. What could it really hurt, wetting a hook and cranking in a third state championship? That's what dynasties do, right? Dynasties, getting ahead of yourself, aren't you Benji? Let's just take one game at a time. Ninety Six would be taking the field soon enough.

Offensive Behavior

Self therapy, Benji Greeson style, appeared to be working. Preseason jitters and those dream state hallucinations were plain and simple, a thing of the past. He had a firm grip on reality now, drooling over the 2017 Panther's offensive reckoning force. As only Benji could frame it,

> "Think about some endearing names you might call your loved ones. Honey, baby, sweetie. You probably would never think to call your special someone a Hogmollie. You might come away with a black eye, right? Well there's one group of young men who want nothing more than to be called a Hogmollie. Being a Hogmollie is almost like being in a fraternity. Offensive linemen never get the spot light, unless they are called for a holding penalty, or for jumping offsides. You are in the trenches every play, on the line of scrimmage, and the Hogmollies set the tone for the entire team.
>
> Think about it.
>
> You can have the best quarterback in the country, the fastest running backs in the world, all the pieces of a dynamic offense that you could possibly have…and if your offensive line is not very good, the rest doesn't matter at all. Everything starts up front with the Hogmollies. Quarterbacks need time to set their feet, find an open receiver and deliver a pass. The Hogmollies are responsible for keeping that quarterback on his feet. They are responsible for keeping defensive pressure off him, giving him a clean view of the field so he can find a lane to throw the ball. It wouldn't matter if Usane Bolt was your running back, if the Hogmollies are not doing their job, opening up running lanes, moving massive piles of defenders, those running backs are going to get hit. More than likely they are going to lose yards.
>
> A good offensive line can make a good offense great and a great offense always begins with the guys up front. The Hogmollies. Now you can't be soft and be a Hogmollie. There may be a string of 5, 6, 7 plays where some positions on the field won't get hit at all. Zero contact. That is never the case for a Hogmollie. Every game, every play, a Hogmollie is hitting someone. The great ones have a nastiness about them. A mean streak. The kinda guy that you wouldn't want to get in a street fight with. Some coaches would say that you must have a guy with "some dawg in ya" or a "war daddy". It's a streak of aggression and a will to win, a will to whip the guy in front of you, every single play. That is what it takes to be a Hogmollie.
>
> Abbeville offensive line coach Wayne Botts was a Hogmollie, and a darn good one. He is now in charge of putting the best five on the field this

season and he has a good cast of Hogmollies to choose from. Connor Nickles, Griffin Lewis, Trey Jones, Jake Hill, DeMichael Williams, Tyrese Harrison, Jacob Stone, Carson Smith and Dae Dae Bowie will suit up for the Panthers this season and take on the coveted role of Hogmollies. You'll see some combination of these guys protecting the quarterback and opening up running lanes for the running backs this season. So, the next time you see a Hogmollie, shake his hand. He's battling every snap to make the Panthers great."

The Hogmollies

Benji mentally prepared for the season opener at Ninety Six. It would be his official debut alongside Wayne Stevenson in the booth. The 100th year of Abbeville Football, the significance he had discovered while excavating in the Abbeville Library, would unfold before his very eyes and under his commentary with Wayne. A sense of pride overcame Benji, just to be part of this historical moment in A-Town. History lurked at every turn, so it seemed. An undefeated season would position Coach Nick at the top, the winningest coach in Abbeville ever, passing Coaches Hite and Botts. Botts currently edged out Hite by two games. Looming larger still, a chance to win a third consecutive state championship, a feat never matched. Twice back to back titles had been accomplished, both under Jamie Nickles watch as head coach. A third, was it even a realistic and obtainable goal? Destiny would determine if a true dynasty existed in A-Town. Some, the true diehards, would argue that a dynasty already existed. Benji, a firm believer in the data and statistics, would wait out the outcome of this compelling argument. A third would indeed be the charm though. First things first, get by those Wildcats, rivals forever.

Game Zero, Ninety Six

Game week finally and Benji had managed to navigate the previous perilous waters with no more eventful revelations. Life had returned to some semblance of normalcy. Well, as normal as normal was in the life of a sports fanatic. One thing for certain, Abbeville didn't need Ninety Six to play the role of season spoiler right out of the chute. Benji laid it on the line as only he could.

> "The slow, painful, football-less July is behind us. The summer practices and scrimmages are behind us. The jamboree season is over. It's game time and it couldn't get here soon enough. The Abbeville Panthers open their 100th year of football with a road trip to Ninety Six to take on the Wildcats. Here's the starting lineup for Week Zero."

Offense

QB #3 Brice Jackson

RB #23 Jermaine Blackwell – #22 Courtney Jackson – #8 Junior Rapley

WR #24 JaBryan Sanders

TE #5 Charles Holback

RT #51 Griffin Lewis

RG #54 Jacob Stone

C #62 Connor Nickles

LG #72 Jake Hill

LT #75 Trai Jones

Defensive

FS #14 David Cobb

SS #4 Malik Leach

CB #2 Kentavious Leach and #11 Ravon Bobo

LB #27 Tyrese Paul – #5 Charles Holback – #32 Charleton "Whootie" Goodwin – #34 Dee Graham

DE #35 Malek Blackwell and #6 Nate Temple

DT #53 Jihad Washington and #68 CJ Rayford

Punter, Kicker, and Kickoff Specialist #41 Dylan Beauford

Benji continued,

> "As famed UFC ring announcer Bruce Buffer would say, "It's TIMEEEEE". Game week is upon us and the greatest time of the year, football season, is merely hours away. Here in the south we have four seasons. Spring, Summer, Football, and Winter. It's a way of life and we wouldn't have it any other way. Let's look at the match up that we'll witness Friday night between the back to back defending AA State Champs, the Abbeville Panthers and the Ninety Six Wildcats.
>
> Ninety Six is welcoming in new coach Andre Woolcock and numbers are up for the Wildcats this season. Woolcock has brought in a renewed enthusiasm. The Wildcats finished a disappointing 2-9 last season. Coach Woolcock is trying to get the returning players to forget about that forgettable season and look forward. Starting quarterback Chad Fairey, a Clemson baseball commit, will be leading the Wildcat offense this year. The strong-armed signal caller will have some weapons around him as well. Braden Bolt will get a ton of carries for the Wildcats and Kentavius Williams, a junior wide receiver should be the key target in the Wildcat air attack. Ninety Six hung tough with a 14-7 loss to Greenwood in the WCTEL Kickoff Classic at Hite Stadium a couple of weeks ago, and they trounced Fox Creek in the Greenwood Jamboree. Already, the Wildcats are looking stronger out of the gates. Bennie Williams will be counted on in the trenches and look for Evan Keller to be in on most of the tackles from his linebacker position.

> The Panthers are riding a long unbeaten streak, back to back state championship wins and a ton of preseason hype. Bryce Jackson will lead a Panther offense that has a stable of running backs capable of going the distance with every touch. Junior Rapley, Courtney Jackson, Jermaine Blackwell and Dominick Washington will get their fair share of carries this year. Each one trying to out rush the other. Competition within themselves seems to be a driving factor for the Panther running backs. Malik Washington and "Dooley" Sanders will be the field stretching long ball threats this season. Starting two sophomores on the offensive line may take the Panthers a game or so to completely gel and be on the same page. Defensively the Panthers will be leaning on "Whooty" Goodwin, Nate Temple, Tyrese Paul and Charles Holback to make plays and slow down the Ninety Six offensive attack.
>
> The Panthers know they have a target on their back. Every team they play wants to be the team that finally beats Abbeville. Can Ninety Six be the one? Is this Panther team mature enough to know how to turn it on when it matters? We'll find out when toe touches leather tonight."

The WZLA 92.9 weekly format would go like this every Friday night starting at 6:30 with the WCTEL Panther Tailgate Show. The Jamie Nickles Coaches Show will follow at 7 and then live play by play action at 7:30. For those not at the game or in the area, streaming the game would be possible worldwide by downloading the FREE app on your smart phone, tablet or computer. The app is called "STREEMA – Simple Radio". Search WZLA once inside the app and you'll be able to listen to every Panther game, all season long.

Game over, Benji summarized it as follows,

> "The Panthers left no doubt when the horn sounded at Wilson-Campbell Stadium in Ninety Six, as to who was the #1 team in Class AA. Abbeville, whom allowed Ninety Six to drive the length of the field on Ninety Six's very first possession, put the clamps down on the Wildcat offense the rest of

the night. The Wildcats mustered very little production after scoring a field goal on their opening drive.

The Panthers did not waste time putting points on the board as Bryce Jackson hit Dooley Sanders on a screen pass, only to watch the speedster out run everyone for a 39-yard touchdown run. On the Wildcats next possession, Nate Temple tips the ball at the line of scrimmage and Tyrese Paul comes down with the interception. The Panthers started their 2nd drive at the Ninety Six 30 yard line. AHS punched the ball into the end zone a few plays later as Courtney Jackson, who scored three touchdowns on the night, walked into the end zone.

The turning point had been when Gabe Calhoun scooped up a Wildcat fumble on the very next possession and returns it 59 yards for a Panther touchdown. The Panthers led 21-3 with 8 minutes left in first half. A fake field goal ran in for a touchdown by Junior Rapley just before halftime put the Panthers on top 27-9 and that was as close as the score would be the rest of the night.

Even though the Panthers are 41-13-1 all-time versus Ninety Six, the electricity was thick in the air. This game is a rivalry and a lopsided one as portrayed by the 54-16 final score. The fans showed up in full force to watch the game as it was standing room only nearly an hour before kickoff. Another evident fact is there are some real burners on the Abbeville team this year. Speed, speed and more speed. More than once, a Panther running back, or receiver would get a glimpse of daylight and you could feel the entire stadium stand to their feet and hold their breath.

The Panthers will travel to Woodruff this coming Friday Night. Kickoff is 7:30pm. Woodruff defeated AC Flora in a shootout 53-45. Check back later this week for a preview of A-Town vs Woodruff."

Benji beamed with delight after his first game with Wayne in the booth. He had been amazed by the texts, emails or calls received from those listening to the Panthers from all parts of the country. Streaming had helped WZLA reach a broader audience of A-Town faithful. Coauthor T. Allen Winn had been listening in from Myrtle Beach.

Those Pesky Spoilers

Anyone who follows Abbeville High School football is certainly aware of one of their all-time nemesis. The Wolverines of Woodruff have forever played a catastrophic role in Abbeville's destiny. Benji framed the picture.

"Woodruff was at one time the thorn in the playoff side of the Panthers for years. In 1972,73',76',78',79' and 1980 the Wolverines bounced the Panthers from the playoffs. In those six games the Wolverines never gave up more than 15 points and pitched two shut outs. Woodruff is long removed from the Willie Varner days now but there is still a little something special in the air when Woodruff comes to town. Or in this case, when A-Town rolls into Woodruff. Which they will do this Friday with kickoff slated for 7:30. Over the last ten years the Panthers and Wolverines have played six times. The record, 3-3. Doesn't get much more even than that. Well, maybe it does. The average score of the last six meetings: 27-26 in favor of Woodruff. Are we in for another nail biting shootout? Or will the Panthers roll like they did last year 28-0? Only time will tell.

What we do know is that Woodruff has a heck of a quarterback. Keegan Halloran, #11, scorched 4A AC Flora last Friday night. The Wolverines trailed 26-7 before Halloran and wide receiver #7 Austin Parks began their onslaught. Halloran threw for 5 touchdowns, three of those caught by Parks, and ran for two more as Woodruff beat AC Flora 53-45. Woodruff head coach Trey Elder likes the spread offense. They will throw the ball 80% of the time. Elder was a quarterback at Byrnes High School before playing college football at Appalachian State.

What we also know is that after one game it appears that the strength of the Abbeville defense lies within their secondary. Tyrese Paul had an interception versus Ninety Six. Gabe Calhoun picked up a fumble and ran it in for a touchdown as well. When hammer meets nail at Woodruff High School Friday night, the matchup to watch is the Wolverine wide receivers versus the Panther defensive backs. Another glaring stat is that the Woodruff defense gave up 45 points to an AC Flora team that could be described as mediocre in their region. They were bounced from the playoffs last season by Hartsville by a 48-10 score. Abbeville quarterback Bryce Jackson only threw four passes last Friday night, three of them complete, one for a score. The one incompletion was a fingernail away from being a touchdown toss as well. How can we not mention the Panther rushing attack? A four-headed monster in Bryce Jackson, Courtney Jackson, Junior Rapley and Jermaine Blackwell produced over 300 yards rushing and they are ready to make another statement this coming Friday. Can Abbeville produce a pass rush to make Halloran uncomfortable in the pocket? Can they contain the fleet footed quarterback? Will we see nearly 100 combined points in Woodruff tonight? Only time will tell. The odds makers like A-town as they are a 16 point favorite heading into the match-up."

In Benji's words, the game wrap-up,

"The Panthers reeled off 35 unanswered points to beat Woodruff 42-19. Abbeville now owns a 25-game unbeaten streak which is best in the state regardless of classification. The Panthers offensive line smothered potential Wolverine tacklers and the fleet footed A-Town stable of running backs piled up 500 yards rushing on 42 carries. (11.9 yards per rush) The Panther defense found their rhythm after allowing 13 Woodruff first quarter points.

Jermaine Blackwell darted 18 yards for a touchdown and gave Abbeville its first lead of the night 14-13. The next play by Woodruff resulted in a fumble that Abbeville recovered. Momentum was heavily on the side of the Panthers at that point. Ole Uncle Mo plopped down on the Panthers sideline for the rest of the game when three plays later Courtney Jackson walked in untouched and gave the Panthers a 21-13.

Junior Rapley and Courtney Jackson capped punishing scoring drives in the 3rd quarter with touchdown runs putting A-Town up 35-13 heading into the 4th. Dooley Sanders out ran everybody on a 24-yard touchdown to put the nail in the coffin.

Up next, the Hite is finally open for business! It seems like an eternity since the Panthers walked down the steps and rubbed the bronze *'Helmet of the Unknown Panther'*. The wait is almost over. Emerald will visit Abbeville September 3rd for the 7:30 kickoff at Hite Stadium-Dennis Botts Field."

Woodruff in the rearview mirror, A-Town could breathe again momentarily. It sure made the ride back to Abbeville a more joyful experience for those supporting the traveling Panthers. Benji looked ahead to the team from the Emerald City of Greenwood. It wouldn't be a conference game, but a loss would hurt just the same when you were accustomed to winning. Benji, happy to be home, would do his best to tread the tranquil waters of his comfortable environment and push back on football thoughts for a while. What one wants and what one gets doesn't always work as one hopes.

Jiminy Crickets, a Caroling We Will Go

It had been a long week and even longer day, the trip to and back from Woodruff. Unwinding, Benji eventually slipped into the world of nocturnal bliss, a head having never been happier to contact with a pillow. Blissfulness would be short lived. Uninterrupted sleep is highly overrated in the Greeson household lately. A whistle got his attention. Not a high-pitched lip whistle or that friendly comforting Andy Griffin theme song, but a referee's whistle instead. What now, he wondered, doing his best to keep his eyes pressed tightly shut. The relentless whistle would have none of it. Why me Lord? Why am I dealing with this life altering vivid dream? Well, it had to be a dream because he was in bed, right? Sticks and stones can mess with my weary bones, but dreams can't really harm me, can they?

Don't do it, Benji boy, he tried to convince himself. Block it out. Think stats, game prep, radio garble, anything but allowing that pesky whistle to reel you in. No dice. The whistle blower would tolerate no resistance. Okay then, he told himself, just one quick little peek to rid the room of its annoying persistence. Tara usually heard sounds more so than he. Why wasn't she stirring? Simple, wasn't it? This obviously wasn't going to be her dream sequence. None lately were. Why now? One eye at a time, just take one tiny peek. What can it hurt? Let me count the ways; locker rooms, washers and dryers, bass boats with Botts and Hite, do I need to go on and on?

"Unsportsmanlike conduct, fifteen yards or what's behind door number two," said the bellowing voice.

Got to look now. There stood in dream state predictable, a zebra striped line judge with yellow flag in hand. What next, wondered Benji. He eyed the man who appeared to be missing his top teeth, reminiscent of that official who had supposedly lost his teeth in the Chestnut street donnybrook many years ago compliments of Bill Ashcraft.

"Come. Please follow me. I must walk off these 15 yards. You don't want another flag for delaying the game, do you, young man?"

"I get it. I'm tired. You're what stands between me and a good night's sleep. Go wave your mustard colored handkerchief in somebody else's bedroom. I don't need the disruption nor the drama."

Benji turned back over, sighed and covered his head with the pillow. The man in the striped outfit was having none of this. The covers were abruptly yanked off, riling Benji this time. He sat up and pointed his finger, about to unleash a tongue lashing when the overhead lights blinded him instead.

"No way. This is impossible."

Benji straddled the fifty-yard line; not just any fifty-yard line. He was slap dab in the middle of Hite Stadium on Dennis Botts Field. Worse still, he was back in uniform, garnet and gold to be specific, sporting his old high school number again, #64. The ref pointed to the score board. The hometown Panthers were holding a 3-0 lead in the third quarter, 3 minutes remaining and with 3 timeouts. The ref told him it was 3rd down and 3. Benji took a deep breath and scanned the stands. They were empty except for one lone folding chair and a figure sitting at the top right corner of the home side. He couldn't identify the person. The scene was a wavy blur for some reason. A player resembling an apparition, a ghostly figure decked out in the Panther colors caught his attention running in from what had just been empty sidelines. The number 84 shown brightly on the jersey.

The ref commented, "Uh, oh, Jiminy Crickets, juice on the loose."

Benji turned just as the ref faded away into nothingness, but at that briefest moment he could have sworn he had caught a glimpse of Coach Hite's smiling face. Poof, just like that, the whistle blower had vanished. He returned his attention to the approaching number 84. A sparkling and twinkling smile drew him in, a face vaguely familiar.

"I'm the player of championship past, proud to meet you Mr. Greeson. Fine job on that book. Indeed, it is all about the 'A' here."

"You do realize that you are plagiarizing Dicken's *The Christmas Story* for the purpose of advancing your football agenda and this dream. And I think I know who you are."

"Maybe you do. Maybe you don't. It really doesn't matter. We were a team, not individuals. This is 1971, our time, our field, our destiny. Remember the Titans, don't you?"

"Larry Ray, it is you, isn't it? You've been called one of the best players in Abbeville history."

"It could have just as easily gone the other way. Coach Cox gave me a second chance and I took it. But, that's not why we're here."

"Just why are we here then?"

"Destiny has more doors yet to open. The 1971 team opened the first, got the ball rolling in the right direction, set the bar so to speak. Game changers, breaking through barriers, making new rules. We were the leaders in changing times in

Abbeville, colored and white on the same team for the same purpose. Montgomery was the first negro assistant coach at Abbeville High. Coach Cox had never been a head coach before arriving here. The 71' team did what they weren't expected to do, small squad, often playing both ways but succeeding in a way no other team had ever. The '71 team won the only 3A state title."

"I am aware of those facts and I, as the entire population of A-Town, are greatly appreciative. That doesn't answer the riddle though. Why me? Why am I here? Why am I being hounded with these dreams, revelations, visions or whatever you want to call them?"

"Destiny chooses. It is wiser than all of us. I just play football to the best of my ability. You were a player. Here, please take this ball. I'm going long. Pass me it to me."

"I played, sure, but I'm no quarterback. Look at me. This is not the body of a Peanut Martin or Billy Woolbright."

"By the way, did you know that Cox was responsible for the block A design."

"Yes. My buddy T. Allen fished that hole. Cox laid claim to it."

The juice was indeed on the loose. He spread wide and then took it down the sidelines before breaking into the middle of the field just inside the five-yard line. Benji shook his head, realizing that he would have to connect on a forty-five-yard pass. He dropped back, now making this a fifty-yard attempt and gave it everything he could. The ball soared through the air like nothing he had ever thrown in his life. It connected. Larry sprinted into the end zone, his empty hand held high over his head, three fingers easily visible. Benji wanted to yell, six, not three but just as quickly number 84 faded and was gone.

Benji was no longer at mid-field but instead was kneeling with the ball in his hands as if he was holding it for the extra point attempt. He stared at the goalpost, befuddled once again. The ball left his hands as garnet pants and a cleated shoe kicked a perfect extra point between the uprights. Benji stood and turned to face another uniformed figure. This kid was nothing like Ray, wearing a white jersey, number 60. He was wide, short but stout, a powder keg of strength under that uniform. Eyes focused on him from underneath the Block A helmet.

"All right, which are you, champion of players, present or future?"

"Bob Winn will do. Thanks for holding the extra point."

"Bob Winn. You played in the 80's."

"Don't rub it in. I wasn't on a state championship team. We did however have one of the best coaches, Coach Hendricks. I loved playing for that man. He taught us about faith, family and football. He won the second state title in 81' in 2A. I just missed being part of that team. See this bruise on my left thigh, got that one in last week's game. You must learn to wear the purple proudly I always say."

"You were a true gamer from everything I have heard. Maybe you can explain why I'm being yanked through this little journey."

"You do love football, don't you? I mean, Abbeville football specifically."

"I do without a doubtful bone in my body. So does almost everyone in A-Town, so what?"

"It's All About the A to you, isn't it?"

"Thanks for the book plug but for some reason I don't think that's why I am here. Care to share your thoughts, Bob?"

"Kids need role models. Especially those struggling through life with threatening circumstances. Faith and family go a long way in the healing process even when healing is not destiny's choosing. Heck, family doesn't necessarily require family connections. Relate, comfort and care I always say. A champion is not necessarily defined by those leading on the gridiron. Anyone can be a champion of anything. One must simply choose and apply. I think you're needed in the booth, Mr. Greeson. Thanks for being my place holder. Maybe next time you can do the same for a three-point attempt. There's something special about those threes." Bob held up three fingers to make that point.

Benji nodded and then diverted his attention to the announcer's booth standing as it always had above the granite bleachers. He now occupied that same booth with Wayne Stevenson. The silhouettes of two figures were there. He recognized both. He turned to Bob to verify just that but #60 had vanished. Benji rubbed his eyes and once again attempted to shake off this apparently well-orchestrated dream. He gathered himself and then made his way up the bleacher steps leading to the booth. Standing now at the booth steps, Benji rolled his eyes, wondering if the next encounter would finally clarify the meaning behind this.

Opening the door, a single figure now occupied the booth. His back was turned to Benji. A notepad was in his hand and he was furiously tabulating stats. No denying it, he had seen this gentleman in action many times, a data crunching machine, football or baseball.

"You're alone. Didn't I see Fletcher Ferguson in here with you?"

"You're here now, Benji. Have a seat. I have the final stats for the Wolverine's game ready for you. The Panthers are off and rolling once again, seemingly destined for a run at a third state crown. I bet you are enjoying your stint with Wayne, aren't you?"

"Honk, just maybe you can be the voice of reason and finally explain my purpose in all of this."

Keith 'Honk' Hall smiled and said, "I've got mine. What about you? I don't need anything for Christmas. I've got my Christmas present, the 2015 State Championship, compliments of those brave boys winning their 7th title."

Benji dropped his head, rubbed his hands over his eyes and prepared his next question. Looking up, Honk was gone. He was in the booth alone. He then heard that Clunk-Clunk sound from somewhere in the stands. He craned his neck out the opening and looked to his left. Two figures sat at the top of the steps in front of the fence, one ringing the bell and the second yelling something about the state and number eight. He had the distinct impression that he was looking at the Dubose, Pidgey and Poops, but before he could confirm his suspicions, he felt an elbow in his side. Benji, like Bob Winn, should wear his bruises proudly, those delivered by his loving wife this time. Tara had again been persistent in waking him from his dream. He did what was best in this situation, just smiled and shrugged his shoulders, seeing no value in recapping the latest for her.

Another connection to the '71 season was not that of dreams or apparitions though. James 'Peanut' Martin, the starting quarterback for the '71 state champs had contacted Benji at the station, airing his disappointment about the way he had been portrayed in the book, specifically the portion about his practice day suspension. Benji listened to his grievances and suggested for him to share them with his coauthor. After all, T. Allen had conducted the interview with Coach Preston Cox and had written the chapters referring to the 71' season.

T. Allen Winn,

> "I had never met Coach Cox until that interview. I called Mr. Martin and spent about an hour on the phone with him. His recollection of the practice event varied from that of his coaches, as did some of the other situations that involved him. He said he was disappointed that he had not been contacted to tell his side as he had been the starting quarterback that year. All fairness, we are not investigative reporters and it never dawned on us to verify interviewers' stories by talking to others involved. Hindsight, we could have done a better job trying to contact as many key players as we could. We do sincerely apologize to Mr. Martin and to any others who feel impacted similarly. We were working to a self-imposed deadline and did our best to follow leads and referrals. Excavating 100 years of history is tougher than most might imagine. We spent nine months start to finish and could have spent years and still might not have talked to everyone.

We're Not in Kansas, Toto

The Panthers continued their season of bulldozering through the competition by defeating those from the Emerald City 56-21. JaBryan "Dooley" **Sanders** has been the fastest person in the stadium each of the first three weeks of the season, evident in his 5 catches for 142 yards and 4 td's. His 70-yard punt return for a touchdown versus Emerald at Hite Stadium. While the team remained focused by beating Emerald, there was no denying the next matchup would be one of the most anticipated.

Benji explains,

> "Well folks, this is one of the weeks that you look forward to, the moment the schedule comes out every spring. This game has been circled on the calendar since the melee that ensued at Larry Campbell Stadium-Buddy Bufford Field last September. The Panthers and the Red Devils clashed in a 7-7 tie and to say it was a physically fought contest would be like saying that grandma's biscuits and gravy are just "okay". It was a war. The pride, the history and tradition of both heavily decorated programs shone through in the grit and viciousness in which both teams played. Are you ready for round two? You better be because it's happening at 7:30pm this coming Friday September 8th at Hite Stadium-Dennis Botts Field.
>
> The Lincoln County Red Devils are a Class A team situated just across the state line in Lincolnton, Georgia. That state line and the Savannah River are just about the only thing that separates the Panthers and the Red Devils. Both have overflowing trophy cases. The Red Devils have won 14 Georgia State Championships. Eleven of those have former head coach Larry Campbell's name on them. The Red Devils are the winningest team in Class A in Georgia High School Football history. LC has done more with less, more so than any other team, maybe in the history of high school football. The Red Devils are on a State Championship drought however. It's been 10 seasons since they last hoisted a trophy (2006) but that doesn't mean they haven't been really good. The respect between both schools is evident and it shows on the field.
>
> This season the Red Devils are 1-1 on the season and ranked 7th in Georgia Class A. Head Coach Kevin Banks spent 19 years as an assistant under Larry Campbell and was handed the keys to the Ferrari before the 2014 season when Campbell retired. Banks is 24-10-1 as the head honcho at LC and he's chomping at the bit to meet the lofty expectations of the Red Devil faithful. You'll see some familiar faces from last season's game as Javon Reid is the starting quarterback for the Red Devils again this season. Last year the dual threat Reid rushed and passed for over 1,000 yards each. Jamal Norman is back in the backfield for LC. He has 168 yards on 27 carries this

season so far. And one of, if not *the* most famous names in Lincoln Co. football history has reemerged on the LC sideline. Gerard Hearst, son of LC, UGA and San Francisco 49er great Garrison Hearst is a running back on this year's team. He has 12 carries for 54 yards so far this season. Can the Panther defense shut down the physical, smashmouth Red Devil attack in front of their home crowd? Can the Panther offense keep clicking against an equally fast and physical LC defense?

The Panthers will start by doing what they do and that's running the football. Pick your poison. Whomever gets the carry out of the Panther backfield this season can take it to the house at any moment. Courtney Jackson, #22, leads all Panther rushers with 26 carries for 271 yards and 5 touchdowns. #8 Junior Rapley has 29 carries for 249 yards and 4 touchdowns and quarterback Brice Jackson has 25 carries for 172 yards and 1 score. Here is where the pick your poison part comes into play. Defenses that play Abbeville must choose whether to commit an extra defender to account for the run or leave an extra defender to keep an eye on JaBryan "Dooley" Sanders who has been the absolute **wow factor** for the Panthers this season. Sanders has been the fastest person in the stadium each of the first three weeks of the season. The Panthers are big, fast and physical. How will they stack up against another elite team in Lincoln County? Game time can't get here fast enough.

Fast forward. So, just what happened you might wonder. Two elite football programs clashed at Hite Stadium-Dennis Botts Field in a game that produced a State Championship type atmosphere. The Panthers and Red Devils traded blows and showcased the athletes that make each program special. Lincoln County received the opening kickoff and the fourth play of the drive saw the very athletic LC quarterback Javon Reid scamper 59 yards for a touchdown. The Panthers, sporting their yella' britches for the first time this season, answered the bell with a Junior Rapley touchdown run on the very next possession.

The Panther defense stiffened and shut out the Red Devils the rest of the first half. Two 2nd quarter Bryce Jackson touchdown runs extended the Panthers lead to 21-7 just before halftime. This one wasn't over until late. The capacity Abbeville crowd got their money's worth. LC scored in the 3rd quarter to close the gap to 21-14. A 24 yard Courtney Jackson touchdown run and an ensuing defensive stand put the nail in the coffin midway through the 4th quarter though. The Panthers extended their unbeaten streak to a state best 27 games.

Next, the #1 ranked back to back State Champs will welcome the Clinton Red Devils to Hite Stadium. Clinton got their first win of the season, defeating Aiken 47-33. This is the last game of the three-game home stand before the Panthers hit the road again on Sept 22nd at Mid Carolina."

Don't Let the Green Grass Fool Ya

Benji would set the stage for the Clinton Red Devils shoot-out. Thinking back to that very first 71' state championship, Clinton posed a concerning bit of stress for Coach Preston Cox. He had been an assistant coach there before taking over the leadership role at Abbeville and implemented the Wing-T offense. Cox had told his team back then that Clinton was not going to lie down for them. They would just as likely bust the Panthers' heads if they weren't prepared to do the same for a win. This was a different era of football but in Cox's words when rereferring to the 71' team 'We were walking the dog'.

Benji lays out the circumstances for the next matchup,

> "Wilson Pickett sings a song called *Don't Let the Green Grass Fool Ya*. That's exactly what comes to mind when thinking about Friday night's contest between the #1 ranked, back to back 2A State Champion Abbeville Panthers (4-0) and the Clinton Red Devils (1-2). Why that song? Well, looking at Clinton's record this season, and looking at their record over the last decade, one could draw a conclusion that the Panthers could merely just go through the motions and take home a victory this coming Friday night. But, as the Sunshine Scooter Lee Corso would say, "Not so fast my friend". Don't let the records fool ya. The Clinton High Red Devils are a big, physical, smashmouth football team who is out to prove a point and to, dare I say, shock the world. Last week Clinton won their first game of the season and they did it behind a stout defense who collected 3 interceptions in the game and turned them all into points. Mark Wise, #5, is a senior running back and linebacker for the Red Devils and against Aiken, Wise rushed for 255 yards and 5 touchdowns. A very big offensive line leads the way for the Red Devils who will try to grind out the clock, and keep the speedy, ultra-talented Abbeville offense off the field. With both teams using the running game as their bread and butter, this game may not take two whole hours to complete.
>
> Meanwhile, the Panthers are rolling along as expected. A state best, regardless of classification, 27 game unbeaten streak is on the line. The Panthers are wrapping up a three-game home stand before taking the show on the road next week. In fact, if you want to see the Panthers at home, you might want to come Friday night as it will be the last home game for the Panthers until October 20th. There is some history between these two teams. Clinton is one of the few teams that hold a win advantage over the Panthers. Abbeville is 8-11 all-time versus the Red Devils. Abbeville has won the last three meetings. Last year's game was a nail-biting 34-31 win for the Panthers. The average score of all 19 contests is 20.1 – 10.8 in favor of Clinton. The Panthers and Red Devils played 12 times between 1956 and

1971 and did not play again until 2002. This is the 20th all-time meeting between the two schools.

The Panthers are led on the ground by a committee of running backs. Rapley (42 carries -329 yards & 4 touchdowns) C. Jackson (33-299-5) B. Jackson (34-258-3) are all averaging over 6 yards per carry. The Panthers have found success through the air this season as well. Bryce Jackson is completing over 65% of his passes for 231 yards and 4 touchdowns. JaBryan "Dooley" Sanders caught all of Jackson's touchdown tosses and is averaging 21 yards per catch this season. The Panther offensive line has been dominating the opposition and this group has "clicked" since jamboree season. The Panther defense has taken a bend but don't break approach this season. Led by Malik Leach (33 tackles – 13 assisted tackles) Dee Graham (19 tackles – 18 assists – 1 sack) Tay Rayford (16 tackles – 6 assists – 6 passes broken up) and Nate Temple (15 tackles – 12 assists – 5 TFL and 2 sacks). This group will look to stop the Clinton ground game and exert their dominance over the bigger 3A school. The Panthers are +5 in the turnover margin this season. They've collected 7 turnovers while only turning it over twice. The Panthers continue their march toward greatness."

Okay, so with all the hype and buildup to a battle with the Red Devils, just how did A-town's best do? Benji sums it up.

"The back to back 2A State Champs have extended their unbeaten streak to a state best, regardless of classification, 28 games. The Panthers rolled Clinton 49-12 last week, and the A-Train rolls into Prosperity, SC this coming Friday night to take on the Mid Carolina Rebels.

Rebel head coach Louie Alexander has his hands full getting the Rebs ready to take on a Panther team that is clicking on all cylinders. The Rebels are winless this season. They were winless last season. In fact, the last game that Mid Carolina won was on October 23rd of 2015 versus Eau Claire High in Columbia. That's 17 in a row. So, Friday night is a game of two streaks, a team on the top of the mountain and a team looking up from the cellar. There's plenty of history between these two schools however. The Panthers are 20-10 all-time versus Mid Carolina. The Panthers have won 8 in a row in the series, with the last Panther loss coming in 1997. Last season the Panthers beat Mid Carolina at Hite Stadium, 37-7. The Rebels participate in class 3A Region 3 with the likes of Chapman, Newberry, Broome, Woodruff, and Clinton. Friday's game versus A-town is the last non-region game on the schedule for the Rebels this season.

The Panthers found some success through the air versus Clinton. Quarterback Bryce Jackson had touchdown passes to Dominick "The Bus"

Washington and a 66 yarder to Jr. Rapley. At the halfway point in the season the Panther signal caller has 16 completions on 26 attempts for 309 yards and 6 touchdowns.

The Panther running backs have had quite a season as well. Here are the midseason stats for the Panther offense.

#22 Courtney Jackson 38 rushes 383 yards 7 touchdowns 10.08 yards per carry

#8 Junior Rapley 46 carries – 362yds – 4tds – 7.87ypc

#3 Brice Jackson 44 carries – 340yds – 4tds – 7.73ypc

#23 Jermaine Blackwell 27 carries – 213yds – 4tds – 7.89ypc

#21 Dominick Washington 29 carries – 166yds – 3tds – 5.72ypc

As you can see there are five players on offense, with a minimum of 20 carries who average over 5 yards per carry. That's just short of amazing. A ton of credit goes to the Panther offensive line for blocking and grinding out those tough yards with the running backs. Connor Nickles, Jake Hill, Griffin Lewis, Jacob Stone and Trai Jones have been consistent, tough and overwhelming to opposing defenses this season.

Defensively the Panthers may have played their best game of the season in game number 5 last week versus Clinton. Malik Leach caused two turnovers, an interception, and a fumble recovery. Which, by the way, he just basically took the ball out of the Clinton ball carriers hands and started running the other way with it. Clinton rushed 51 times in that game and averaged less than 3 yards per carry. Defensive leaders at this point in the season look like this…

#4 Malik Leach 40 tackles – 16 assisted tackles – 2 tackles for loss – 2 recovered fumbles and 1 interception.

#34 Dee Graham 30tkl – 24 assisted tackles – 1 sack – 1int

#6 Nate Temple 18tkl – 16 assisted tackles – 5 TFL – 2 sacks

#5 Charles Holback 18 tackles – 13 assisted tackles – 1 TFL

While it would be easy to do, the Panthers must not overlook Mid Carolina. The most important game of the season is the next game. That's the mentality that the Panthers must take into Friday night's matchup. Everyone not on staff or not wearing a helmet on Friday night is already giddy with excitement about the matchup on September 29th at Newberry College when the Panthers will take on a revenge minded Hartsville team."

Magic Shoes

Benji continued to be in his element, sharing the broadcast booth with Wayne Stevenson and providing game previews and their results for the loyal A-Town fans. He hadn't experienced any of those ghostly encounters or dream state disruptions in recent weeks. Hopefully this signaled that these nerve racking encounters were a thing of the past. Omens they had been, possibly. Abbeville was sure clicking on all cylinders in their quest for a three-peat, no denying that fact. Now to matters at hand, Benji lays the groundwork for the next gridiron encounter.

"Surely everyone has watched the movie *Forrest Gump*. In one scene, while sitting on a park bench, Forrest is telling the story of his childhood. He had to have braces on his legs. His mama called them his "Magic Shoes." She said they'd take him anywhere. After Forrest's legs strengthened, he ran right out of those braces. And from then on, he was "Run-ning". That seems to be the theme for this year's edition of our A-Town Panthers. They are "Run-ning".

This past Friday night at Lon Armstrong Stadium the Panthers ran around, through and right by the Mid Carolina Rebels. How much so? The Panthers put up 597 yards rushing. That's an insane number of rushing yards. Some teams may not rush for that many yards in an entire season. The Panthers did it on 61 carries. Big gaping holes created by a big physical offensive line and selfless running backs have allowed these gaudy numbers to jump off the sports page at you. As a team the Panthers are averaging 373.17 yards rushing per game. That's an average of 8.81 yards per rush. To put that in perspective, the Panthers are averaging a first down every other play when they hand the ball off. Of their six opponents so far this season the Panthers have played four 3A schools, one 2A school and Lincoln County, the winningest team in Georgia high school football history. It's not like the Panthers are running up and down the field on Sallie Mae Catholic School for Orphaned Girls. Through six games the Panthers are averaging 45 points per game while giving up 14 points per game.

The Panther defense seems to have found their stride as well. The Panthers have allowed 88 points this season. They have faced spread teams who throw it every play. They've faced balanced teams who can mix the run with the pass. They've faced running teams who like to line up and test your manhood. They've passed every test with flying colors. With only four regular season games remaining, can the Panthers maintain their elite level of play? The next test is a big one.

Most Panther fans had two games circled with a big red marker when the schedule was announced in the spring. The first game was versus Lincoln

Co. The second game was Hartsville. That game is upon us and you can feel the excitement building in the air as we inch ever so close to kickoff this coming Friday night.

Last season the Panthers came into the neutral site game at Newberry College as a 27-point underdog to the 4A Red Foxes. The Panthers trailed 21-7 in the first half before unleashing an offensive explosion and ultimately whipping the Red Foxes by a final of 32-21. This season the odds makers have the Panthers as a 4-point favorite heading into this non-region matchup. The Panthers and the Red Foxes are two of the most decorated high school football teams in the state. Hartsville is led by head coach Jeff Calabrese, who holds a career record of 124-36 over his 12 years at the helm. Hartsville is 4-1 on the season. The lone loss was a 35-21 defeat at Conway. Hartsville has won in a lot of different ways this season. A touchdown as time expired propelled them over South Florence. They've blown out a couple teams and been in a couple of closer games as well. Hartsville is very similar to Abbeville in that they like to run the ball.

They will line up under center 99% of the time and employ their version of the double wing option. Big, fast and physical are the only three adjectives that come to mind when describing the Red Foxes. Their offensive line averages 6'2" 250lbs. Playing in 4A-Region 6 with the likes of Crestwood, Lugoff-Elgin, Lakewood and Darlington, this game is their last non-region contest of the season. Hartsville has four state championships in their trophy case ('81 – '87 – '88-'12) and they have played for three more since 2010. Most recently, last season. This season they average 30 points per game offensively while giving up 17.4 on defense. If there was ever a David vs Goliath narrative in a football game, this is the one. Hartsville has an enrollment just a shade over 1,400 students, while Abbeville's enrollment is 487.

The Panthers, well, they don't buy into the David and Goliath storyline. They stood toe to toe with the 4A powerhouse last season and came away victorious. This season, riding a wave of confidence and a 29-game unbeaten streak, the Panthers are no longer the hunted. They are the hunters. The Panther offense led by quarterback **Bryce Jackson** and a pick your poison group of skill players, has shown that they can hang with anybody this season. Leading rusher **Courtney Jackson** has 512 yards rushing this season, complimented by 9 touchdowns. He sports an unbelievable 12.19 yards per carry. Nipping at the leading rushers heels is **Junior Rapley** with 439 yards and 5 touchdowns. The Panthers offense is averaging 45 points per game while only giving up 14.6.

Defensively the Panthers have answered the bell each and every game. Leading tackler **Malik Leach** has 66 total tackles on the season. He has recovered 2 fumbles and he also have an interception. The A-Town defense will need to play fundamentally sound against a big, strong, option-oriented Hartsville offense. The Panthers will be playing without budding sophomore star defensive end **Carson Smith**. He broke his hand last week versus Mid Carolina and is having surgery Thursday morning. The defensive line and linebackers will have to play a very smart, fast and physical game to limit the Red Fox offense, who can grind out first down after first down on the ground while milking the game clock.

This is a big one. Can the Panthers do the impossible again? Will the revenge card come into play? Can the Panthers keep the state's longest unbeaten streak alive? Panther fans heading to Newberry; The Panther are the home team this time around, so sit on the home side, and get ready for an electric, playoff type atmosphere."

Beat to Smithereens, Phase II Begins

Revenge is a powerful motive indeed. Benji recaps the Hartsville game, one leaving a despicable aftertaste in the Panther's mouths.

> "A well-deserved bye week has the Panthers licking their wounds and trying to heal after Coach Nickles described the health of the team as, "Beat to smithereens" entering their bye week. Summer workouts, 7 on 7 camps, summer practice, numerous scrimmages, jamborees and seven consecutive games have the Panthers tired yet still hungry.
>
> The Panthers lost their first game in nearly two seasons versus Hartsville (28-21) on September 29th. That game seems like it was played two months ago, not two weeks ago. The Panthers who nearly overcame a 'perfect storm' and stuck around with the #3 ranked 4A Red Foxes. Three turnovers, costly penalties, a special team's touchdown and losing their leading rusher to injury after just one carry, would be a recipe for disaster for the top ranked 2A Panthers. So, what was lost in that game on the pristine field at Newberry College? In one word…Nothing.
>
> Everything this team set out to achieve is firmly in front of them. I for one, am eager to see how the Panthers will respond coming off the bye week.

Did the loss alleviate any pressure that the team may have felt? Pressure to be perfect, pressure to not only win, but win by way of blowouts? Will the Panthers experience a hangover game on the road versus Liberty? Will the loss ignite a fire in the team and Liberty is standing in the way of a 26th Region Championship?

The Panthers enter now Phase two of the season. Region play. Phase one is the non-region and subsequently Phase three is the championship phase. The non-region schedule is behind them and the boys from A-Town boast a 6-1 record. There are three good teams left on the schedule. The last road game of the season is this coming Friday night versus Liberty High School. Liberty is 5-2 on the season. We will post a full Liberty game preview later in the week. Here are some cumulative stats thus far this season.

The Panther offense is averaging 38.5 points per game. That includes 350.7 yards rushing per game and 62.7 yards per game passing. They total 413.4 total yards per game and have outscored their opponents 291-116 this season.

The Panther defense is giving up 16.5 points per game while allowing 185.5 rushing yards per game and 148.8 yards per game through the air, for a total of 334.3 yards per game average.

The Panthers also come out of the gate running. They have outscored their opponents 84 – 30 in the first quarter of games this season. The Panthers are +3 in the turnover margin for the season. They have 10 takeaways and have turned it over 7 times. The Panthers have not attempted a field goal yet this season but are 33-39 on extra point attempts."

It would be time to cherish the bye week and lick their wounds. The Liberty game would come regardless, ready or not.

The Spirited Panther Mascot

Benji, exhausted like everyone else, the Hartsville game had sucked the life out of most watching or listening on the radio. The game really meant nothing in the big picture, the quest for the state championship. It hadn't even knocked Abbeville out of the number one spot in the 2A standings. Still, losing a chance to go undefeated still wore on the hearts of the devoted Panther followers. Nightmares and dreamscapes, déjà vu.

Benji woke, or thought he had, to the sounds of a marching band. He was perched in the booth at Hite Stadium, overlooking Dennis Botts Field, the lights brightly shinning on the Abbeville Marching Band. No, at a second glance, this wasn't the usual band. Benji rubbed his chin, thinking, was this the Facebook throwback Thursday version. Performing on the gridiron was the acclaimed Grenadier Marching Band. In its heyday it had won countless championships before the football team had won their first in '71. The kilts and bagpipes were the bands' trademarks. This wasn't real, just another one of those idiotic premonitions. What the heck, thought Benji, might as well enjoy the show, the vintage version had performed before my time.

A large trophy rested center field on the fifty-yard line, apparently their latest. A banner waved proudly, signifying that the Grenadiers had just won the '71 state championship. Now Benji knew something was fishy, even if he hadn't already suspected it. He was back in dream world for sure. The band faced the A-town stands and began playing the school's alma mater. Benji rose to his feet and sang along. A panther mascot in the end zone held up a sign that said, 'Forever to Three.' Benji thought, what a bozo, he misspelled 'Thee'. The Band Director, Sandy Scott held up three fingers and pointed his director's stick toward the score board.

A flash, maybe lightening, temporarily blinded Benji. Blinking, he attempted to regain his focus, the booth swaying and moving underneath him. He quickly took a seat, afraid he was about to lose his balance.

"Don't you have any common sense, boy? You need to keep your butt planted while fishing in my boat. And there you go again, where did you put your rod this time?"

"Come on Coach Botts, leave the kid alone. He's struggling, can't you tell. That loss has rattled his cage, made him unsure and fearful of the season yet to come."

"Now Coach Hite, I know your heart is in the right place but I'm the captain of this boat. I call the shots. One loss does not ruin a season."

"Eleven of them will though, won't they?"

"Cheap shot, even for you Coach. That was just one bad season, my first."

"Coaches, I'm not upset over the loss to Hartsville. It doesn't really count in the bigger scheme."

"That's the spirit, son. Wins and losses happen. Getting to the finish line is what counts."

"Unless the losses keep you out of the state title, right, Coach Hite."

"Touché, good dig, even for you, Coach Botts."

"Those boys are banged and battered up something fierce though. Lost their top running back. You don't have enough piss to repair all those injuries, Coach Hite."

"Benji, son, this will be your first state championship from inside the booth, won't it?"

"Yes, Coach Hite. And it would be awesome to be part of history."

"Championships are earned with blood, sweat and tears. There are no silver platters out there. To be the best, you have to beat the best or be the best everyone else is trying to beat."

"Coach Botts, I think this team is the best."

"Opinions are put up or shut up opportunities. Bragging and boasting just gets your butts kicked otherwise. I think you have a nibble there, Coach Hite."

"I assume I am here so that you two gents can offer me a glimmer of hope about the 2017 championship. So, do we win or not?"

"Boy, you don't know nothing. We're here to fish. Got a bet with Coach Hite, who wins this time."

"Right," winked Benji. "Who wins. And who do you think will win it all this time, Coach Hite."

Hite stood up and held up three fingers.

Botts shouted, "Sit down, you, old coot before you swamp us. And stop showing off those broken fingers of yours. I've heard that story from your playing days too many times already."

Lightening flashed.

"Time to get off this water before we become crispy critters," said Botts.

Benji was standing at the goal line with the uniformed panther mascot. The band was no longer on the field.

"Okay, what say you oh great Panther, I saw your Forever to Three sign earlier."

"I'm Bobby Leon Smith."

"Yoda?"

"No, I'm Bobby Leon Smith."

"Why in the world are you wearing the mascot outfit, Bobby? You were a water boy, not a Panther mascot."

"Had to. Lost rock, paper, scissors three times in a row to Jerry Winn. Loser had to wear this costume. And we're managers, not water boys. Jerry gets to be the manager in Friday's game while I wear this on the sidelines."

"Sorry. Three times, you say. By the way, Jerry was a manager years ago, long before your time,"

"Three times, what are the odds of that? Managers are managers, now and then. I lost. He won fair and square. I'm the mascot, not the manager this time."

"You're sure more talkative than I've heard you were, Bobby."

"And you look different that how you sound on the radio."

"Thinner, I've been told."

Benji's ribs ached something fierce. Tara asked him had he been dreaming about Star Wars with all that mumbling about Yoda.

Benji just grunted, "Something like that."

All Aboard the A-Train

Back to business for Benji. He couldn't explain the dreams and decided to just keep them his little secret. Sharing them would be like admitting he had spotted Bigfoot down at Parson's Mountain. Most called it Little Mountain. Explaining them could add no value to his life. He certainly didn't need to be portrayed at a Looney Tunes to his listeners, friends or family. He'd just take it in stride and hope there was meaning behind them. Too many threes, how could they not be some sort of good luck charm, or maybe just wishful feelings.

Give me Liberty or give me death, time for Benji to prepare the A-town readers for his next installment.

> "The bye week came at a great time. The Panthers were battered and bruised and honestly, just tired. Tonight, the A-Train rolls into Liberty with renewed enthusiasm and for the first time this season, something to play for. Liberty marks the first region game of the season. Kudos to the Panther coaching staff for getting the team prepared to show up week in and week out, playing seven non-conference games. Games that honestly mean nothing in the grand scheme of things. The region games decide playoff seeding and let's be honest. The playoffs and the road to the state championship are the ultimate goal every season. Let's look at Liberty, the third set of Red Devils that the Panthers will face this season.
>
> Liberty Head Coach Kyle Stewart has the Red Devils sitting at 5-2 on the season. Like most teams these days they will run a balanced spread offense. Balanced, meaning they will run out of the spread and try to throw using play action. That is, if the run is working for them. But offense isn't what Coach Stewart hangs his hat on. The Red Devils have used a stingy defense over the last couple of seasons to impose their will on their opponents. Liberty averages 27.2 points per game offensively, while giving up 12.8 points per game on defense. Last season that defense led them to a quarter finals appearance versus Saluda, who ultimately won and faced Abbeville in the Upper State Championship game. Can the Red Devils slow down the speedy A-Town offense? That's a tall task.
>
> Liberty got some help slowing down the Panthers by way of Hartsville. Sounds weird I know but hang with me here. In the Hartsville game the Panthers leading rusher Courtney Jackson (43 carries -525yds-9tds-12.2ypc) left the game after just one carry. He was examined on the sideline. Jogged up and down the sideline a few times and went back in the game briefly before coming right back out. What we didn't know then is that Jackson had suffered a season ending knee injury that will require surgery. That's a

tough break for an outstanding football player and an even better kid. Best of wishes and a quick recovery for #22. So, what now? Well, to say that the cupboard is full of running backs would be an understatement. The Panthers will have a starting backfield that looks like this; The wingbacks will be Junior Rapley (69-498-6-7.22) and Jermaine Blackwell (38-284-4-7.47) and Dominick Washington (45-245-3-5.44) will start in the fullback position. And of course, the Panther quarterback Bryce Jackson (63-503-7-7.98) is a big run threat as well. He's currently the Panthers leading rusher. The Panthers have had a handful of near misses in the passing game. Literal fingertip misses that could have blown games wide open and padded the passing stats for the season. Even still, Jackson has connected with Dooley Sanders (11 catches 246yds 5tds) on a regular basis. Robin Crawford (16-143-1) and Cruz Temple, who has been moved up from the JV team will bring added depth to the running back position.

Here's the storyline or the questions in the air about tonight's game at Liberty. Did the loss take some pressure off this Panther team? Did the loss light a fire and create a sense of urgency? Have the Panthers completely flushed the loss vs. Hartsville and moved on? Everything this team wanted to accomplish this season is still in front of them. They have a chance tonight to make a statement and prove that the road to the Region 2 2A championship still squarely runs through Abbeville."

Give me Liberty, the results of life according to Benji,

"I think many of us had a preconceived notion that the Liberty game was going to be a cake walk. That was not the case at all. Liberty is a much-improved team with a big, strong, physical defense. They will make a run in the playoffs this season. Mark my words on that one. In fact, Liberty is a couple skill players away from being a real threat in the Upperstate brackets. And how about those facilities? I can't say enough good things about their stadium, concessions, bathrooms, press boxes. Maybe one-day Panther fans…maybe one day. Now on to the game.

There was not a lot of running room for the Panthers in the interior. The Panthers had to take their game to the edges. Junior Rapley (74-529-7) had an ESPN Top 10 type run early in the 2nd quarter. He zigged and zagged his way to the end zone for the Panthers first score of the night. Bryce Jackson also connected with Rapley on a 50-yard TD pass in the 2nd quarter to extend the Panthers lead to 20-3. Other than a 30-yard Jermaine Blackwell (45-347-5) touchdown run in the 4th quarter, that was about all the offensive highlights on the night. The Panthers were held to a season low 131 yards rushing on 33 rushes. However, 9 completions on 15 attempts for 171 yards and touchdown pass off the arm of Bryce Jackson was just what the doctor ordered for a stifled A-Town offense.

The defensive player of the game without a shadow of a doubt was Charles Holback. He flew to the ball carriers and played with a reckless physicality that was unmatched on the field. Holback, #5, showed up and showed out. He had 18 total tackles, 4.5 sacks and a fumble recovery in this game alone. On the season Holback has 32 tackles, 27 assists, 2 tackles for loss, 4.5 sacks and one fumble recovery. The Panthers defense held Liberty to 47 yards rushing on 40 attempts and caused 3 turnovers. That Panther D is only giving up 16 points per game so far, this season and a total of 282.75 yards per game.

The Panther defense will have to play their best game of the season this coming Friday night as the Southside Christian Sabers come to Hite Stadium for a top 5 matchup. You'll never get a coach to admit it, but folks, ***this is the Region Championship game***. Your #1 ranked Abbeville Panthers vs the #5 ranked, undefeated, Southside Christian Sabers. You don't want to miss this game."

Sharpen Those Sabers, Claws Out

Clash of the undefeated, it just doesn't get any better than this for A-town loyalists. In front of a hometown crowd, what better setting to settle this thing. Come one, come all, the honorable Benjamin Greeson proclaims this "The Game" of the season and spreads the mustard his way.

"This is one of my favorite times of the year. Games that matter. Games that have a purpose. Games that lead you in a certain direction. Games that add to the trophy case. And that is exactly what we have in front of us tonight at Hite Stadium – Dennis Botts Field. The undefeated and 5th ranked Southside Christian Sabers (8-0) make the trek down from Greenville County to take on our #1 ranked, back to back defending state champion Abbeville Panthers. Call it what you want but the Region 2 AA championship is on the line tonight in a winner take all showdown. Let's see how the teams stack up against each other.

Southside Christian has historically been a 1A team. The last round of realignments bumped them into the 2A ranks and landed them in the region shared by Abbeville, Ninety Six and Liberty. Since there are only four football playing schools, it only takes a couple of weeks to find out how the region seeding's will unfold. Abbeville defeated Liberty (26-13) last week, and Southside Christian defeated Ninety Six (31-6). That sets up tonight's match-up, the only two undefeated region opponents left. Call it a winner take all, call it the fight for first, call it what you will, but tonight's game has huge playoff implications.

SSC runs a spread offense and they like to throw it around the park. Quarterback JW Hertzberg has 1,307 yards passing and 17 touchdowns to just 4 interceptions. The 6'3" sophomore QB has some help in the run game as well. Anthony McFadden and Mallory Pickney are both fast and effective ball carriers.

McFadden is a transfer from 5A Hillcrest High in Simpsonville. Both running backs have over 400 yards and they have combined for 21 rushing touchdowns on the season. You won't see SSC under center on the night. Three, four or five wide receivers will be their base offense and they will try to test the A-Town secondary. SSC's average score for the season is 43.6 while giving up 9.5 points per game.

The boys in Garnet are ready to go trophy chasing again. The Panthers could secure their 26th region championship with a win tonight and a Ninety Six loss. The Panthers defeated Liberty last week in a very businesslike fashion. There was not a lot of glitz and glamor within that game. Some spectators even suggested that the Panthers were flat or looked as if they were just going through the motions. It's going to take more than just going through the motions to get a win tonight. A championship is on the line and the players and the crowd should be at full throttle come game time. The Panthers will do what they do. A steady dose of the run game and some play action will stretch the SSC defense. Does SSC have the athletes to hang with A-Town? They think they do. SSC is coming into the game with a "disrespect" chip on their shoulder. Social media posts even suggest that SSC is calling tonight's trip into Hite Stadium a "statement game". So, who will make the statement tonight? Will SSC bring more energy and just want it more? Or will the Panthers prove once again that the road to the state championship runs through A-Town?"

Home is Where the Heart Belongs

Teams usually pick other teams that they feel confident they can defeat for homecoming. Maybe not in A-Town. The Wildcats are not only in the Panther's 2A conference, they have also played them once in zero week. Sometimes rolling those dice a second time can be a chance with odds not necessarily in your favor. Benji isn't one that often pays must attention to odds makers. He just calls them like he sees them. So here goes.

"Where has this season gone? It seems like Week Zero was yesterday and Panther Nation was gearing up to take on the Ninety Six Wildcats in the season opener. Friday night will mark the end of the regular season, but there is one common denominator. The Ninety Six Wildcats. The 2017 season has been polar opposites for the Panthers and Wildcats. Abbeville has lived up to its potential sporting an 8-1 overall record and a 2-0 region record, while Ninety Six is currently 3-6 in head coach Andre Woolcock's inaugural season.

Last week, Ninety Six knocked off a very tough Liberty squad by a 24-17 score. Reid McKellar picked off two Liberty passes and Evan Keller, who recently was moved to quarterback threw for a touchdown to beat the Red Devils on Senior Night at Ninety Six. The Wildcats, who are starting their third QB of the season because of injuries, have collected two of their three wins during the month of October. Still tough defensively, the injury bug has bitten the Wildcats and fielding a fresh eleven on offense and defense, just won't happen. The Wildcats will be playing many players both ways and that has been an issue for the entire season. Ninety Six is scoring 18.5 points per game while giving up 31.1 defensively for the season. Yet the Wildcats have an upset on their mind and would love nothing more than to swipe a Region Championship from their rival Panthers.

The Panthers are far from healthy either. Aside from losing then leading rusher Courtney Jackson, the Panthers have been dinged up pretty good. Trai Jones, sophomore starting offensive tackle, who has started every game this season, has a lower leg injury and is questionable for the Homecoming contest this coming Friday night. A myriad of other small, nagging injuries are starting to test the depth of this Panthers squad. As Coach Nickles would say, "We're beat to smithereens, but that's football"

The Panthers answered some questions coming off the bye week last week versus Southside Christian. The defense is still able to shut down what teams do best. And the Panther offense is still able to stress opponent's defenses on the interior and on the edge. Gabe Calhoun intercepted a Southside Christian pass and returned it 101 yards for a touchdown, only to have it called back because of a block in the back penalty. Nevertheless, that play swung momentum the Panthers direction and they never looked back, beating a very good SSC team 33-14. Quarterback Bryce Jackson had his best rushing performance of the season vs SSC and he will prove to be a big weapon for the Panthers rushing attack as we move into the playoff portion of the season. Before we look ahead to the playoffs, there is a region championship to play for. That happens Friday night at Hite Stadium, Dennis Botts Field. How fitting is it that the Panthers get a chance to win their 26th Region Championship at home, on homecoming versus one of their biggest rivals. The Panthers are 41-13 all-time vs. the Wildcats. These teams are very familiar with each other as this is the 7th meeting between the two schools on the gridiron in the last three years. Tons of playoff implications are at stake in this game. A Panther win clinches a #1 seed, a Region Championship and basically gives A-Town home field throughout the playoffs.

Will injuries and the pump and circumstance of Homecoming distract the Panthers from their task at hand? Will Ninety Six have enough left in the tank to upset the #1 ranked Panthers? We'll find out soon enough at Hite Stadium-Dennis Botts Field."

Regionally terrific, Benji deals a winning hand,

"The Abbeville Panthers secured their 26th Region Championship this past Friday night with a dominate 42-7 victory over region rival Ninety Six. The Panthers left no doubt as they scored early and often. Bryce Jackson saved his best passing game of the season for the Homecoming showdown with the Wildcats. Jackson finished the night 8-10 for 242 yards and 3 touchdowns. Running back Junior Rapley caught two of those touchdown tosses which covered 101 yards collectively. Rapley also moved ahead of Dooley Sanders for the leading receiving spot on the stat sheet. Rapley has rushed for 607 yards and 8 touchdowns this season. He has caught 15 passes for 389 yards and 4 touchdowns. Also, Rapley has added 239 punt return yards and 79 kickoff return yards on the season. His grand total yards from scrimmage is 1,314 total yards and 12 total touchdowns. The numbers and accolades are a testament to the scrappy, never-quit, fighting for every inch, tenacity that Rapley plays with on every down. Touchdown runs were added by Jermaine Blackwell, who has stepped in very well for the injured Courtney Jackson, and another touchdown run was added by budding star Dominick "The Bus" Washington. Congrats to Malik Washington on his first touchdown reception of the year as well.

The Panther defense was just plain nasty Friday night as well. Big hits, constantly playing behind the line of scrimmage, tight coverage in the secondary, running in packs to the football. It's a defense coordinator's dream scenario. Defensive Coordinator Tad Dubose put the Panthers in position to give up less than 200 total yards of offense and held the Wildcat quarterbacks to 3 of 14 passing for a miniscule 8 yards. That kind of defensive dominance is what will take you deep into the playoffs. The Panthers will be leaning on leading tacklers Malik Leach (99 total tackles), Dee Graham (98 total tackles), and Nate Temple (64 total tackles) to keep up the focused pressure on future playoff opponents. The Panther defense is only giving up 15 points per game. When you have an offense dropping 39.2 points per game, that spells wins. And let's not fool ourselves, Abbeville has played one of the toughest schedules in the state regardless of classification. The Panthers have played and beaten three 2A playoff teams, a #4 3A playoff team (Clinton) and beaten a #1 3A seed (Emerald). Lincoln Co will make the Georgia State playoffs and the only blemish on this this year's record is a seven-point loss to #1 seed 4A Hartsville. You've all heard the cliché, "Defense wins championships". Well this team has been tried and tested by fire and walked out smelling like a rose. Needless to say, I like our chances.

The Panther will host the St. Joseph's Catholic Knights on Friday night. I'll post a full round one preview later in the week. I've also attached a bracket for you to refer to has the playoffs progress.

I'd be remiss if I didn't say, a big congratulation to Emily Anna Smith (Maid of Honor) and Meg Botts, our 2017 Homecoming Queen. What an honor to be crowned the Queen on a field that bears her grandfather's name."

The Playoffs, Are You Ready for Some Football?

Phase 3, Round 1, there are seasons and then there are seasons. Abbeville has managed to navigate the waters mostly unscathed, 4A Hartsville being the only blemish. The season has not been without key injuries and pothole filled roadways. Thus far, persevering, the Panthers have managed to claw their way, their sights still on the golden ring, a third state title. Benji unable to help it otherwise, thinks about all the premonitions pointing to just that. Fact or fiction, one cannot say. Dreams are usually just dreams. Few have significant impact in your life. Pursuing fairy tale endings are not for the faint at heart. Benji prepares for the playoffs, his words, his way,

> "It's time to turn the page to Phase 3 of the season. It's playoff time. All those February days in the weight room. Those spring conditioning drills. The hot summer days at practice, melting away under the sweltering sun. All those days matter. They matter because they lead you to this time, this place, this phase. *The Playoffs*. Win or go home. Sudden death each and every week. Who has the will to continue? Who has the will to push through bumps and bruises? Who can handle adversity and pressure packed situations? 32 teams start their march tonight. But only one can hoist that State Championship trophy on December 1st. Only one team can have their names written forever in the history books. That march starts tonight at Hite Stadium – Dennis Botts Field as the back to back defending State Champ, #1 seed Abbeville Panthers will host the #4 seed St. Joseph Catholic Knights at 7:30pm.
>
> St. Joe's will come into The Hite tonight with a first-year head coach Brandon Bennett. Some of you will recognize that name. Bennett was a running back for the University of South Carolina. He also played in the NFL for the Cincinnati Bengals and the Carolina Panthers. His Knights will be bringing a 4-6 record with them. They finished 3rd in Region 1 AA. The Knights will spread the field offensively, meaning they will line up with four and five wide receivers. Yet their main goal will be to run the football. Their feature back is a 6'1" 210lbs running back by the name of Brandon Bennett Jr. The coach's son wears #2 and he will get the bulk of the carries. The Panthers and the Knights have two common opponents on the season. Both squads have played Southside Christian and Woodruff. The Panthers defeated both SSC and Woodruff while St Joes dropped both contests 51-13 to SSC and 49-13 to Woodruff. St. Joe's is limping in the playoffs. They have had some injuries like most teams this time of year. A depleted roster and a lack of depth have caused them to lose their last three. The Knights have averaged 22.1 points per game this season and given up 29.3 points per game. The Knights will have to bring their A+ game tonight to deal with the speed, size and physicality of the Panthers.

A-Town is beat up. Point blank period. There will be a handful of starters that miss tonight's game due to injury. Some more serious than others, however, a true test of quality depth will be on display tonight. Trai Jones and Jake Hill will be game time decisions. Both are college quality offensive linemen. Dooley Sanders, the lightning quick wide receiver and kick returner, who did not dress out last week, will also be a game time decision. The Panther defense will be counted on tonight to stop the St. Joe's attack and put the offense in good field position. On the flip side, the Panthers will try to control the line of scrimmage and methodically chew up game clock by running the football and imposing their will physically. The winner of the game will get to play the winner of the Chesterfield/Fox Creek.

So, the matchup will be, inquiring minds wish to know, Benji?

"The Panthers pound St. Joe's. The first round of the 2A playoffs have come and gone and the Panthers took care of a pesky St. Joseph's Catholic Knights squad by a score of 42-6. St Joe's didn't just lay down and accept their fate though. They came out swinging and in typical fashion, the Panthers had to answer the bell and establish themselves after the first couple of series. If you've paid attention to the ebbs and flows of the Panther games this season you've noticed that the Panthers are almost like a boxer that must get hit a couple times before he wakes up. It's worked for them thus far, as the Panthers now sit at 10-1 on the season and are squarely in the driver's seat, determining their own fate for the rest of this season. It's playoff time, win or go home. The Panthers want to keep playing awhile longer.

A-Town got on the board first with a Junior Rapley 51-yard touchdown run with 10:24 to go in the first quarter. Jermaine Blackwell followed that up on the next drive with a 23-yard TD run to put the Panthers up 14-0. St. Joes responded in the 2nd quarter with a touchdown run of their own. But that was the first and last time the Knights would visit the end zone as a stingy Panther defense dug their claws in and shut out the Knights for the rest of the game. The Panthers had three different backs go over 100 yards on the night. QB Bryce Jackson had 145 yards and touchdown, Rapley had 125 yards and two scores and Dominick "The Bus" Washington had 133 yards on just 12 carries. Collectively the Panthers had 557 yards on the ground.

It's been well documented just how banged up the Panthers are right now. Trai Jones and Jake Hill, offensive line starters did not play. Neither did wide receiver JaBryan "Dooley" Sanders, the fastest player on the team. Courtney Jackson hasn't played since week 6 of the regular season and that's just on the offensive side of the ball. Defensive starters are banged up and missing reps as well. So, what do ya do? Well, you call up some JV players and give them a shot. Folks, we've got some very young but very talented players just waiting to get their shot at the Friday night lights. Offensively we saw Cruz Temple get 5 carries for 62 yards and a touchdown. The freshman found an opening, sprinted down the sideline, gave a head fake, did a juke and rumbled for 59 yards before he was finally caught. That play set up a Quadarius Guillebeaux 28-yard touchdown run on the very next play. Not bad for a freshman and a sophomore. Guillebeaux's first varsity carry resulted in his first varsity touchdown. These guys, if they remain focused and hungry, will be stars on the gridiron very soon.

Defensively the Panthers saw the usual cast of characters impose their will. You also saw a first-time varsity player jump off the field at you. That player is freshman #43 Luke Evans. Some people are just football players. He's that guy. Still very young and has a lot to learn but the natural Linebacker instinct is there. He collected five tackles, five assisted tackles and one tackle for loss in limited defensive snaps and on the kickoff coverage team. Again, with focus and time in the weight room, the upside of Mr. Evans is tremendous. The Panthers will host the #2 seed Golden Rams of Chesterfield (9-2) next at Hite Stadium-Dennis Botts Field."

A Basketball Game on Grass

Now don't get your britches in a wad. The Panthers are not using medical marijuana to mask the pain of any injuries. Coach Hite had the solution for that and it didn't require a prescription. Times have indeed changed since those *Hitemen* days but not to the point that the players will be marching onto the field in a drug induced state. Coach Jamie Nickles was quoted as saying, "If you want to see a basketball game on grass, come out to Hite Stadium Friday night. These two teams are going to be ripping up and down the field."

Benji expands on this premise.

> "There is one thing that you can count on this time of year. Everybody left in the playoffs is a good football team. The field of 32 was cut in half last week. The 2nd round of the AA State Playoffs will continue this Friday night and the Panthers will face an outstanding Chesterfield team led by maybe the best overall athlete that the Panthers have faced yet this season.
>
> Savion Watson is the name you'll hear Panther PA announcer Craig Gagnon announce into the chilly night air from the historic press box in Hite Stadium. #15 Watson, a 6'1" 205lb senior, is the definition of a dual threat quarterback. He's thrown for 3,215 yards this season. He's also tossed 38 touchdown passes against only 9 interceptions. Watson is a running threat as well with 474 rushing yards and 11 touchdown runs. If you haven't done the math yet he's accounted for 49 total touchdowns so far this season. The cast around him his good too. Ricky Lockhart is a 6'0" 200lb wide receiver and he's hauled in 43 of Watson's passes for 1,028 yards and 10 touchdowns this season. The main receiving target on the Golden Rams offense is Shyhiem Rivers. He has 60 catches for 1,054 yards and 12 touchdowns. The Golden Rams, as you can see, likes to throw it around the park. Yet, they are still balanced offensively. James McBride is small in stature, but the 5'3" running back has amassed 915 rushing yards and punched it in the end zone twice this season. The Rams average 39.3 points per game while giving up 20.9 points on defense.
>
> Taking what Coach Nick has so eloquently stated, that tells you about all you need to know. The Panthers attack defense a little differently than their 2nd round counterparts. Panther fans near and far know that the boys from A-Town like to run it left, right and up the middle. They run it at you, around you and if need be, through you. The Panthers have four ball carriers averaging 6.5 yards per carry or better. All with over 70 carries on the season. The Panthers are averaging 39.4 points per game while giving up 14.1 points per game on defense.

That yards per carry average will be a big stat to watch Friday night. With Chesterfield having such an explosive, quick strike kind of offense, the Panthers will use their pound and ground to chew up the clock and control the tempo of the game. The Hogmollies will be counted on heavily in this game. The Panther offensive line should be back to full strength Friday night. Trai Jones and Jake Hill should return from injury, joining their Hogmollie brothers Connor Nickles, Griffin Lewis and Jacob Stone. The Panther defense will face a big challenge as well. Maintaining their pass rush lanes and keeping the Golden Rams QB in the pocket will be a key to victory. Watson is dangerous when he escapes the pocket and still has a run/pass option.

Pack the Hite Panther fans. Chesterfield is travelling over 3 hours to be here. That tells me they won't bring a huge crowd. Let's give our Panthers the best home field advantage possible, as they continue their march to their third straight State Championship and 9th overall. But, you can't win State without winning Round 2."

Final Four Madness

It's not supposed to look this easy, right? To reap the rewards, you must work for it. That doesn't mean the Panthers haven't earned every inch of turf. They certainly have and then some. One can never get too cozy when the season has advanced to this point though. Get too cocky and over confident, it can cost you as easily as becoming to comfy and complacent. Not to fear, the Panthers remain focused. Benji puts it in perspective with his view from the booth.

"The Panthers breezed through the first two rounds of the South Carolina 2A State Playoffs by a combined score of 103-41. We are down to the Upperstate's final four teams. So basically, the best of the best is what is left. Saluda and Lee Central will play in Saluda Friday night for a chance at an Upperstate Championship game appearance against the winner of the Abbeville – Cheraw game. This is a rematch of last year's quarterfinal game that was played in Cheraw. A game that Abbeville dominated 42-14. This season, the Braves will make the four-hour ride to Hite Stadium for a chance to keep their season alive.

The Cheraw Braves are 9-3 on the season. They finished tied for 3rd place with Chesterfield in Region 4-AA. Because of their finish, they picked up a #3 seed in the playoffs. Cheraw beat Gray Collegiate 28-18 in the first round and they whipped Blacksburg 40-6 last week. The three losses on their record came by way of an AAAA Marlboro County team who finished with a 3-8 record. They also lost two region games. The first to Lee Central, who won their region by a 14-7 score and they also lost to Chesterfield 38-21. In his 2nd year at the helm of the Braves, head coach Andy Poole has a 19-6 overall record. Now that you are a little more familiar with Cheraw's season, let's look at the players that will be on the field Friday night.

Bradley Holliman is the senior quarterback and catalyst of the team. His numbers don't wow you, but he's a good game manager that doesn't turn the ball over. He's thrown for 1,493 yards with 18 touchdowns and 8 interceptions on the season. He's completed 54% of his passes. Most of those have gone to #7, sophomore wide receiver Jalen Coit. He has 46 catches for 858 yards and 9 touchdowns on the season. The Braves offense is very balanced and very multiple. You may see them with 4 wide outs one play and in the wishbone the next play. The ball cow for the Braves is 5'11 170lb junior running back Quan Pittman. He has 256 carries for 1,542 yards and 17 rushing touchdowns on the season. He has ten 100-yard rushing games so far this season. Cheraw likes to feed Pittman the ball, draw your defense in tight, and then hit Coit on a play action pass. That's their bread and butter offensively. The real calling card for the Cheraw Braves however is their defense. Allowing 16.6 points per game, they are a tackle for loss machine. The Braves have a big, physical defensive line that usually eats up the offensive blocking and allows their linebackers to roam freely. Nick Dozier. #5, has 48 tackles and 21 tackles for loss this season. Starting linebacker #44 Tallon Campbell has an amazing 145 tackles on the season so far with 11 tackles for loss.

The Panthers have faced nearly every possible type of offense this season, so Cheraw won't do anything they haven't seen before. The biggest question for the Panthers is if they will have enough players to fill the roster. Nate Temple broke his arm in last week's game. The junior starting defensive end has 79 tackles, 9TFL and 2.5 sacks on the season. His status is doubtful this week. The Panthers offensive line is banged up. Dooley Sanders is a game time decision and so is starting quarterback Bryce Jackson who is dealing with a leg injury. JD Moore will get the start at quarterback should Jackson not be able to play. Moore is a very capable athlete when given the opportunity. Coach Nickles stated that this is the most injury plagued season that he can recall since his first season as an assistant in 1993. The game of football isn't for the faint of heart, that's for sure. The Panthers will have to match the physicality of this Cheraw team and just do what they do best. Run the ball, control the clock and try to get out of this game without any new injuries. It should be a great game and a great atmosphere with an Upperstate Championship game appearance on the line."

Julian McWilliams of Greenwood's Index Journal featured a story November 11th with the Panthers heading into the matchup with Cheraw. He reported that Abbeville baseball's Brice Jackson made it official, signing his national letter of intent to attend College of Charleston on a baseball scholarship. He had verbally committed to them in August. In the article, Bryce said,

> "It feels good knowing you don't have to worry about the (recruiting period) anymore. You know where you're going, and you can just work on getting better. And just to know you're going basically for free is good, too."

In the article, McWilliams stated that the College of Charleston didn't have a football team and that Brice's last game on the gridiron would be when Abbeville's season is finished. In the article it stated that with a love for both baseball and football, the future of being on the diamond only didn't seem to bother him as much as it once did after suffering a knee injury in Friday's 61-28 playoff win against Chesterfield. Brice was quoted as then jokingly saying,

> "After that hit on my knee, I don't want to play football (after this year). Anything can happen in football, easy."

Expanding on his role on the college diamond, Brice said that he just expected to go down there, get better and just work on getting better for the future and earning a spot. He will join former Erskine head coach Kevin Nichols, who is entering his first year as an assistant under first-year head coach Chad Holbrook. Holbrook resigned from his position as head coach at USC before coming on with the Cougars. According to Jackson, there has been a shift in culture at College of Charleston under the tutelage of Holbrook and Nichols, who are going to be vital in the reshaping of the program after former Cougars head coach Matt Heath was fired this offseason.

McWilliams included this statement from Brice, who was the South Carolina Baseball Coaches Association 2A State Player of the Year last season.

> "I read an article that said the players weren't really wanting to go to practice with the previous coach. But with the new coaches, they said they're liking it and enjoying it and having fun. The coaches are making it fun, and everyone wants to get better. So, I feel like I will go down there, get better and have fun."

Those present for Brice's signing were Christi Jackson, Coach Jamie Nickles, Abbeville principal Dr. Charles Costner, Meg Botts, Abbeville athletic director Tad DuBose, former Abbeville head baseball coach Mark Smith, Abbeville baseball head coach Nick Milford, Brad Jackson, Brooks Jackson, Kelly Jackson, Bryce Jackson, Carol Jackson and Steve Jackson.

Not by the Hair of My Chinny-Chin-Chin

Someone from Saluda posted a photograph on Facebook of goats grazing on a field implying Abbeville was preparing the home gridiron for the upcoming matchup. That wasn't taken too well by the A-Town loyalist. All is fair game in big games and rivalries, anything to push the buttons of opponents, get under their skin and inside their heads. Sometimes this works. Sometimes it backfires and just riles them up instead. Sometimes it is best to not get sucked into the hype and allow the game to play out without all the silly distractions.

Let's just be thankful and return this chapter over to Benji and his Upperstate Championship forecast.

> "Abbeville is rich in history and tradition. That's not exactly a bold statement or a new revelation. Just as sure as you'll eat turkey and dressing on Thanksgiving, it's become almost a safe bet that on the morning before you stuff your face, the Panther coaching staff will be orchestrating their yearly walk through inside Hite Stadium. That is good news for Panther players and fans alike, because that means that you're playing for an Upperstate Championship. That is the case again this season as the 12-1 Abbeville Panthers will host the 12-1 Saluda Tigers for the chance to play for the State Championship.
>
> That last sentence should sound familiar. This will mark the 3rd consecutive season that the Upperstate Championship game will come down to a battle between the Panthers and the Tigers. Abbeville has won the previous two meetings 36-14 in 2015, and 21-16 last season. It's a remarkable feat, the same two teams meeting for a chance to play for it all for three straight years. It's so rare that it's never happened in the 100 year history of Abbeville football. This will be the 19th Upperstate Championship appearance for the Panthers since 1950 and the 7th for the Tigers in the same time frame.
>
> Saluda has won 12 straight games this season after dropping their opener in Week Zero to Strom Thurmond 35-6. The Tigers cruised to a perfect 5-0 region record and captured the Region 2-AA championship and a #1 seed in the playoffs. The Tigers led by head coach Stewart Young (36-14 overall record) in his 4th season has become a mainstay in the playoff conversation as of late. The Tigers are averaging 33.3 points per game while giving up 16.5 points per game defensively. Sophomore quarterback Noah Bell, a lefty, gets a lot of the attention with his dual threat skill set. However, the Saluda defense is the calling card of this team. Big, fast and physical are the words that Abbeville head coach Jamie Nickles used to describe the Tiger defense. The Tigers found their way to the Upperstate Championship game

by defeating Pageland-Central 24-21 in round one. They beat rival Ninety Six 28-14 in the second round and knocked off Lee Central 30-26 last week in the Quarterfinals. They are now tasked with stopping the vaunted A-Bone offense and a Panther defense that is playing its best ball of the season.

The Panthers and Tigers are no strangers, not only in the playoffs, but they were once region foes, and will be again next season after realignment. The Panthers hold a 29-15 all-time record vs. Saluda. Ten of Saluda's 15 wins came before the 1970 season however and the Panthers have owned the series of late. The last Saluda win versus the Panthers came in the 2003 season, in a regular season matchup. The Panthers injuries have been well documented and slowly but surely the Panthers should be getting most of their starters back in some capacity this week. Quarterback Bryce Jackson, who did not play last week, will be a game time decision. Sophomore JD Moore filled in nicely for the injured Jackson in last week's 14-7 Quarterfinal win versus Cheraw. Moore carried the ball 22 times for 84 yards and commanded the offense well. It'll take another complete team effort to make it back to Benedict College."

Streaming is not for Wussies

Benji has laid out the pregame and postgame weekly and has done a wonderful job, hasn't he? Applaud him for this. Sometimes, however, there are those who can't be there that must rely on the colorful commentary delivered to us so effortlessly over the airwaves. As coauthor and pal, living at Myrtle Beach doesn't pose too many opportunities to make the weekly trek to A-Town or other destinations where the Panthers are playing those Friday nights under the lights. I did make it for the WCTEL Classic and the first home game though. The remainder of the games I utilized the streaming link on the WZLA website to listen in to the Panthers. Wayne and Benji were my eyes on the ball from the booth. I missed but one game streaming and that was the previous game because we were at New York City in a play. I texted my bud, Benji for updates.

Saluda versus Abbeville, now that one almost gave an old man a Fred Sanford, 'coming to see you Elizabeth moment.' I'm going to paint this canvas from my perspective, as a listener from 4 ½ hours away. I must say again that the boys in the booth did an excellent job in scaring the you know what out of me down the stretch. Here goes.

Saluda had taken an early 3-point lead, kicking the field goal on their first possession. Abbeville eventually pulled away, leading them 20-3 with as I remember it, 1:56 remaining on the game clock. They managed to score but missed the conversion, 20-7, no problem, right? Well it doesn't take a rocket scientist to figure out that Saluda is going to try an on-side kick. They did and Abbeville recovers. Saluda has no time outs. Game over, right? Abbeville can just run out the clock. Not so fast, Pilgrim. Saluda forces the fumble and quickly marches down the field for another score/ They go for two and fail to covert, score 20-15 with not that much time remaining. But, we know, there will be another on-side kick try coming.

Now let me be the first to tell you, it isn't fun sitting in front of a laptop, wearing a headset, visualizing something coming unraveled. Those in the booth refer to how many ways you can come up with three scores, no timeouts and less than two minutes remaining in the game. My bud, Benji made a comment at that 1:56 time that it was probably a good time to order those Benedict College tickets and set the GPS, the Panthers were heading back to the state title matchup. Wayne added that the Saluda faithful were heading to the gates. Now Benji was back tracking on that call, stating over the airways that he wished he hadn't said it. I'm sitting at the beach wishing the same thing, my gut tied in knots, envisioning the unimaginable.

As predicted Saluda kicks that dreaded on-side boot and this time recovers it. Still, no timeouts only make me feel marginally happy. Touchdown before that last second ticks off the clock makes it a 21-20 Saluda win and they are heading to the state championship game instead. You can't make this stuff up. Abbeville is this close to potentially being knocked out of a chance at a three-peat. Not wishing to be too pessimistic but the omen demons are beating the drum loudly about this time. Nothing for a coach potato to do but listen and hope. Saluda moves the ball ever so close, somehow milking that clock for all it is worth.

And guess what, Abbeville holds, game over. Now, buy those tickets and set that GPS. The Panthers are headed back to Benedict College and their attempt to make history. Ole T. Allen is just glad this puppy is over. I am sure a stadium full is breathing a sigh of relief too. Panther football, it just doesn't get any better.

The Booth

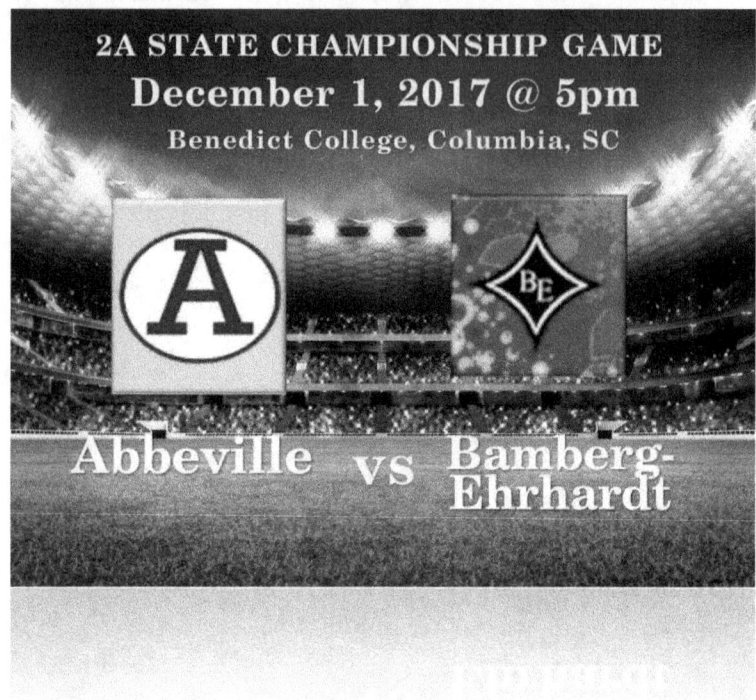

Benji sets up his first state championship stint with WZLA at Benedict College in Columbia, the state capitol.

> "When I was a kid, I didn't know that I was practicing. I was just having fun. I didn't have the foresight to know that what I was doing would eventually, years later, turn into a job that I absolutely love. Starting at about eight years old, I would turn the volume down on the TV in my room. I'd watch a Braves baseball game and instead of listening to Skip Carey or Don Sutton, I'd do the play by play myself. I had the roster memorized, the batting averages, home runs and RBI's were there on the screen. I had everything I needed in my bedroom to call a baseball game. Baseball season turned into football season and I'd do the same thing. Especially with the NFL. I looked up to Clemson's play by play voice Jim Phillips. I wanted his job. I wanted to travel with the team and be the voice of the Tigers. How cool, I thought.
>
> Fast forward to today, nearly 30 years later and here I am. Doing play by play for a few different media outlets and enjoying every second of it. I started doing full time play by play for McCormick High School football. My broadcast partner and good friend Bobby Hamby helped us land that gig

and we thoroughly enjoyed our time with the Chiefs. An opportunity presented itself in the spring of 2017. Sadly, the voice of Abbeville Panther baseball, Keith 'Honky' Hall had passed away the previous September. His voice floating over the airwaves of WZLA will never leave my thoughts and my heart. Honk was a dear friend and he's missed terribly. I had the chance to be Honk's color commentary partner on baseball broadcasts the last year that he got to call Panther baseball. I learned so much from him. The following season I was asked to take over the play by play duties in Honk's absence. Talk about big shoes to fill. I was nervous at first, but then the flow of the game naturally takes the nerves away. Fast forward to the 2017 football season and the powers that be asked if I would step into the booth as the color commentary partner of The Voice of the Panthers Wayne Stevenson. Wayne has called every Abbeville football game since Abbeville football hit the airwaves in 1992. It was an honor and such a fun season to broadcast the games with Wayne. It's like I was living out a dream. I was getting to do the job that I love doing, for my alma mater. I just felt so blessed that I was given that opportunity.

When you follow a team for 15 weeks, funny things happen from time to time. I inadvertently caused one of those funnies and it happened during the State Championship game. Abbeville Athletic Director Tad Dubose emailed me the name and number of the person that I needed to contact at Benedict College, the site of the 2017 State Championship game. I needed to tell the media director at Benedict College what all we needed to preform our broadcast from their facilities. It's common practice, so I thought "No big deal". When I called the Media Director, he asked a few questions about our needs."

> "Do you guys need a dedicated phone line?"

> "No sir. Our system runs off Bluetooth. We don't need a phone line at all."

> "Do you guys need a dedicated internet line?"

> "No sir, we have a hot spot available if we need it. We are pretty much self-sufficient, other than a power supply." (an outlet – somewhere to plug in a phone etc.)

The Media Director continues,

> "Okay well I tell you what. I know you're the home team, so you should get the home radio booth. But your opponent's radio team needs all that stuff. They need a phone line and an internet line, so I'm placing them in the home radio booth. But we'll take care of you. You'll be in a nice area of the press box. Oh, and you can't use

the visitor radio booth. Television cameras and whatnot will be in there. But don't worry. I got you covered."

"This was my first experience of calling a game at the State Championship site, so I didn't really know what I was or was not agreeing to. I was just happy to be there. Now, fast forward to game day.

We show up early, get our media passes at the gate and make our way to the press box area of Benedict College after exchanging hello's down on the field with other Panther faithful, players and coaches. We got on the elevator and went to what we thought was the media floor of the press box. You've got to understand, we are not accustomed at all, to being in press boxes with elevators. We are calling 2A football in South Carolina, okay. Some schools have very nice facilities, some not so nice. Honestly, the facilities at Abbeville High are in serious need of upgrading, but we'll save that conversation for another day and another book.

Long story short. We got off on the wrong floor. We were walking around the school's President's personal box. Quickly after realizing that, and in hopes that we were not going to get arrested for trespassing, we found the media floor of the press box. We passed the home radio booth. We passed the PA announcers booth. We walked through the lobby and past the TV and away radio booth. We saw nothing noting where we were supposed to be. Did they forget we were coming?

A nice gentleman emerged from around a corner and you could tell he worked there at the college. We asked him where our designated broadcasting area was located. He pointed at the windows there in the lobby area. We were in the newspaper/print media area. Some people call it the "bull pen". There is a long table top desk with nice chairs. About 20 writers could comfortably sit and work there. There was ample room for a laptop or a note pad. Just in front of that and down three steps were the exact same desktop and chairs. This work area was affixed to the windows of the press box/ This is where we were to do our game broadcast from. Most broadcast teams prefer to open the windows of the press box to get a feel for more of the game atmosphere. You can hear the hits, you can hear the fans erupt in cheers, all the ooohhh and aahhhhs come through much better when the windows are open. So, we slid open the big impressive college press box window, just like we would at any game.

Being new to the whole media world I didn't realize that there are certain unwritten rules of the press box. Pretty much anything is fair game if you are sequestered in your own personal area. Like in the home or visitor's booth. You have a door that you can close, and you can whoop and holler as much as you want inside your own personal room. However, the Bull Pen is a little different. It's mostly newspaper and website media members. Except for Abbeville's Henry Green, who was there covering the game for the Press and Banner, the other writers are not attached to either school. In other words, they didn't care who won or lost. They are just there doing their job. One of the unwritten rules that I mentioned earlier is there is no "cheering" or outbursts allowed in the Bull Pen. It's supposed to be like a library. Sure, people are talking and saying hello, but outbursts and pulling for a certain team is frowned upon.

Fast forward to the game.

WZLA expanded their coverage of Abbeville Football this season for the first time. Presently, The WCTEL Panther Tailgate Show airs an hour before kickoff. Bobby Hamby and Jerry Catoe host that show and they do a great job of interviewing fans, players, coaches, and giving the run-down of games around the state. They preview the Panthers opponents and set the stage for the upcoming game. After the Tailgate Show ended, Bobby and Jerry sat behind us, at the elevated desk top and watched the game. The game was a defensive struggle. Neither team could find the endzone and the game was scoreless into the 4th quarter. We pick it up in the forth quarter. The following is the transcript from the booth coverage, Wayne Stevenson and Benji Greeson, condensed and commercial free."

Wayne,

> "The Panthers have to punt, and Bamberg prepares to receive the punt back around their own 37-yard line. Panthers need a good snap to Beauford and it's a good snap. It's a nice high kick to the 25 and it takes an Abbeville bounce and is picked up there at the 18-yard line. It's taken to the outside yard line and nobody is there and down the far side of the field. There he goes. That's going to be the first score of the ballgame. It's a touchdown on the punt return from Bamberg-Earhart. They draw first blood at the 9:34 mark in the football game, leading it 6-0.

Benji,

> "What an absolute beautiful punt off the foot of Beauford, the best all night. We're thinking we are about to pin them back inside the 10-yard line right here. Instead, they picked it up and there was no coverage on the right side of the field."

Wayne,

> "This is the type of game that a punt return can make or break the difference in the ballgame. The try for the point afterwards is good. With 9:34 to go in the football game it's Bamberg 7, the Panthers

nothing. We'll take a break. When we come back the Panthers will get the football with 9:34 to go in this football game."

Wayne,

"With 9:34 to go Bamberg leads with a score of 7 to nothing. Rapley and Sanders are deep to receive the kick from Bamberg. They're standing around their own 20-yard line. Here's the kick. It's a short kick recovered by one the Panthers at the 30-yard line. That's as far as we will go, right there. The Panthers now with their backs to the wall, they'll have receivers on the nearside and Jackson will work out of the shotgun. On a reverse to Sanders from the right side and Sanders is off and running. He falls at the 50-yard line with nobody in front of him. The turf monster got him at the 45-yard line. He would have scored easily on that play and we would have had a tied game, nobody around him and he gets tripped up and falls down."

Benji,

"We have everybody in this stadium on their feet."

Wayne,

"Abbeville will have it at the Bamberg 46-yard line. This time off the left side…"

Benji,

"Junior Rapley had a good carry there. With 8:50 left in this ballgame you don't have to panic. It's not a two-minute warning situation. You don't have to score right this second, but the points have been at a premium tonight. Calm down. Relax. Play our game."

Wayne,

"Second down and six yards to go from the Bamberg 43-yard line. Brice Jackson with the ball picks up the first down, down to the 35-yard line."

Benji,

"That punt return for a touchdown woke up the Abbeville crowd. That run from Rapley really got them going."

Wayne,

"Again, Abbeville at the 35-yard line, split to the right side, down to the 25-yard line, first down, Abbeville."

Benji,

"Blackwell, one of the faster running backs here, can run it to the wide side of the field. He's the team leader in touchdowns. They rattled this Bamberg defense. I think they're going to take a time out here."

Wayne,

"We'll take it with them. With 7:59 to go in the football game, it's Bamberg 7, the Abbeville nothing. This is Panther Football on WZLA."

Wayne,

"First and ten, Germaine Jackson on a run to the 16-yard line; he'll get 8 yards out of that. Second down and two yards to go, Panthers at the 16-yard line of Bamberg. And this time on the quarterback keeper, Brice Jackson will be tripped up before he can get back to the line of scrimmage. This will bring out third down and they'll lose a couple back to the 18-yard line. It'll be third down and four. 7:11 left in this football game. Bamberg leads it 7 to nothing. Panthers will go with a receiver to either side. Jackson with the football, he'll look to the right side and dive to the 15-yard line. It'll be short of the first down."

Benji,

"It's forth and a yard for the Panthers. I don't think they have a choice right here. They've got to try to punch this one in with about 6 1/2-minute left in this state championship football game. Here they go. They're lining up. Let's do it."

Wayne,

"Yeah, they might not get another chance. It's fourth down and one for the Panthers. Rapley starts in motion. He'll reset on the right side. The Panthers will take a time out and we'll take it with them with Bamberg 7, Abbeville, nothing."

Wayne,

"It's fourth and one for the Panthers with 6:15 to go in the football game. Abbeville is down 7 to nothing. The football is in the middle of the field at the Bamberg 15-yard line. Panthers send the offense back out."

Benji,

"That is a full yard that they have got to get right there, Wayne."

Wayne,

"Rapley on the right side, Blackwell on the wing on the left side, Dominick Washington is the full back. They need a yard. This time they give it off to the right side and we've got the ball inside the ten to Germaine Jackson, first down Abbeville, first and goal."

Benji,

"Got the ball on a little sweep there and we barely found a hole for a 10-yard gain."

Wayne,

"First and goal on the 5-yard line. Blackwell is in motion and he's got it. He's tripped up and gets back to the line of scrimmage. And, that's all. Second down and goal."

Benji,

"There's all world linebackers coming up to make the stop for Bamberg. What a game! What a game!"

Wayne,

"5:37 to go in the football game. It's second down and goal from the Panther's five. Rapley and Blackwell on the wing, and it's Rapley in motion with the football and he turns it up inside, down to the 1-yard line. Junior Rapley was the ball carrier and its third and goal."

Benji,

"You need three feet right here. What do you do? It's third down and a yard, maybe a yard and half. It looks like they are going to put the ball right at the 1-yard line. It will be a full yard here. You got let the big dogs eat. The offense line has been stellar all season. Just tell them to go get it boys."

Wayne,

"Two plays to get a yard, 4:50 in the football game. It's third down and goal from the one-yard line. Sanders split out wide to the right side. Rapley in motion. He's got it. Touchdown Abbeville! Junior Rapley takes it in with 4:33 to go in the ball game. Now they have to try the all important extra point to tie the game."

Benji,

"I saw a ref on the right side drop a beanbag and I held my breath. I thought there may have been a fumble after seeing him drop it but Rapley goes in for the score with 4:33 for the Panthers first offensive touchdown."

Wayne,

"What a critical extra point. Bryce Jackson to hold it for Dillon Beauford to try to tie this football game with 4:33 to go. Conner Nickles to snap it back. It's a good snap. Beauford's kick is in the air. It's good! With 4:33 to go, it's Abbeville 7, Bamberg 7."

Benji,

"I tell you what, that young man right there, you talk about ice water in the veins, staying cool and collective with the championship riding on an extra point. And, he kicked it through like he's been doing it for 50-years."

Wayne,

"Center of the goal posts too."

Benji,

"True. Very True."

Wayne,

"Dillon Beauford, a sophomore, kicker for the Panthers…wow! 4:33 to go in this football game and we're tied at 7."

Benji,

"I tell you. We have a barnburner here. If there has ever been an old fashion donnybrook, we got it."

Wayne,

"Dillon Beauford, the man, the man that just kicked the extra point and now he's kicking off for the Panthers. Receivers back deep for the Red Raiders. It will be interesting to see what the Panthers do with this kickoff. They want to prevent the return and it's short, high, good kick. It's taken by one of the upbacks at the 25-yard line. He'll be knocked down when he comes…fumble! Panthers have the football! The Panthers have it! It's the first turn over of the football game by either side."

Benji,

"You've got people going crazy here in the stands!"

"Wayne,

> "Abbeville has the ball at the 30-yard line of Bamberg-Earhart with 4:21 to go in the football game."

Benji,

> "They are ninety feet away from making history right here, Wayne."

Wayne,

> "Receivers split wide, Blackwell to left, Rapley to the right; first and ten from the Bamberg 30-yard line. Motion to the right side, Blackwell. Jackson punches his way to the 25-yard line. They'll mark it at the 26. We'll go for 4, grind it out"

Benji,

> "Absolutely. Don't leave a second on this clock if you can help it, man."

Wayne,

> "Bamberg is out of timeouts."

Benji,

> "They cannot stop it except for maybe an injury timeout. They are trying to get him off the field right now. That's one of their wide backs, number 33. He's been making plays left and right all night. He's played both ways all night as well. He limps off the field."

Wayne,

> "Second down and six yards to go for Abbeville. We have it at the Bamberg 26-yard line. Sanders set out to the left side. Rapley is in motion. Rapley's got the football. To the outside, the ten, five…touchdown! Touchdown! Junior Rapley! Junior Rapley! Junior Rapley! Takes to the house. Abbeville leads 13 to 7."

Benji,

> "Unbelievable change of circumstances! They are celebrating on the Abbeville sidelines right now."

Wayne,

> "I admit. I got a little excited."

Benji,

> "If you are here and you're not excited, you're dead. Something's wrong with you. This is amazing."

Wayne,

> "Brice Jackson to hold it for Dillon Beauford, to put up point #14. The snap is back. The kick is good! With 3:32 to go in this football game, it's Abbeville 14, Bamberg 7. We'll take a break and then the Panthers will kick it off."

Wayne,

> "Wow, 3 ½ minutes to go. Wayne Stevens here with Benji Greeson and we're both out of breath."

Benji,

> "I'm worn out."

Wayne,

> "A nothing to nothing football game with about six minutes to go in the fourth quarter, and here's Abbeville leading it 14-7. Dillon Beauford to kick it off for Abbeville. He has it teed up at the 40-yard line with 3 ½ minutes to go."

Benji,

> "Looks like it's going to be another pooch kick by Beauford."

Wayne,

> "They put everyone up and Beauford to kick it for Abbeville. He kicks it over everybody's head and it's into the end zone for the touchback. Nice call right there."

Benji,

> "Three yards from the ball and what a toe to put it in the end zone."

Wayne,

> "You have to remember, Dillon is just a sophomore."

Benji,

> "That's unbelievable."

Wayne,

> "With 3 ½ minutes to go, Bamberg with the football at their own 20-yard line, and Abbeville hanging onto a 14-7 lead. Abbeville is trying to clinch their third state championship in a row, but they have some work to do.

They've got to stop this Bamberg team. They'll have it on the hash mark on the far side. It's a quarterback keeper. He finds a little running room for 10-12 yards off the right side. It moves the chains, gets out of bounds and it stops the clock with 3:25 to go."

Benji,

"Williams is the leading rusher for this Bamberg offense. He has over 900 yards rushing for the year."

Wayne,

"He's about the only one for that offense. He picked up 14 on that play. It's first and 10 from their own 33-yard line. They'll put two and two split out wide to either side. Williams is in the shotgun. Williams to his left. He'll take the football and they ride it off straight ahead and he'll pick up about 4 or 5 yards. Clock runs with 3:15 to go. Bamberg is out of timeouts. They got 5 on the play. It will be second down and 5."

Benji,

"Well he's getting in the turf there. I want to see how quick they can get this play off. This is just hurry up and go mode."

Wayne,

"We're under 3 minutes to play and they are taking their time, which is not an offensive tool to go to. It's second down and 5 from their own 39-yard line. Williams is in the shotgun. Takes the football and hands it off straight ahead and they picked up the first down at the 45-yard line. That will stop the clock momentarily while they move the chains at 2:36."

Benji,

"34 seconds it took from the time Williams went down until the ball was snapped; 34 seconds in between plays."

Wayne,

"That gives you about six plays if they keep that up. They start the clock with 2 ½ minutes and counting, and they still haven't come to the line of scrimmage. First and 10 from their own 46-yard line. Three receivers to the left side, one to the right. Williams will get the football and he'll take it himself. No, actually Williams handed it off that time and I thought he had been knocked down for at loss, but they went straight ahead with it, picking up 7-yards."

Benji,

"Tyris Falls and Nate Temple thought he had it too because they rode him down pretty hard in the backfield. The tackle was made out there by Carson Smith, in again on the tackle for the Panthers."

Wayne,

"It's second down and 3 from the Abbeville 47-yard line, minute and 54 and counting. It's a quarterback keeper to the right side. Williams is dragged down as he gets to around the 41-yard line. They'll get the first down. There's a flag down. This may be holding against Bamberg. It stops the clock with 1:42 to go. The flag was thrown back at the 44-yard line. It's going to be holding against Bamberg. I don't think there is a person in the stadium sitting down right now."

Benji,

"Yeah to that. Everybody is on the edge of their seats with 1:42 left."

Wayne,

> "They'll mark off the penalty to the Bamberg 46-yard line. It will be second down and inside 10-yards to go with 1:42 to go in this football game. Two receivers wide to the left, one to the right side. Williams will hand it off straight ahead and they don't have much running room. They'll pick up about 3. The clock is ticking, under a minute and a half to go."

Benji,

> "Temple absolutely lowered the boom on the running back. That was a hard 2-yards he just picked up. Somebody stopped the clock."

Wayne,

> "Somebody did top the clock. Maybe Bamberg had a timeout remaining that they had missed on the scoreboard. I don't know why but we'll take it with them, a quick break, with Abbeville leading 14-7. We'll be right back.

Wayne,

> "Abbeville called that time out to get their defense thinking alike. Bamberg has got to think about making a first down. They're a third down and 20 with a minute, 21 to go. They are at their own 48-yard line. Williams is out of the shotgun with three receivers to the short side, one to the wide side. Williams with the football, wants to throw, with one on one coverage down field. A receiver out there, ball batted away. A beautiful defensive play over there on the far side by Rayford. You can't play one on one defense any better than that. It's forth down and 8, the game rest on this play right here."

Benji,

> "Rayford on an island out there by himself, and you said it, Wayne; you can not draw better coverage than that. He ran stride for stride with the wide receiver, the ball was in the air; he turned around and looked for the ball, goes up and knocks it away. Absolute, fundamental coverage."

Wayne,

> "If they don't make this first down, Abbeville wins the state championship for the third time in a row. They need 8 yards. They have three receivers wide to the left side. Quick toss to the right side, intercepted at the 35. He'll put a knee down and the Panthers are going to win the state championship. We have 1:04 to go. The Panthers have won this championship, having gotten up off the deck. Come from behind."

Benji,

"Oh, my goodness, I don't even know what to say. I'm at a loss of words here. This is historical, in their 100th year history of Abbeville football. No team has won three in a row."

Wayne,

"And I got excited and didn't pick up the number during the interception."

Benji,

"I think that was JD Moore, if I'm not mistaken, number 15."

Wayne,

"All the Panthers have to do now is come out and get in the protect formation and win their third state championship in a row.:

Benji,

"Unbelievable. Ninth state championship in their school history. It's unbelievable. I want to talk about, Wayne, we can do it. Let's talk about a dynasty. This is unbelievable. This team has accomplished so much all year long. What an incredible testimony to the coaches and everyone who has worked so hard this year."

Wayne,

"In the protect formation here's the snap. The clock goes under one minute and counting. They may have to do that one more time. You can hear the Abbeville crowd down here as that clock runs down to 45-seconds. Clock is running with 40-seconds, it's third down. Coach Nickles just received a little bit of a Gatorade bath. Tony Temple just got the full force of a bath."

Benji,

"Looks like they just got Wayne Botts over there on the sidelines."

Wayne,

"There's not enough Gatorade down there to go around."

Benji,

"Coach Debose just took a bath. Unbelievable. What a historical night here a Benedict College."

Wayne,

"The clock winds down and Abbeville wins it by a score of 14-7, three state championships in a row, back to back to back. Congratulations to Coach Jamie Nickles and his staff, to the players, and just like that; it's unbelievable when you think about that. A come from behind to get this win; what can you say but congratulations Panthers. We'll take a quick break and then we'll wrap this one up for you. You're listening to Panther Football on WZLA-FM."

Benji explains,

"Bamberg returned a punt for a touchdown and took the lead by scoring the first points of the game with 9:34 to play. Abbeville marches down the field on their very next drive and scores to tie the game. Obviously, we, the radio broadcast crew got a little excited when the Panthers scored. I didn't think anything of it. On Abbeville's next possession, All Star running back Junior Rapley broke free for a 26-yard touchdown run to put the Panthers ahead with very little time remaining in the State Championship game. The Voice of the Panthers Wayne Stevenson is calling the action by shouting,

"Touchdown Panthers!!!! Touchdown Panthers!!! Junior Rapley!!! Junior Rapley!!! Oh My Gosh!!!! Junior Rapley!!! The Panthers lead!!! The Panthers lead!!!"

Through all the commotion, you can hear Jerry Catoe, co-host of the Tailgate Show screaming in the background,

Bobby Hamby is shouting

"He's high stepping into the end zone, touchdown, touchdown, touchdown"

All four of us are jumping up and down, high fiving, basically screaming like the thousands of Panther fans in attendance. The roar from the crowd at that moment was nearly deafening. All that noise was rushing in through the open press box window. Right into the Bull Pen, where four Abbeville radio guys are doing everything we can to unknowingly break the unwritten rules of the press box. We were just short of doing cartwheels and back flips in an area that is supposed to be like a library.

No one reprimanded us. Actually no one even looked up at us. They probably thought we were a bunch of backwoods idiots, but we didn't care. Our Panthers had just brought home the 9th State Championship in school history and the 3rd in a row in dramatic fashion. You couldn't tell us anything. We were on cloud nine and never gave the Bull Pen rules a second thought. I do know one thing is probably a given. Should the Panthers make it back to Benedict College for another State Championship game, we'll probably be gifted with our own radio booth. With a door that shuts.

Hamby-Cato-Stevens-Greeson

Stevens and Greeson in the Benedict College Booth

And now, here's Benji.

"2017 State Champions, **Dynasty**. That's the adjective that is being used after the Abbeville Panthers won their third consecutive AA State Championship, and rightfully so. The boys from A-Town endured a physical, knockdown, drag out slobberknocker of a game Friday night at Charlie W Johnson Stadium on the campus of Benedict College in Columbia. Athletic Director and defensive coordinator Tad Dubose celebrate a 3rd straight state title."

Let the celebrations begin…

Coach Tad Dubose in a magical moment

Coach Jamie Nickles, choking back tears with five or six television cameras in his face, described his team as having a "heart of a champion". No truer words have been said. Starting at a 7-0 deficit, after giving up a punt return for a touchdown, late in the fourth quarter, the Panthers decided that their season was not over, and they were not going out in any other way, then a champion. The Panthers found a way to get speedster Ja'Bryan "Dooley" Sanders the ball on a reverse and flipped the field position, on their way to the first offensive touchdown of the game. A fumbled kickoff recovery on the ensuing kickoff followed by a 26-yard sprint by Junior Rapley for a touchdown put the game away. The Bamberg defense grabbed all the headlines leading into the game. Only allowing 79 points for the entire season, they were without a doubt the best defense the Panthers had to play all season. However, the Panther defense overshadowed the Red Raider defenders in Friday's Championship bout. The Panther defense allowed only 89 total yards and pitched a shutout. By a 14-7 score, the seniors on this 100th season of Panther football etched their name in the history books by becoming the first class at AHS to ever win three straight State Championships. The numbers that this class has put together are staggering.

Through their three-year state championship run, the Panthers has collected a 40-3-1 overall record. The Panthers have not lost to another AA team since a loss to Strom Thurmond in 2015. This group of Panthers have also won 15 straight playoff games, again another school record. They have defended their home field as well. The last time that the scoreboard in Hite Stadium didn't reflect a Panther win was October 17, 2014. That's a streak of 26 consecutive home games without a loss.

As a program, the Panthers won their 5th State Championship in the last 7 years. The Panthers are tied for 2nd place with Dillon for all-time playoff wins (82). The Panthers now have NINE Football State Championships which ranks them 3rd all-time in the state regardless of classification. Only Byrnes (11) and Lake View (10) have more championships. The Panthers won their 25th Region Championship this season, which ranks them 5th all-time in the state and the Panthers finished with a 14-1 overall record giving them their 28th 10+ win season, which is good enough for 2nd most all-time in the state. Head Coach Jamie Nickles won his 5th State Championship as head coach of the Panthers. The win ties Nickles with Hall of Famer, the late Dennis Botts with 147 wins, the most in school history. The win also moved Nickles into a 4th place tie in all-time state title wins in the history of South Carolina High School Football. One word can sum up the state of the Panther program.

Elite…

The Panthers, as you can see have been rich in history and tradition for many years. 100 to be exact. This group of seniors upheld the winning tradition of Abbeville football, and raised the bar to a new level of expectation. It's been a pleasure covering this fine group of young men and coaches all season long. It's sad to see this journey come to an end, but what a way to go out. Back to Back to Back State Champions has a nice ring to it. We are only 256 days until we kickoff the 2018 season, Week Zero at Lincoln County and begin the march for that pinky ring.

Stay tuned for more AHS sports coverage all year long. Also, a big thank you for reading our coverage. Since the beginning of football season atownpanthers.com has received over 12,000 reads. We appreciate all the dedicated readers and fans near and far. Until next time"

As posted in the Greenwood Index Journal

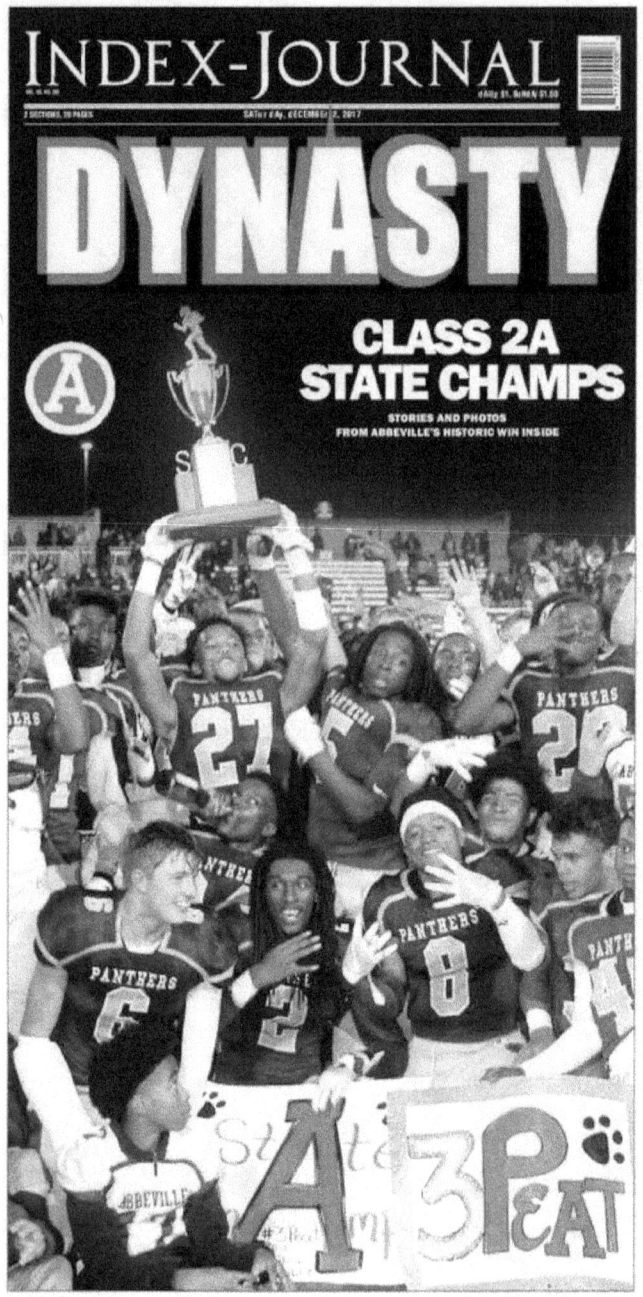

Legends Never Lie, A Wayne's World Moment

Benji, for reasons he could not explain, had this urge to ride by the stadium. Nearing dusk, a nasty day had been brewing, a winter storm named Benji by the Weather Channel, dumping snow from Texas to northeastern states. He pulled into the parking lot above Hite Stadium and sat there for a couple of minutes reflecting. His first season stint in the broadcast booth had been one he'd not soon forget. Before he realized what he was doing, Benji stood at the back gate with key in hand, unlocking it. Taking a deep breath, he entered and walked over to the steps leading to Dennis Botts field.

Benji marveled at the scoreboard, eight years of state championships displayed beneath it. Soon there would be a 9th. This place oozed with greatness and history. Traditional values were grown and nurtured here. Sure, the coaches had done it their way for generations, all successful in their own way. Football was not just a game here. Boys became men, men with values, respect and faith. The wind whipped up suddenly, almost whisking Benji's hat off his head. This was not an ordinary wind though. Benji sensed something magical. Possibly he was just getting caught up in the moment, the realization of three straight championships and the dawn of a football dynasty. Still, special moments deserved to be cherished.

The scoreboard suddenly came on, oddly aglow. It was strange to see it lit when the field lights were not on. Even more bizarre, the scores of the final game played in Columbia were displayed. The Chicago Bulls music blared loudly over the speakers. Benji craned his neck, looking up at the booth, figuring this smelled like a Hamby trick. This required a full investigation, Benji making his way to the booth's stairs. Climbing the steps, he would have the perpetrator cornered and red handed. That ah-ha moment didn't happen. The booth was completely empty. Talking about just a tad bit spooky. Benji leaned out of the booth, again staring at the scoreboard. Odd, an eerie mist hoovered just below it almost at ground level. He watched as this blanket of fog drifted onto the football field, a misty blob making its way center field hash mark by hash mark.

Benji couldn't take his eyes off this supernatural feeling phenomena. It moved the full length of the field hoovering in a defined formation. It then passed underneath the field goal at the opposite end of the field and up the hill towards the athletic building. Impossible, fog doesn't move like this, thought Benji. He glanced back at the scoreboard and just like that the music stopped and the scoreboard went blank. Benji quickly turned his attention back to the opposite end of the stadium. His jaw dropped.

Just under the Panther on the back wall of the athletic building, nine figures formed from the mist. Scarier, as they took shape he recognized them. From left to right were Fletcher Ferguson, Coach Tommy Hite, Coach Dennis Botts, Larry Ray, Bob

Winn, Yoda (Bobby), Poots and Pidgy Dubose, and Honk. Each held their right hand over their heart and their left hand in the air, three fingers clearly in view. So surreal, blessings indeed, thought Benji. Spirits of the past had guided him through the season, confident history would be made and now there they were, united, paying a final A-Town tribute.

"2017, the best team ever to play for Abbeville," came a spiritual whisper from behind, one belonging to Asa Griffin.

Benji nodded before turning to see what he expected to see, nobody standing there. When he returned his attention to the hilltop, the nine figures and fog were gone. The pressure on his chest became too much to bear. Bouncing and laughing, his daughters woke him from his slumber on the couch. Benji smiled and grabbed them, enjoying the reprieve before the quest would begin for number 10 and a fourth consecutive title, the dawn of a dynasty in full throttle.

Reflections, Accolades and Honors

Greenwood's Index Journal on December 25, 2017 voted the Number 1 Sports Story in the Lakelands Abbeville's second-half surge against Bamberg-Ehrhardt to win its third consecutive state championship. The article written by David Roberts states that the state title is Abbeville's fifth of the decade and ninth in program history featuring the two best teams in Class 2A, adding that the game seemed to have two of the best defenses in the state.

Roberts wrote, Abbeville couldn't crack Bamberg-Ehrhardt's defense and Bamberg-Ehrhardt was unable to solve Abbeville's defense, and that the two teams carried a 0-0 tie into the fourth quarter, where the Red Raiders and Panthers combined to score 21 points. Bamberg-Ehrhardt's 79-yard punt return for a touchdown was the first score of the game, which was 10 yards fewer than Bamberg-Ehrhardt's total yards in the game.

Roberts continued in his article stating how Abbeville running back JR Rapley had been instrumental on the Panthers' two scoring drives. He had gotten the ball to the goal line on the first score before fumbling it into the end zone. Luckily wide receiver JaBryan Sanders fell on the ball to tie the game. The Panthers caught a break on the kickoff when Red Raiders wide receiver Jerrald Manigault, who scored on the 79-yard punt return earlier in the quarter, muffed the kickoff, which led to a Rapley touchdown from 26 yards out.

Roberts reported that with 3 ½ minutes remaining in the game, Rapley knew the 14-7 lead would hold. Rapley was quoted in the article as saying,

> "I knew on the next possession my defense was going to put a stop to their offense. I just knew it. We put them on our back and they put us on their back. It was a team win."

Roberts made the following comments in the Index in closing,

One interesting note about Abbeville's three consecutive state championships is the team's flexibility at quarterback. Joseph Battle led the Panthers to a title at the position in 2015, then Jamie Gray took over in 2016. Bryce Jackson moved from wide receiver to play quarterback this year, meaning the Panthers have broken in a new quarterback each of the last three years. And they'll have to do it again next year too. Can the Panthers make it four in a row?

Julian McWilliams from the Index interviewed Rapley and he reflected on how he had looked for answers as to how to finally break free of the stifling Red Raiders defense. Rapley had needed some alone time to sort this out so he walked over to the sidelines. Not one to throw in the towel with only 17 yards rushing in the first three quarters, he had to figure out how he was going to right this. He had dedicated the state title run to his uncle who had been recently involved in a car accident. He also wanted this for his teammate, Cortney Jackson who had suffered a year ending injury. The chance to three-peat loomed large. From the sidelines on the 30-yard line, Rapley said,

> "I just go over there and get away from the noise and just focus on the game. Anything bad that happened, I just keep my mind focused on the game and get in the end zone."

In the article, Coach Jamie Nickles was quoted as saying,

> "That's the relationship JR has with our coaching staff. We knew to leave him alone and let him get his thoughts together. It's the heart of a champion. We started building up kids."

Nate Temple was interviewed by McWilliams and he added,

> "Coaches said don't flinch. They said we have a ballgame and have to play. We bucked up, put our hands in the dirt and scraped it up and played."

Rapley told McWilliams,

> "It's amazing, man. I can't put any term or words on it. We're forever going to be the 2018 class that three-peated first."

Coach Nickles became the winner of the John McKissick Coaching Excellence Award and was voted 2A Coach of the Year. Junior Rapley was selected Player of the Year. Making the All Region Team were the following Panthers.

Brice Jackson QB

Jermaine Blackwell RB

Kentavious Rayford DL

Charles Holback DL

Nate Temple DC

Dee Graham LB

Ravon Bobo DM

Looking to the Abbeville farm club, the 2017 young panthers of the 12U Rec Team also won their 3rd straight state championship in Bluffton.

The following was is an excerpt reported by the Index Journal staff Nov 18, 2018

The reigning Class 2A state champion Abbeville Panthers account for six players on a list of 28 players who will be honored during Monday night's All-Lakelands banquet. The 23rd annual banquet, which recognizes the top football players in the Lakelands, starts at 7 p.m. Monday at St. Mark United Methodist Church in Greenwood. Abbeville's two Shrine Bowlers, seniors Cortney Jackson and Nate Temple, lead the way for the Panthers.

Jackson finished the regular season with 677 yards and 12 touchdowns on 68 carries, adding four receptions for 96 yards and a touchdown. Jackson also returned one kickoff for a touchdown. Temple led the team in sacks with seven. He logged 57 tackles during the regular season, including nine tackles for loss.

Temple is joined by fellow defensive lineman Carson Smith, a junior who had 65 tackles, including 10 tackles for loss and four sacks. Senior Gabe Calhoun represents the Panthers in the defensive backfield after tallying 29 tackles and six pass break-ups. Senior Jake Hill is a three-year starter along an offensive line that allowed Abbeville to rush for more than 3,000 yards in nine games. Abbeville placed at least one player on offense, defense and special teams, with junior Dylan Beauford rounding out the Panthers' selection after recording 41 touchbacks and an average of 39 yards per punt.

Dawn of a Dynasty Year 101

The Panthers had made history by winning three consecutive state titles and their 9th state title in 100 years. What could this season, the beginning of the next 100 years, hold in store? Could it be conceivable that a fourth championship be within their grasps? Benji Greeson wondered if he would again receive any unworldly signs of things to come. The off season had been quiet, not spiritual encounters. He wasn't sure if he should have regrets or be thankful. So far though he had heard no clanking cowbells or experienced the sounds of cleats marching down the sidewalk. Coach Hite had not whispered in his ear offering to pee on any new injuries. There had been no dreamy bass fishing adventures with him sandwiched between Coaches Hite and Botts. Benji nearly panicked, thinking that the absence of these might be a sign of bad omens. If the spirits of the nine had not intervened yet, possibly this spelled that a 10th championship was not in the cards. There would be no fourth in a row. Nope. It was too early to be thinking this way. The season hadn't even started. This was not a time to give up or become pessimistic. No diehard Panther fans, the players or the coaches would condone such thinking. He quickly pushed it from his mind. Still, positive signs were welcome.

Four and half hours away on the Grand Strand, T. Allen Winn anticipated the upcoming season, also hopeful of another championship. He had become an avid streamer. He rarely missed a game from Myrtle Beach, listening on WZLA to the dynamic broadcasting duo of Benji Greeson and the veteran voice of the Panthers, Wayne Stevenson. Bobby Hamby, Mister Statistician, could taste football in the air too. Readying for another season of Abbeville Panther football was old hat for this seasoned trio. Anticipating a fourth run at another state title would get any of the A-Town faithful's juices flowing. So accustomed to winning, losing never entered the thoughts of those breathing and bleeding the garnet and gold, off and on the gridiron. The town rolled up the streets and packed it in on Fridays or any other days Abbeville was scheduled to play. Football frenzy didn't begin to describe the attitude in A-Town come gameday. This year's schedule would be different, a realignment tossing familiar foes into the same conference. For the Panthers, business as usual would prevail.

Spring (Football) Fever 2018

Benji begins with his first entry on the A-Town Facebook page, previews of events and games to come, and recaps of outcomes. In Benji's words…

I realize that I am one of the handful of folks that never really lets football season die. It's a constant with me. I mean it kind of must be, as it is part of my job. My thoughts are never too far away from rosters, starting line-ups, players leaving, players returning, road trips and schedules. This time of year usually gives me just enough of a football fix to tie me over through a grueling hot and boring sports summer. Spring football practice started last Monday. As I watched a few practices stretched out over the last week or so, I could feel the excitement and anticipation of the 2018 Panther football season brewing in my blood. I also had an opportunity to sit and talk with Abbeville head football coach Jamie Nickles and Panther Athletic Director and defensive coordinator Tad Dubose. I sat for about an hour, picking their brain and asking questions about the upcoming season and their thoughts on most everything.

Coach Tad Dubose,

"Spring practice is a really good time to evaluate some younger players. I gotta give Coach Nickels some credit. Some people go hog-wild during spring practice but you're not going to win a state championship in the spring. You get 10 days of contact, so however you wanna turn it. Rain got us one day last week and it ran us off the field one day too. We get to look at some players in some positions and places on the field and see how they take to that role. We try to develop some good depth. If we have a slot to fill in, let's say the…nickelback role, well we can try some people in that area. Spring is a really good time for evaluations and it gives the kids a little shot of confidence to ride into summer 7 on 7's and weight lifting and all that."

Coach Jamie Nickels,

"Ya know, I really like where we are right now. The kids have been energetic and hungry to get back out on the field. They'd play a game tomorrow, but we're nowhere near ready to play yet. It's fun to see the growth between spring and summer practice. Some kids really grow up in a couple of months when they know there are going to be counted on this fall. I really love our team this year. We've got some new pieces that I'm excited to get plugged in and we've got some veterans that are going to be the leaders on this team."

Benji asked the coaches what position group would be the strength of this year's team and the two agreed that both offensive and defensive lines should be solid this season.

Coach Nick,

"We've got depth and good leadership across both lines. It all starts up front, so we're excited to have guys like Jake (Hill) and Tre' (Jones), Connor (Nickels) and (DeMichael) Johnson. Nate (Temple) and Carson (Smith) are back on the D-Line too. We've got college scouts at every practice now watching these guys, and others too. We'll just have to wait and see how it all plays out."

Another scenario that still must play out is this year's actual football schedule. Yes, I know it's been done and posted and set in stone for a few months now. Not so fast my friends. Remember the whole uproar about re-alignment last summer? Well, the schools that got denied their appeal to stay put or move elsewhere in the re-alignment process has now embarked on what's called an "Injunction". That's basically a fancy legal word meaning that they are still appealing the process. A whole new group of people will decide if things stay like they are now, or if we'll revert back to the Regions that we played in for the last two years. So, by June 1st we will officially know the fate of our schedule. If things stay put, the Panthers will be in the Region with Batesburg, Fox Creek, Silver Bluff, Saluda and Ninety Six. If they decide to go back to the last re-alignment, the Panthers are again in a four team Region with Liberty, Southside Christian, and Ninety Six."

Spring is a time for figuring things out and getting organized. A lot of info will come out between now and kickoff in August. Keep an eye out for more summer schedules and football tidbits as we near the start of the 2018 Football season. The Spring Game is scheduled for Thursday May 24th, at 6pm. The game is held at Hite Stadium and is free to the public. Coach Nickels will have a parent meeting before the game to get paper work filled out as well.

As always…God Bless and Go Panthers!

Fifty and Counting

Benji does the math his way for his next A-Town entry.

Fifty, no it's not the number of laps around the field that Coach Nickles runs on his lunch break. It's not the number of games in a win streak or the number of trophies in the trophy case. Fifty is the exact amount of days before you will see the boys in Garnet and Gold take the field for the West Carolina Kickoff Classic. The unofficial beginning of the 2018 football season is only fifty days away. It seems like just yesterday the Panthers were hoisting the AA State Championship trophy at Benedict College. Yet, here we are. Only a hot, humid southern summer away from starting over, and competing for what could be a very historic season.

The Panthers will break in a fourth starting quarterback for the fourth year in a row. I've tried to find information to see if any team has ever won three straight State Championships with three different starting QB's. As you can imagine, that info is impossible to find. We know it's happened at least once, as the feat was completed back in December. Joseph Battle was the Panther QB in 2015, Jamie Gray was the signal caller in 2016, and Bryce Jackson last season.

This year it's JD Moore's turn to lead the offense. Moore, a Junior, filled in nicely last season while Jackson was injured. Specifically, JD Moore stepped in and led the Panthers to a third-round playoff win versus Cheraw. Not an easy task for a first-time starting sophomore. He handled the pressure with ease, and we got a glimpse of what the future will hold for the Panthers. Let me be the first to tell you. The future is very, very bright. Moore, not as big in stature as the previous three QB's, but Moore may be the fastest of the championship bunch. The 7 on 7 season has begun already, and Moore is getting his timing and chemistry with his wide receivers down pat. The Panthers are primarily a running team, but the presence of a passing attack opens up the running lanes for the bevy of talented Panther running backs.

Speaking of talented running backs. I'm sure the Panther coaching staff is chomping at the bit to unleash Courtney Jackson this season. As most of you know, Jackson suffered a season ending knee injury last season during the Hartsville game. He played in 6 of 15 games last season and amassed 525 yards rushing and 9 touchdowns on just 43 carries. He also returned a kickoff for a touchdown. His understanding of the blocking schemes of the offense, his determination and shear speed alone will be a huge asset for this Panther offense. The offense lost a lot of production to graduation. Jr. Rapley, Bryce Jackson and Jermaine Blackwell combined for 2,967 yards and 42 touchdowns. That's good enough for 62% of the total rushing yards and 68% of the rushing touchdowns from last season. But, if you've been paying attention. The Panthers don't really rebuild. They just reload.

Joined in the backfield with Jackson this season will be a 3 or 4 or 5 headed monster. Dominick "The Bus" Washington will play a big bruising role, as will Robin Crawford. Combined, last season Washington and Crawford ate up nearly 1,000 yards and scored 7 touchdowns. Expect to see the blazing fast JaBryan "Dooley" Sanders taking handoffs this season, as well as stretching the field from the wide receiver position. Jhalyn Shuler will have a bigger role offensively this season as well. He's a physical specimen that is drawing a lot of attention from the numerous college scouts that are camping out at most practices. The Panther offensive line is big, mean, and experienced. Jake Hill will be the Senior leader of this group. Hill at 6'3" 260+ is getting a lot of college love in the off season as well. Conner Nickles and Trai Jones are road graders that will be anchors up front for the Panthers. Add in Tillman Allen at the Tight End position and the Panthers may be deeper, and bigger across the offensive front than at any time in recent memory.

Graduation took a few long-time starters off the defensive side of the ball. I must admit, it'll be a little strange not seeing Whoodie Goodwin on the field. The same goes for Charles Holback and Tae Rayford. Those guys left a proud defensive legacy and set the bar for the next group of Panther defenders. Don't start feeling sorry for Panther DC Tad Dubose just yet. He has talent and experience to pull from this season. Nate Temple and Carson Smith are poised to have stand-out seasons on the defensive line. Malik Leach and David Cobb will be key pieces to the defensive backfield too. They combined for 184 tackles and 4 interceptions last season. It's been rumored that Cruz Temple may see time at linebacker this season, add in sophomore Luke Evans, and that will be a fun group to watch terrorize ball carriers this season.

The roster is always a fluid, every changing and evolving work in motion during this time of year. Half of what you just read could change pretty quickly. We'll keep you updated as 7 on 7 camps come and go and summer practice gets underway. The Panthers will practice at Strom Thurmond on June 19th, and the FCA 7 on 7 tourney will start at 8:30am on June 26th at Grace United Methodist, before taking to the practice fields and Hite Stadium. Summer practice officially starts on July 30th.

Check back often as we will get you ready for the 101st season of Abbeville Panther Football.

God Bless and Go Panthers!

Preseason Preview Vol. 1

Benji makes his preseason predictions, matching up the Panthers with their opponents as only the big guy can. Still looking over his shoulder though, wondering whether those angels, visions or whatever you want to call them, might instantly appear and offer some insight in a season quickly approaching. No cow bells yet. No wetting a hook in the Bott's bass boat. No apparitions haunting his dreams. He's on his own thus far but ready to take the reins. The summer of dreams has begun. The Dynasty is real. Benji pens and posts his first preview…

For football junkies, July is one terribly awful month. Sure, the weather calls for lake days, pool parties and beach trips, but the thought of football season being so close yet so far away is brutal. The magazine racks are full of pre-season college and NFL football previews. The sports networks are beginning their annual "media days" and the "Talking Season" has officially begun. So, to bridge the gap between now and August 3rd, which is the date of the WCTEL Kickoff Classic at Hite Stadium, we'll begin our pre-season previews. Over the course of the next three weeks I'll break down each game on the Panthers schedule and give a hypothetical preview or prognostication as to how I see the games playing out. Let's get started…

Week Zero at Lincoln County

Has there been a more physical match-up over the course of the last few years? The history, tradition and pride that these two teams take with them onto the field is evident from the opening kickoff. It's like watching the Steelers and the Ravens just pound on each other. It's big boy football at its best. The last time the Panthers traveled to historic Buddy Bufford Field, the Panthers and Red Devils played to a 7-7 tie. Coach Nickles described the game as a "blood bath" and a "physical beating". Last season the Panthers won at home by a score of 28-14. Will we see the same kind of contest this year? Two sledge hammers pounding on one another until the other breaks, or gives up? You bet you will. Will Lincoln Co. be out for revenge? You bet they will. Can the Panthers match the physicality of old fashion smash-mouth football? You bet they can. In another slobber knocker, I'm taking the team with a big experienced offensive and defensive line. That team wears the A on their helmet. A little extra motivation might help spark the Panthers as well. A win will make Abbeville Head Coach Jamie Nickles the winningest coach in school history.

Prediction: Panthers 20 – Red Devils 17

Week One versus Newberry

Other than a couple jamborees and maybe a 7 on 7 tournament, Abbeville and Newberry have been somewhat strangers on the football field. Newberry's move to

3A in the last few re-alignments have taken them away from the A-Town schedule, yet this year they will meet for only the 7th time in school history. It's the home opener for the Panthers in a non-region match-up that should provide some fireworks. Newberry finished 11-2 last season behind Head Coach Tyon Williams. I think the interesting match-up in this game will come down to the speed of the Panthers offense and the size of the Newberry defense. Can the Panthers run around the Bulldogs, stretch them from sideline to sideline and wear them out as the game drags on? That's my guess. The Panther defense won't be seeing anything they won't be prepared for and I can envision A-Town getting off to a 2-0 start.

Prediction: Panthers 42 – Newberry 20

Week Two at Emerald

The Vikings are coming off a season in which they won their region championship and played for the 3A Upperstate Championship. They are also coming off a season in which they lost to Abbeville 56-21 inside historic Hite Stadium. It'll be interesting to see how the Vikings handle losing so much of their offensive production from a year ago. Running backs Chamberlain and Settles are gone from a team that lined it up and ran it straight down the throats of most of their opponents. Tight End, Auburn commit Luke Deal grabs all the headlines, but this Emerald team has more questions than answers. Can they be consistent offensively, and can they match the speed and physicality of the A-Town squad. Unfortunately for the Viking faithful, the answer to both questions is more than likely, NO. Abbeville's personnel matches up very well against Emerald's. Speed kills and when you can control the line of scrimmage as the Panthers can, that doesn't bode well for the opponent. The Panthers move to 3-0 on the season after this one.

Prediction: Panthers 40 Vikings 14

Benji had digested phase two in the season, running the scenarios and potential outcomes. Continuing his *Lone Ranger* assessment, all without paranormal intervention and assistance, he wasn't sure if he should be relieved or disappointed. The mission defined, putting it all out on the line was a big part of the fun this time of year. Nobody loved this part any better than Benji Greeson.

Preseason Preview Vol. 2

The anticipation of the 2018 season is almost hitting a fever pitch. We are only a little over a week away from the WCTEL Kickoff Classic at Hite Stadium. That's right, August 3rd at 6pm you will get to hear the pads popping and whistles blowing at Hite Stadium for the official kickoff of the 2018 season. Last week we gave our preseason predictions for the first three weeks of the season. Today we'll look at games four, five and six on the Panthers schedule.

Week Three: Panthers at Southside Christian

Southside Christian has made major strides as a program over the last ten years. The Sabre's at one time were playing in a lot of homecoming games. In 2014 they strung together a 6-5 record and have yet to have a losing season since. In fact, the Sabre's won a Class A State Championship in 2015. A bump up to the 2A ranks in 2016 yielded another 6-5 record, but the Sabre's went 10-2 last season and have some momentum headed into this year. What does that translate to as far as the Panthers are concerned? Well, not much. You'll see varying styles of play on September 7th. The Panthers will grind it out on the ground while SSC plays a spread, up tempo style of offense. In their only two meetings the Panthers have won 42-21 and 33-14. I expect to see a similar outcome this go-round. The Panthers might have their hands full in the early stages of the game, only to wear out the Sabre's with a physically punishing rushing attack and solid interior line play.

Prediction: Panthers 40 – Sabre's 20

Week Five: Panthers at Hartsville

After an open date on September 14th, the Panthers will travel across the Palmetto State to one of the most iconic stadiums in South Carolina high school football. Kellytown Stadium is the sight for what is sure to be an old-fashioned donnybrook. A real slobber knocker. A bloody nose kind of game. The Panthers and the Red Foxes of Hartsville have put on quite a show over the last couple of seasons. Each team winning a game on the neutral field at Newberry College, both in dramatic fashion, has set the stage for what is sure to be an exciting contest. Round 3 of a heavyweight fight is what this one already feels like. The Panthers only loss last season came to the 4A state runners-up by a score of 28-21. So, what happens this year? My guess is much of the same. You'll see two teams who love to physically dominate their opponent, bash each other until one team folds. The problem is, neither team ever folds. Last season the Panthers lost by a touchdown, but they turned the ball over four times. With their backs against the wall, in a hostile environment, the Panthers win one for the history books.

Prediction: Panthers 31 – Red Foxes 30

Week Six: Panther vs. Batesburg-Leesville

They'll turn the lights on at Hite Stadium for the first time in over a month when the Panthers of Batesburg-Leesville visit A-Town in the first Region game of the year. To anyone who's been paying attention over the last 30 or 40 years these two teams are fierce rivals and they love to beat up on each other. The last time they played, all the marbles were on the table. The Panthers won their 2nd consecutive State Championship in 2016 versus B-L by a score of 44-21. B-L handed A-Town their worst home loss in decades in 2014 by a 46-0 score. Abbeville then bounced B-L from the playoffs that same season, beating them on their own turf 34-28. B-L finished 7-6 last season, but made a run in the playoffs, losing to Barnwell in the 3rd round. B-L hasn't been the model of consistency lately with a few coaching changes over the last few years. The boys from A-Town will be protecting a long home game winning streak by the time this one rolls around. Expect standing room only as this rivalry renews. I guarantee the Panthers will win this one. (see what I did there) But my guess is the Panthers in Garnet and Gold will grab the bragging rights this season.

Prediction: A-Town Panthers 36 – B-L Panthers 23

We'll wrap up our Preseason Preview next week with Volume 3 covering the last four games of the regular season. As always…God Bless and Go Panthers!

Benji's ribs remained unbruised and his dignity in tack. Tara had launched no elbows waking him from those uncanny nightmares. Those filled with the antics of locker room washers and dryers, phantom announcers and him being suited in his old football uniform. This continued to dog him though. If they didn't intervene, was this a sign of ominous things to come this season for the Panthers and their faithful. Pressing forward, Benji dismissed the premise and didn't allow it to interfere with what his gut was telling him, predictions wise.

Preseason Preview Vol. 3

The boys are back in town! Yes, that's a hit song from 70's rock band Thin Lizzy, but it's also what comes to mind as Fall Camp began this past Friday. Seeing the boys back on the practice field, running though individual drills and getting ready for the season put a smile on my face. Football season is inching closer and closer by the minute.

Over the last couple of weeks we've previewed the first six games on the Panthers schedule. Today we'll look at the last four games that the Panthers will have to navigate during the regular season.

Week Seven – Panthers @ Fox Creek

This will be the first ever meeting for the Panthers and Predators on the football field. This game has already been moved to a Thursday night, October 4th, by request of the Fox Creek head coach Derrick Quinn. So, a little Thursday night football in North Augusta, why not? What can we expect on the field? Fox Creek hasn't given any reason recently that this will be a close game. Last season the Predators finished 6-4 in the regular season before being bounced in the first round of the playoffs by Chesterfield. The Panthers, on paper, seem bigger, faster and more experienced. Will that translate onto the scoreboard? My guess is yes.

Prediction: Panthers 52 – Predators 17

Week Eight – Panthers vs Silver Bluff

Hite Stadium will be open for business once again as the Panthers welcome in the Bulldogs of Silver Bluff. These two proud programs usually put on quite a show when they meet. The last couple of meetings have come via a State Championship game appearance. In 2015 the Panthers defeated the Bulldogs to bring home the first of their three consecutive State Championship trophies. The Bulldogs beat the Panthers in Williams Brice Stadium to win the 2000 State Title. The Bulldogs have been down the last couple of years. A 5-7 record last season and a 3-7 record in 2016 is very uncommon for a program with five state titles, a ton of region championships and a handful of NFL alumni. Word on the street is that Silver Bluff is back on the upswing and the team has some renewed enthusiasm with new Head Coach, Silver Bluff alum De'Angelo Bryant. The upswing is coming for the Bulldog fans in Petticoat Junction, but the Panthers are already where the Bulldogs are trying to get to.

Prediction: Panthers 38 – Bulldogs 13

Week Nine – Panthers @ Saluda

Three years in a row the Panthers and Tigers have met in the Upperstate Championship game. Three years in a row the Panthers have beat the Tigers on their way to three straight State Championships. This year, a regular season region match-up in Saluda should provide some fireworks. There's been no love loss in this game over the last few years. Hard fought, tough games that have come down to the waning moments. This game will be no different. Likely there will be a region championship on the line. Playoff implications, home field implications. The tension will be high. The stakes will be higher. I expect a sellout crowd in mid-October. I also expect a heck of a game with a playoff atmosphere. Can the Panthers endure a hostile environment and do what they do? Which is physically impose their will against a team that is hungry to take the next step? I tend to lean on experience in big games, the Panthers will have played on the road at sold out Lincoln Co, Emerald and Hartsville before this contest. Give me the battle tested Panthers in a nail biter.

Prediction: Panthers 24 – Tigers 21

Week Ten – Panthers vs Ninety Six

It'll be homecoming for the Panthers in the last week of the regular season and they will host familiar foe and rival, the Ninety Six Wildcats. Second year head coach Andre Woolcock seems to have the Wildcats on the right path and improving with every passing week. The match-up has been lopsided over the last few years. The Panthers have won five straight, including last year's two games 54-16 and 42-7. Will Homecoming be enough of a distraction to keep the Panthers from being focused? Can Ninety Six spoil what could be another region championship and playoff run for the Panthers? Not this year. Quality depth is likely the culprit that will catch up to the Wildcats in this one.

Prediction: Panthers 48 – Wildcats 10

That concludes our preseason previews. Bookmark this page and check back often as we will continue to provide weekly previews, analysis and recaps of each and every game that the Panthers play this season. We'll be starting with an article later this week previewing the WCTEL Kickoff Classic, which will be held at Hite Stadium this coming Friday, August 3rd at 5pm. Football season is here!! Finally! And as always…

God Bless and Go Panthers!

Benji, bewildered yet ready, prepares the A-Town followers and staunch believers for the season opener. Bewildered because those so persistent in haunting his dreams prior to the 2017 season have remained deathly quiet. Deathly quiet, thought Benji, with the slightest of smiles. Bad vibes, bad omens, just what did this mean, wondered the man preparing to share the WZLA broadcast booth a second season with Wayne Stevenson. 'More Cow Bell' could go a long way about now. No 'clunk-clunk', not from the angel, Pidgy Dubose. Not his time. Where were the likes of Yoda, Honk and the Juice when he could use a little friendly 'don't worry' nudge? Ghosts of football seasons pass would be a welcome sight about now. Last year the ordeal, truth or imaginary, had been a bit troubling and confusing. Now that he had endured that ordeal and understood the significance, the spirits had abandoned him so it seemed. The real season was just a blink away now. Time to toss out closing Benji thoughts…

August 8th This Week in Panther Football

We are now just 10 days away from the start of the regular season. The Panthers will be traveling "Across the River" to Lincolnton, Georgia on Friday August 17th for their week zero match-up versus the Lincoln County Red Devils. The Panthers are hard at work sharpening their skills and getting ready for the regular season. Today we'll look at some of the preseason activities the Panthers have been up to over the last week.

Last Friday night Hite Stadium was buzzing with anticipation as the West Carolina Tel Kickoff Classic began sharply at 6pm. A rain storm earlier in the day provided a soggy turf, and under the late afternoon sun, very humid conditions. The Panthers played in the third contest of the night, playing against the 3A Crescent Tigers. It was hard to gauge the Panthers offensively, as the majority of the Panthers starting offensive line was in street clothes on the sideline for various reasons. In all there were five or six players that participated very little or not at all during the contest. Even without some key contributors, the Panthers controlled the game from start to finish.

Ja'Bryan "Dooley" Sanders was moved from wide receiver to running back this season. He took a handoff from quarterback JD Moore and blew past the Tiger defenders for a 44-yard touchdown run for the first score of the evening. Moore hit Quad Woods on a 34-yard pass on the next possession and set up a Robin Crawford one-yard touchdown run. The extra point kickoff off the foot of Dylan Beauford, sailed through the uprights to give the Panthers a 14-0 lead. A stifling Panther defense kept Crescent at bay the entire game. The Tigers crossed the 50-yard line once, briefly, before they were held to another punt. Malik Leach scampered into the endzone from 10 yards out to finish the scoring for the Panthers as they defeated Crescent by 20-0 score.

Fast forward to Tuesday of this week and the Panthers hosted 5A Lexington High to Hite Stadium for a preseason scrimmage. It was a situational scrimmage where each team possessed the ball the same amount of times, from the same yard lines. They worked on goal line situations and the kicking game. The size of the Lexington team looked intimidating. The Panthers however, didn't look intimidated. Had they kept score, it would have been in the range of 35-7, in favor of Abbeville. Courtney Jackson, coming off an ACL tear last season, looked crisp in his cuts and as fast as ever. The glaring difference from the WCTEL Kickoff Classic was having most of the offensive lineman participating. The Panthers dominated the line of scrimmage against the much bigger Wildcats. Defensively the Panthers gave up a pass here or there, but ultimately shut down the Lexington offense.

The last segment of practice was the goal line segment. Each team had four downs to score from the ten-yard line. Abbeville Head Coach Jamie Nickles could be heard shouting, *"It's overtime in Georgia boys. Let's see what ya made of."* Lexington turned the ball over on downs at the six-yard line. Linebacker Jhalyan Shuler is a difference maker on this defense. He's big, fast and seeks out contact. Luke Evans, a sophomore starter at linebacker, plays with a recklessness that is fun to watch. Just find the ball, and you'll find Evans near it. Starting defensive end, and Middle Tennessee commit Nate Temple was held out for precautionary reasons after getting banged up in the WCTEL Kickoff Classic. His D-Line counterparts held their own during the scrimmage. Coach Nickles said, *"Our lines are probably going to be our strength this year. We've got some good ones on both sides that will help us this year."* Carson Smith is coming back for his junior year and will be a terror for opposing offenses. Jihad Washington and Ar'Darius Burton are both big, physical defensive tackles that will be counted on as well. David Cobb, Tyreke Campbell, and Gabe Calhoun are all experienced, athletic contributors in the defensive backfield as well.

The Panthers will get to play the first contest in the Greenwood Jamboree this coming Thursday night. Their opponent will be the Ninety Six Wildcats. The Jamboree will start at 6pm. JW Babb Stadium has implemented a clear bag policy this season, as well as metal detectors at the entrances. Get there early in case there are longer lines due to the new policies. Next week we'll begin our weekly regular season game previews and reviews. Hold on just a little longer, the 2018 season is almost here. As always….

God Bless and Go Panthers!

Goose bumps and giddiness prevailed. The first game of the season was almost here. The spiritual world maintained their code of silence. Benji's dream world had been uneventful or at least normal when it came to a peaceful night of slumber. Maybe everything had just been wishful thinking on his part last year, an over active imagination, him just caught up in the hoopla of wishful supporters seeking that third championship in as many years. He kept his thoughts to himself. Crazy thoughts and crazy talk had no place, even in a season of high promise and uncertainty. Hite peeing on anxiety had never been tested. On to the task at hand, preparing the loyal following for opening day.

Week Zero vs. Lincoln County Preview

Can you believe it's finally here? We made it. Football season has finally arrived. The talk is over, the pre-season is done, the scrimmages and jamborees that mean absolutely nothing has come and gone. It's 'go' time. For the duration of the season we'll be posting weekly preview and review articles following the Panthers on their journey through the 2018 season. Let's get started.

When AHS Athletic Director Tad Dubose showed me the schedule back in April, I laughed out loud. That was followed by an "Are you kidding me?". This season is no cake walk for the three-time defending 2A State Champs. This, in my opinion, is the toughest schedule I have ever seen assembled. It all starts Friday night with a "trip across the river" to a small Georgia town called Lincolnton. Lincoln County High School is the type of program that millions of schools across the country strive to be. A perennial power that brings a toughness and a will to win to the field week in and week out, without fail. The Legend of Larry Campbell will live on forever. Coach Campbell graced the LC sidelines from 1972 to 2013. He won 11 state championships. He won 33 region championships and amassed a ridiculous career record of 477-81-3. He had multiple undefeated seasons and put multiple players in college and the NFL. Lincoln County under Campbell was the cream of the crop.

Campbell retired after the 2013 season and longtime assistant Kevin Banks took over. Being the next guy up, after a legend retires, is a job that few people would want. Banks collected a 30-15-1 record in four seasons. The Banks led Red Devils never made it out of the 2nd round of the playoffs and that just doesn't cut it in Lincolnton. So, after having one coach for 42 years, the Red Devils find themselves with their 2nd coach in five years. Michael Pollock was named the LC head coach in March and he's been handed the keys to a program that is steeped in winning history and a tradition of championships. Last season the Red Devils finished 7-5 and lost in the 2nd round of the playoffs. It's hard to know what exactly to expect from this years Red Devils. I do know that no matter who the coach is, a game versus Lincoln County is usually a 48-minute war. The pads will be popping Friday night at Larry Campbell Stadium-Buddy Bufford Field.

The Panthers have experienced success like few have ever seen. Especially over the last decade. Since 2010 the Panthers have played in 6 of 8 state championship games. They won five of those. This year's senior class has never lost a playoff game. That's just short of impossible. The Panthers have also won three state championships in a row, (5'10" 180) a junior, is the big man on campus now, and the coaches are pleased with his progress.

"JD is a very capable quarterback. He's improving every day. He takes control of the offense and has a good grasp of what we want to do. His passing is improving every day and he's a hard worker. We're blessed to have such a great young man on our team," said Head Coach Jamie Nickles.

Moore isn't all alone in the Panthers backfield. Returning this season is Senior Courtney Jackson, a four -year varsity player. Jackson (6'1" 205) was the leading rusher last season when he tore his ACL versus Hartsville in week six. Jackson looks to have fully recovered and brings blazing speed and big-time division one college size and tenacity to the vast stable of running backs. Ja'Bryan 'Dooley' Sanders will join Jackson in the backfield. Sanders was utilized as a wide receiver last season. He routinely brought the fans to their feet with uncommon speed and separation ability. All he needs is a small crease, and he won't be caught. Joining Jackson and Sanders is Dominick "The Bus" Washington. Maybe the most physical runner of the three, "The Bus" ran for over 700 yards and 6 TDs last season. Robin Crawford, and Malik Leach will get carries as well as Cruz Temple. The running backs are only as good as their offensive line. Led by seniors Jake Hill (6'3" 260) Tre' Jones, and multi-year starter, juniors Connor Nickles and DeMicheal Johnson. The Panthers O-Line is big, strong, physical and they play with a mean streak. Throw in the strapping Tillman Allen at Tight End. Senior Jake Hill leads the Panther offensive line. End and a field stretcher, Quad Woods at wide receiver, and you've got, on paper, a very explosive and physical offense. Offense wins games and defense wins championships. If that old cliché holds true, we might be playing on Thanksgiving again.

The coaching staff will tell you that the defensive line may be the best position group on the entire team. Scary, right? Nate Temple grabbed all the headlines in the offseason. The 6'5" 230lb defensive end was heavily recruited by tons of colleges and he made his decision to play a little closer to home by choosing Mid Tennessee as his college of choice. Nate will be joined by Carson Smith who had a breakout year a season ago collecting 68 tackles. Smith will be joined by Ar'Darius Burton, Arthur Wideman and Jihad Washington. That's about 1,000 pounds of block eating nastiness. They will allow sophomore Luke Evans, who will get the nod at Linebacker, to roam the field freely. Evans plays with a recklessness that's fun to watch. Cruz Temple and Tyreke Campbell are ball seeking missiles as well. The defensive back field will also be a strength this season. David Cobb returns after a 57 tackle, 3 interception junior season. Jhalyan Shuler is a physical specimen that can and will play all over the field. Gabe Calhoun will bring experience and more speed to an already speedy defensive backfield. Throw in a sure-footed kicker in Dylan Beauford and you've got a really solid team from top to bottom.

So, what to expect Friday night? Expect to see a war. A physical, bloody nose kind of game. When you beat an anvil with a hammer, something has got to give, eventually. Can the Panthers get off the bus with the attitude that they have something to prove? Can they bring a physical nastiness with them to Larry Campbell Stadium? They better, if not, the Red Devils are a very capable team who are looking to make a statement. The target is always on the back of the Panthers, they get everybody's best shot. How will the 2018 Panthers respond? Only time will tell.

God Bless and Go Panthers!

Christina Margaret Nickles

Prior to the opening game the Nickles' family faced a horrific loss.

Christina Margaret Nickles, 29, of Donalds, died Tuesday, August 14, 2018 at Greenville Memorial Hospital due to injuries sustained in an automobile accident. She was born in Greenwood to Smitty and Margaret Wilson Nickles. Christina, a 2006 graduate of Dixie High School, was also a 2008 graduate of Piedmont Technical College. She was employed with TCC Communications in Anderson and a member of New Spring Church. Christina had a passion for life and loved her family and friends superlatively. She cherished each day with her most recent nephew and niece, Christopher and Bella.

Christina is survived by her parents of the home; two brothers, Jamie Nickles (Misty) of Abbeville and Brent Nickles (Jaimee) of Donalds; two sisters, Sherrie Dansby (Bob) of Abbeville and Monica Patterson (Carey) of Greenwood; nieces and nephews, Connor, Addison, Dale, Matthew, Cameron, Christopher, Bella, Makenna and Logan, uncles Marshall Wilson (Chris) and Joe Nickles (Georgeanne) and extended family and Matt Cole (Ann) and their daughter, Tamara.

August 18th Posting: Historical Dominance

There were a few thousand people that can now say they saw history made before their very eyes. The Abbeville Panthers dismantled the Lincoln Co Red Devils 57-0 in Friday night's much anticipated contest. The score itself holds historical significance. Lincoln Co. had never allowed 57 points to an opponent on its home field. The Panthers also broke a record that stood for 65 years. In 1953 Lincoln Co lost to Warrenton High by a score of 54-0. That 54-point margin of defeat was the largest in school history. Until the Panthers came to town. The 57-point margin of victory for Abbeville is the new record at Larry Campbell Stadium, marking the worst loss in Lincoln Co High School history.

Another piece of Panther history that unfolded before our eyes is the record that Head Coach Jamie Nickles set. In his 15th season at the helm of the Panthers, Coach Nickles is now the winningest coach in the 101-year history of Abbeville Panther football. Nickles' career record is now 148-39-1. He passed the late Dennis Botts, whose record he tied with the 2017 State Championship win at Benedict College vs Bamberg last December. Nickles (148), Botts (147), Hite (145) and Hendrix (103) are the only coaches with 100+ wins in school history.

Now to the game itself. When the point spread was released a couple of weeks ago, many scoffed at the idea that Abbeville was a 20-point favorite, on the road, at Lincoln Co, in the opening game of the season. The Panthers surpassed the 20-point mark early in the 2nd quarter. Panther quarterback JD Moore took the first Panther offensive play from scrimmage and zipped 66 yards, virtually untouched, for a touchdown. Moore's night ended in the 3rd quarter, with a comfortable lead, after he rushed for 137 yards on 10 carries and finding the endzone three times. Courtney Jackson scored twice, Dominick Washington added a touchdown run and 95 yards on the ground as well.

The Panther offensive line was dominate as well. Jake Hill, Conner Nickles, Tre Jones and company manhandled the severely out manned LC defensive line. Panther ball carriers totaled 348 yards on 41 carries. They averaged 8.5 yards per rush and completely controlled the game from the opening kickoff. Speaking of kickoffs. How nice is it now to see the football land five to seven yards deep in the endzone on nearly every kickoff. Dylan Beauford has improved his leg strength and accuracy in the offseason and he is not only an asset to this team. He's a weapon on special teams.

When you look at the rushing numbers, you might think that the 348 yards isn't the biggest number you've seen recently. That is a true statement, as the Panthers have rushed for over 500 yards in multiple games over the last few seasons. The number isn't indicative to how dominate the offense was. That number is indicative however to how dominate the defense was. The Panther defense punished the Red Devil offense for the entire game. They forced punt after punt and set up the

Panther offense with a short field. A shorter field to work with equals fewer total rushing yards, but a big number on the scoreboard.

Let me say this. There was not a single player that was wearing a Lincoln Co jersey Friday night that could block Ar'Darius Burton. He absolutely dominated the line of scrimmage and was a nightmare for the Red Devil offense. He disrupted every single play, in one way or the other, for every play that he was on the field. The combination of Nate Temple, Carson Smith, Jihad Washington and Burton may be the most dominate starting defensive line that the Panthers have had in a very long time. Quadarius Guillebeaux scored twice Friday night. The long rangy safety scooped up a LC fumble and glided 79 yards to pay dirt to extend the Panther lead to 36-0 with 1:11 left before halftime. That was the quintessential nail in the coffin for the Red Devils. They never crossed the 50-yard line again for the remainder of the game.

Ooohhhss and aaahhhhsss filled the humid Georgia air as Tyreke Campbell did his best (insert hardest hitter in the NFL name here) impersonation. Campbell laid out a LC blocker on a kickoff. He then delivered a thunderous hit near the A-Town sideline that drew a penalty, even though the hit looked clean. David Cobb and Tyrell Hadden were flying all over the defensive backfield as was Jhalyn Shuler. I know it's early in the season and there's a lot of football left to play, but this defense has the potential to be a very special unit moving forward. Defensive Coordinator Tad Dubose has got to be pleased with the talent that he gets to help mold this season.

Benji preseason prediction: Panthers 20 – Red Devils 17. A win is a win but both Benji and Wayne proclaimed on the broadcast that they never saw this outcome coming. Benji had professed he would have lost the house and the farm betting against this score and spread.

The Panthers will host Newberry this coming Friday for the home opener at Hite Stadium. Kickoff is 7:30. Abbeville has instituted a clear bag policy this season. Purses, bookbags, and any bag that you bring into Hite Stadium must be clear. They are also subject to be searched. There is zero exception to this new policy, so please decide before attending the game to avoid any delays at the entrances.

God Bless and Go Panthers.

Week one under his belt and a win for the Panthers, a startling and unexpected lopsided one at that, Benji looks ahead to the next contest. This one would be in the warm surroundings of Hite Stadium - Dennis Botts Field. Would the two coaches bookend him again in a dreamland fishing adventure? He almost wished they would. It was a fantasy come true, him with the two legends in an unforgettable dream sequence. Unfortunately, you just can't will dreams to be speckled with the dead you're hopeful of visiting. If it were that easy, people would forever visit their long departed loved ones. While the bass fishing events had been memorable last season, real or not, they shed no light on what this season held. Time to just move on and preview the Newberry game.

Week One vs Newberry August 23rd Preview

Hite Stadium will be open for business on Friday night. It's the home opener for your Abbeville Panthers as they welcome in the 3A Newberry Bulldogs. The Bulldogs are coached by legendary Head Coach Phil Strickland. He's been around the block and has produced great team after great team for the last 31 years. Strickland has coached at Ridge Springs-Monetta, Brooklyn Cayce, Batesburg-Leesville, Gaffney and now Newberry. His 319-99 overall career record speaks for itself. His teams have played for eight state championships and won five of those. In 31 years, his teams have only posted two losing seasons. Newberry is coming off a 10-2 record last year. They did not play in Week Zero, so this is their first regular season game of the year.

The Panthers and Bulldogs have not met since 2013. That game ended with the Panthers losing 14-0. This is the seventh meeting all time between the Panthers and Bulldogs. In fact, the Panthers have a 2-4 overall record against Newberry. One of the few teams that the Panthers have an all-time losing record against. The last Panther win in the series was a 38-27 win in October of 2012.

Newberry is a big, physical team. They want to control the line of scrimmage and run the ball. In the preseason they were playing a lot of "I-Formation" sets on offense. They can also line up with four wide receivers and throw the ball if they must. With nearly 900 students, they have a good pool of players to choose from. #1 Josh Mathis is a Senior Wide Receiver that gets a lot of attention. The same can be said for #2 Zymere Epps. It will be an interesting match-up watching the Panthers defensive backs and the Newberry wide outs Friday night. KT Robinson, #20, is the workhorse at running back for the Bulldogs. A senior heavy offensive and defensive line will be a good test for the Panthers.

As for the Panthers, they are going to do what they do. And that's a heavy dose of the run game. Last week versus Lincoln County the Panthers ran up and down the field at will. They rushed for 348 yards on 41 carries. That's an 8.5 yard per rush average. JD Moore led all rushers with 10 carries for 137 yards and 3 touchdowns.

Dominick "The Bus" Washington averaged 15.8 yards per carry. He had 95 yards on 6 carries and a touchdown. Courtney Jackson added 50 yards on 9 carries and two touchdowns as well. The talent is evident and plentiful for the Panthers. The Panthers will also be protecting a 26-game home win streak. They have not lost at home since October 17th, 2014 to Batesburg-Leesville. This game will be won or lost on the line of scrimmage. Newberry will put much bigger, faster and stronger athletes on the field than what the Panthers saw last week. That means that the offensive and defensive lines are going to have their hands full. Can the Panthers dominate the line of scrimmage versus a much bigger team? Friday's game should be a good one.

Kickoff is at 7:30, and Abbeville School District has implemented a 'Clear Bag Policy' for all events in the district. Get there a little earlier than usual in case there are delays at the gates with the new security policies in place. And as always….

God Bless and Go Panthers.

This is it, thought Benji. Time to put up or shut up. He was still flying solo, no voices or images from those long-passed entities to provide reassurance that the Panthers were destined for a historical season. Four consecutive state championships seemed improbable, maybe unattainable and impossible for most high school programs. Abbeville wasn't like most high schools. Those strapping on the helmets and sporting the school colors were work horses, determined and proud. They had already shattered many records. Why should this season be any different than the past three? Look what they had done against Lincolnton. The seniors had a mission and were determined to keep their streak intact. They had won three straight titles and had never lost a playoff game in their reigning three years. A dynasty sought its destiny. Benji set the table for those salivating and hungry by recapping game two.

AUG 25 Welcome to The Jungle

Black Panthers are indigenous to the jungles of Asia and Africa. They are apex predators with an innate desire and instinct to stalk and hunt their prey. You see where I'm headed with this, right? The Garnet and Gold Panthers have established themselves as the apex predators of South Carolina High School Football. They've successfully defended their home turf 27 consecutive times as of about 9:45 pm last night. The opponent is faceless and nameless. They play the same team every week. Themselves. There's real belief within the program that if they do what they do, to the best of their ability, the scoreboard will take care of itself. In a nutshell, it's working.

The Panthers moved to 2-0 on the season and the fashion in which it happened is still a little jaw dropping. The Panthers won the coin toss and deferred to the 2nd half. The combination of Dylan Beauford's booming kickoffs, and the relentless Panther defense has spelled trouble for their opponents. It's becoming a deadly one-two punch here early in the season. Newberry went three and out to start the game and the tone was set. The Panther defense allowed 3 yards per rush on the night. They forced and recovered three fumbles, made Newberry punt six times and held the Bulldogs to 1 of 13 on third down. That's a 7.7% third down conversion rate, if you're keeping score at home. Continuously facing an 80-yard field, Newberry could muster very little offensively. The Abbeville defensive line was constantly disrupting the Bulldog running backs and quarterback. The defense helped the offense by providing them with great field position the entire game. The A-Town offense's average starting field position was the Newberry 48-yard line. Newberry's average starting field position was their own 18.

Ja'Bryan 'Dooley' Sanders made the most of his carries on the night. He had 2 carries 83 yards and 2 touchdowns. Talk about making the most of your opportunities. All told the Panthers rushed for 291 yards and 5 touchdowns. JD Moore flexed his passing skills as well. The junior signal caller finished 3 of 4 for

57 yards and 2 TD's. First, he connected with Quad Woods for a 37-yard score, and then Robin Crawford pulled in the second TD pass from 21 yards out. A 21 point 2nd quarter slammed the door on a Newberry team that had no answers for the swarming Panthers. Courtney Jackson and Himize Rayford added additional rushing touchdowns and the Panthers strolled out of game two with a 49-0 victory.

Benji's preseason prediction for this one, Panthers 42 – Newberry 20, had been close. Back to back shutouts had not been foreseen though. Benji nor Wayne wanted any part of betting the bank on these odds, the Panthers by far exceeding anyone's expectations, especially this early in the season. No spiritual intervention by those predicting last year's three-peat was required, so thought Benji, joyful and jubilant to say the least.

Emerald is next on the schedule. After being ranked #2 in 3A in the pre-season polls, Emerald is still looking for their first victory. TL Hanna beat the Vikings 47-7 Friday night dropping them to 0-2 on the season. Frank Hill Stadium in Greenwood is the location, and kickoff is at 7:30.

As always... God Bless and Go Panthers!

Benji, juiced and excited beyond description, readied the rally for the upcoming contest against Greenwood county rival, Emerald. There would be no yellow brick road leading to this Emerald City though and the voice of the all-powerful OZ wouldn't intervene. The Panthers would play the roles of the Lion, Scare Crow and Tin man, courage, brains and heart. Everything rested squarely on the shoulders of those wearing the pads and sporting the Block A helmets. Benji frames the matchup as only he can.

AUG 29 Week Two @ Emerald: Preview

Game three of the 2018 season has the Abbeville Panthers (2-0) facing off against a familiar foe. The 3A Emerald Vikings (0-2) campus sits only about 14 miles from Abbeville's. Separated by a county line, it's a natural rivalry game for the two schools who have played each other every year since 1996. The Panthers own a 16-7 all-time record versus the Vikings. All but two of Emerald's wins have been at home, inside of Frank Hill Stadium, the site of Friday night's match-up. The Panthers took care of the Vikings last season with a 56-21 win at Hite Stadium. Emerald made a run to the 3A Upperstate Championship game later that season, after winning their Region, and eventually losing to Chapman, capping 10-4 season.

The Vikings have been tasked with replacing nearly 3,700 yards of offense from last season. With Keshawn Settles and Treshawn Chamberlain gone, the Vikings are still trying to find that one-two punch in the backfield that led to last season's success. The Vikings were ranked #2 in the pre-season polls, just behind the unanimous #1 Dillion. Two losses to open the season now has Emerald looking for answers and hoping for a game that can turn their season around. Luke Deal got a lot of the press this summer with his announcement to play college football at Auburn after a lengthy recruiting process. The 6'5" 240 pound tight end/linebacker is surrounded by other talented players that possess what you'd want in a team, size, speed and experience.

With 29 upperclassmen on the roster, it seems like it's only a matter of time before Head Coach Tim McMahon finds the right recipe to get Emerald back on the winning side of things. McMahon who is 59-50 in his 10th season will be leaning on a "power I" offense and a defense that is big and multiple. Zack Amerson, a Liberty University commit will get the bulk of the carries while Jamil Martin, a senior speedster is their change of pace back. Martin was injured and did not play in their 47-7 loss versus TL Hanna last week. Kedarren Dean, #1, is the senior quarterback that directs the offense and #24 Nick Sheets is a big contributor on defense. Emerald is big, really big. Multiple 300 pounders are the reason that Coach McMahon pointed toward his offensive line in the offseason as the strength of his offense.

The Panthers meanwhile have sailed through their first two games. They've averaged 53 points per game and have yet to allow a point. The loaded offensive backfield for the Panthers have barely broken a sweat this season. JD Moore, junior quarterback has 15 carries on the season, which leads all players in carries. That's an unusual stat,15 carries is hardly a heavy work load for one game, much less two games. The Panther defense have been so disruptive and physically dominate this season, that the Panther offense has rarely had to navigate a drive starting on their side of the field.

Panther Head Coach Jamie Nickles never misses a moment to test and teach his team. The message this week is adversity. "I'm curious to see how we respond to adversity. It could come on the first drive versus Emerald. It could come late in the 4th quarter. You just never know, but every team will face adversity eventually and that's how you can judge the fabric of a team, how they respond to adversity." Coach Nickles said.

Can the Panthers keep up the impressive start to the season? Will they respond positively, should adversity strike? Only time will tell. Kickoff is set for 7:30 PM at Frank Hill Stadium on the campus of Emerald High School.

As always, God Bless and Go Panthers!

Benji-Wayne mantra stood fast yet again as, *we didn't see this coming*.

Wayne recapped his adventure on trying to enter Emerald Stadium through security for the listening audience.

> "I set the metal detector wand off. I took off everything I could take off and it continued setting off the alarm. Finally, they got another wand and I passed inspection."

Benji commented on the slow start to the beginning of the game. Delay of game achieved new heights at the hands of the referees. Nobody was providing an explanation so Benji came up with his own.

> "We can start now. Henry Green just entered the stadium. Apparently, the refs were waiting on scoop Green to get here."

The A-Train Rolls through Emerald

The Panthers rolled into week 2 of the regular season undefeated, and they rolled out the same way. Big plays, an unrelenting defense and more speed than the law should allow, propelled Abbeville to a convincing 52-17 win over the Emerald Vikings. The Panthers moved to 3-0 on the season, as Emerald remained winless at 0-3.

Note: The first drive was stymied, and Abbeville punted for the first time this season.

Dylan Beauford started the scoring onslaught for the Panthers when he hit a career best 46-yard field goal with 6:37 to play in the first quarter. The kick would have been good from 50+. Junior quarterback JD Moore added a 35-yard touchdown run just a minute later to put the Panthers up 10-0. The tone was set, and the game was pretty much in the bag from that point forward. The Panther defense never allowed Emerald to get in a rhythm by applying constant pressure from their defensive front. Nate Temple, Ar'Darius Burton and Carson Smith harassed the Viking quarterback to the point that he finished 1-9 passing for 49 yards and an interception, courtesy of Quadarius Gullibeaux.

The next Viking punt pinned the Panthers back to the 3-yard line. The second play from scrimmage saw Panther senior Courtney Jackson catch another gear and out race everyone for a 93-yard touchdown. Jackson wasn't done with the afterburners yet either. After a 37-yard Emerald field goal, Jackson took the ensuing kickoff 85 yards for a touchdown. Jackson finished the night with 4 carries for 112 yards and a touchdown. Giving him 197 total yards and two TD's for the game. JD Moored added to his passing touchdown tally on the season as he hit Quad Woods and Ja'Bryan Sanders for TD tosses of 28 and 38 yards respectively. A blocked punt recovered by Ar'Darius Burton for a TD, right before halftime made the score 45-10 and completely out of reach. A continuous clock in the second half was the only thing that slowed the A-Train down. 52-17 final.

Benji had envisioned a 40-14 victory for the Panthers in his preseason prediction. He nailed it, the final just a tad more lopsided. So far, his predictions had mirrored the 3-0 start. No heavenly help had influenced his, not that he was aware of.

Here are some excerpts from Greenwood's Index Journal 09/01 and 09/02/18, articles by staff writer Greg Deal.

Before the game hype 9/01/18:

Tonight's game between Abbeville and Emerald features two of the greatest forces in Lakelands football this year: Abbeville's bruising running game and Emerald's rugged defense.

Abbeville coach Jamie Nickles, who has led his team to two straight blowout victories to start the year, said he's watched plenty of tape on Emerald and expects a challenge up front.

Coach Nick was quoted as saying the following about Emerald,

> "They are so big. Their defensive line is almost *unblockable*. They have the skilled people to go along with that. If we don't do the little things on the offensive line, they'll be in our backfield on each and every play. If we don't play with good fundamentals on our defensive line, they will blow us all the way back to Abbeville.
>
> Running backs are worth their weight in gold, especially in our offense. The more you have, the better you are going to be.
>
> How do we respond when things don't go our way? That's when I'll evaluate our team and see where it goes."

Emerald coach Tim McMahon's shared his perspective with the Index,

> "We're excited about a great team coming to play us, and I do mean great. We've got a lot of respect for Abbeville High School. They do it right. It's a

great challenge for our kids physically. I think our kids are excited about it. But anytime you face a team with the quality to do things the right way, it's exciting.

Obviously, we're going to take steps forward. The biggest thing is, we're facing a physical challenge. And we need to improve by growing up and seeing if we can face that physicality."

More comments in Index 09/02/18 after the game, by Coach Nick,

"That Emerald team came ready to play. That first quarter was quite a battle. It felt like a playoff game. They were playing more players both ways than us. I really saw that in the second quarter, but that first quarter was a brawl."

Coach McMahon summarized the game,

"We made some mistakes. We had some missed assignments on both sides. We made mistakes that set them up, and they're a good football team. We made a few steps forward. We were physical in the first half and we played well on defense."

Benji ended with closing comments,

The Panthers will be on the road again next as they travel to Southside Christian. The Sabers are 2-1 on the season, losing by one-point last week to Woodruff. This game will be fun as two completely different offenses will take the field. The Panthers with their pound and ground attack, versus Southside Christian's fast paced, spread aerial attack.

With the Panthers now 3-0 on the young season, the WZLA radio host and football announcer, prepared his preview for what might be the Panther's ultimate test. If he ever needed more Pidgy cow bell or wisdom from Hite and Botts it could be now. No dreams, no visions, no wispy fogs or ghostly reflections in window fronts contributed though. He and Wayne would be in the booth without spiritual oversight from Fletcher Ferguson or longtime pal Keith 'Honk' Hall. Nothing to do but lay out the preview for the Panther-Sabres matchup.

Week 3 vs Southside Christian Preview

A new week brings new challenges, and more questions. The main question is; When will the Panthers be tested this season? Abbeville has rolled through their first three opponents by a total combined score of 158-17. All three games have basically been over at halftime. Will this week be different? Let's look at the Panthers Week 3 opponent, Southside Christian.

The Sabres, who are 2-1 on the season are a great looking group of young men. Big across both offensive and defensive lines, they have experience at all the key positions and most importantly, they are hungry. Led by Head Coach Mike Sonneborn, the Sabres are ready to prove they are among the elite in AA football. Sonneborn has some tools to work with. Southside Christian plays an up tempo, spread offense like you'd normally see on Saturday's watching college football. JW Hertzberg, #7, a junior quarterback is big (6'3" 220lbs) and has a cannon for an arm. He's a good decision maker and has playmakers on the outside. Bryson Cheek, #4, is a regular target for Hertzberg.

The match-up between the Sabres wide receivers and the Panthers defensive secondary will be a fun one to watch. SSC also has a couple of running backs that they utilize for a balanced attack. Mallroy Pickney, #44 (6'0" 205lbs) is a bruising running back who gets tough yards between the tackles, while #6 Anthony McFadden is their change of pace back (5'7" 180lbs) who can get to the second level of a defense in a hurry. The Sabres dropped a heartbreaker last week as they lost 28-27 to Woodruff. The Sabres are outscoring their opponents by an average of 30.6 to 14 this season. Defensively, SSC is again, big, fast and experienced. #42 JR Schroeder (6'1" 215lbs) is a four-year starter at linebacker and holds a lot of college offers. Overall the Sabres return 15 starters from a team that finished 10-2 last season.

Meanwhile, your back to back to back AA State Champ Abbeville Panthers have adopted a very workman like approach to this season. They seem unphased by their opponents or any hype that comes along with them. The theme last week from Head Coach Jamie Nickles was "adversity". He wanted to see how the Panthers would respond to adversity. I'm not sure punting twice in three games constitutes adversity, but the Panthers seemed to respond. After blanking Lincoln County and Newberry, the Panthers gave up their first points of the season last week at Emerald. To say that the Panther defense is playing with a chip on their shoulder would be a mild understatement.

This team doesn't just want to win games. They want their names mentioned among the best that ever wore the Garnet and Gold. They're off to a good start. The Panthers average final score in its first three games are 52.7 to 5.7. The defense is led by leading tackler #36 Tyreke Campbell who has 23 tackles, 2 tackles for loss, a recovered fumble and a blocked punt. #53 junior defensive lineman Carson Smith has collected 21 tackles, 5 for loss, a sack and a fumble recovery. Nate Temple leads the team in sacks with four. Another amazing stat from this Panther team is that they are +11 in the turnover margin. Defensive Coordinator Tad Dubose has his group playing a very fast and physical brand of A-Town football.

Offensively the Panthers have hardly broken a sweat. Averaging 301.7 yards rushing per game at a 9.6 yard per carry clip, the Panthers have distributed the ball among 12 different ball carries this season. Leading rusher, quarterback JD Moore (23 carries-265 yards-5 TD), has proved to be the perfect ball distributor in Offensive Coordinator Mark Smith's offense. Senior running back Courtney Jackson (17-197-4) is averaging 11.6 yards per carry this season, while fullback Dominick "the bus" Washington (15-154-1) and Ja'Bryan 'Dooley' Sanders (7-139-3) round out a dangerously explosive four-headed monster in the backfield for the Panthers. Sanders is averaging a ridiculous 19.9 yards per carry.

The air attack has been a pleasant surprise for the Panthers this season as well. They can do more than just ground and pound. JD Moore has connected with Quad Woods (5 rec-77yds-2tds) Sanders, and Robin Crawford on touchdown passes this season. It's a pick your poison scenario for opposing defenses. Stack the box with 9, or 10 defenders and the Panthers are capable of throwing it over the top. Only play 7 in the box to defend the pass and the Panther will pound out run after run with their big offensive line and stable full of running backs. It's a great time to be a Panther.

Southside Christian will be having "Salute to Heroes Night" at Sabre Stadium. There will be free admission to all past and present First Responders/Military, their spouses and children. There are not very many seats on the visitor's side, so get there early and be loud and proud. As always…

God Bless and Go Panthers!

Definition for Expectations: a strong belief that something will happen or be the case in the future.

The hype and expectations were achieved last Friday night at Southside Christian. Benji best summarizes the first real test of the season.

Southside Christian Sabres Review and Bye Week Thoughts

Sheewww… I think that's what most everyone wearing garnet and gold muttered Friday night as the clock struck zero at Sabre Stadium in Simpsonville. The Panthers found themselves in a dog fight and in true A-Town fashion, they never quit. The Panthers prevailed 43-28 against a very tough, very big, very well coached Southside Christian football team. It almost felt like you were trying to chop down an oak tree with a sledge hammer. Hit after hit, fighting for every yard, every inch. Without a doubt, SSC is the best team that Abbeville has faced thus far this season. A great, yet exhausting game, that will only make the Panthers better as a team moving forward. Here are some highlights.

JD Moore and Dooley Sanders hooked up on a 76-yard touchdown pass on the second play from scrimmage. The Panthers led 7-0 early. SSC answers with a 19-yard TD pass to tie the game. As the 2nd quarter began, JD Moore sprinted 58 yards for a TD to give the Panthers the lead once again. Two minutes later SSC ties it back up with a halfback pass. JD Moore breaks the tie with a 5-yard TD run and then right before the half, he completes a 2-yard TD pass to Sanders to give the Panthers a 28-14 halftime lead. A Courtney Jackson touchdown run was sandwiched between two SSC TD passes and the score stood at 36-28 until JD Moore put the nail in the coffin with a 39-yard TD run with 31 seconds remaining. The Panthers won 43-28 and moved to 4-0 on the season.

JD Moore was recognized as the Index Journal Player of the Week for his five-touchdown performance. Panther linebacker Tyreke Campbell was recognized as Defensive Player of the Week by the Greenwood Touchdown Club for his game versus Emerald. Congrats to those two Panther student athletes.

Rest and mental preparedness are what this bye week is all about. Bumps and bruises will be healed. Soreness will fade. The Panthers will mentally get ready for next week as they travel to Kellytown Stadium to face the #1 team in 4A, the Hartsville Red Foxes. The coaches will self scout this week as well. They will watch film of themselves and see if they notice tendencies that other teams may pick up on and possibly tweak their offense or defense accordingly. It's a week of mental focus and physical rest. They will evaluate players and positions and make adjustments there as well. They will also start in on preparing for teams that they may face down the road.

After a trip to Hartsville, A-Town will be back home for just their 2nd home game of the season, the region opener versus longtime rival Batesburg-Leesville. A Thursday night contest at Fox Creek will get us into October. Then the Panthers will be home versus a much-improved Silver Bluff team. On the road at Saluda and then back to the Hite for homecoming versus Ninety Six will end the regular season. The Panthers next game will mark the halfway point in the season. It sure goes by in a hurry.

Here are some stats at the (almost) midway point in the season.

Points per game – Abbeville 50.3 vs 11.3

3rd down conversions – Abbeville 15/31 – 48.4% vs 7/47 – 14.9%

Turnovers – Abbeville 1 vs 13

Rushing – Abbeville 1288yds (322 per game) vs 567 (141.8)

Tackles for Loss – 28 (7 per game)

Sacks – 9 – 5 QB pressures – 10 recovered fumbles – 1 interception – 2 blocked kicks

Individual stats

Rushing (players with over 10 carries) – JD Moore (43 carries – 438 yards – 8 touchdowns) Courtney Jackson (31-273-5) Ja'Bryan Sanders (18-217-3) Dominick Washington (24-198-1)

Passing – JD Moore 9 of 15 for 229 yds 6 TDs and 1 interception

Receiving – Ja'Bryan Sanders (3-116-3) Quad Woods (5-77-2) Robin Crawford (1-21-1) Courtney Jackson (1-19)

Defensive stats (only players with over 20 tackles)

Tyreke Campbell – 35 tackles-2 tackles for loss-1 sack-2 recovered fumbles-1 interception

Carson Smith – 27 tkls – 5 tfl – 1 sk – 1 caused fumble – 1 recovered fumble

Luke Evans – 24 tkls – 1 tfl

David Cobb 23 tkls – 2 tfl

Nate Temple – 21 tkls – 5 tfl – 4 sks

Joc Norman – 20 tkls

Gabe Calhoun – 20tkls – 1 tfl

It's been a great season so far and we're looking forward too many more games this year. Check back next week for a full preview of the Clash of the Titans. Your #1 AA Abbeville Panthers versus #1 AAAA Hartsville Red Foxes. And as always…

God Bless and Go Panthers!

Only Hurricanes and record-breaking floods can slow the Panther momentum.

T. Allen Winn,

> "We've lived in the Myrtle Beach area since 2005. Two years ago, 2016, Hurricane Matthew, a Category 1 made land fall. Only Zone A on the immediate coast were issued mandatory evacuation. We are in Zone B and remained at home. As the hurricane weakened and made landfall, we thought we had dodged disaster. That's when the backside of the storm slammed us, bringing winds that downed trees everywhere, including our neighborhood. We were hemmed in the first day, trees blocking our exit. We lost power for four days but hunkered down at home with candles, propane cookers water and food. It wasn't easy but thankfully we were not in a flood zone and were spared the flooding that impacted so many.
>
> Fast forward to 2018, Hurricane Florence approaching the coast as a Cat 4, just shy of a 5. Mandatory evacuation was issued for all three coastal zones, A, B and C. This was a first by the governor. We didn't hesitate and evacuated. This one was a devastating rain and flood event. We dodged another bullet thankfully. Prayers were with the many thousands that didn't fair so well, too many losing everything. I'll be the first to admit it. Abbeville Panther football was the furthest from our minds. Lives and homes were at stake. The storm had remained almost stationary for days over the Carolinas churning and dumping record rainfall. Coastal South Carolina would also have to cope with the flooding from North Carolina yet to make its way down the rivers on its way to the ocean. Life would forever be altered in Horry and surrounding counties. Even now, as I write this, five months later, the recovery continues for far too many. Some lives have returned to some semblance of normalcy while others have yet to overcome the tragedy that altered their lives.

Through both these hurricanes I have witnessed sights I could have never envisioned while living in Abbeville. We thank the Lord above for sparing us and we continue to pray for those needing of our prayers. We're not promised anything in this life we live. One thing for sure, material things can and will be replaced. One life lost is too many. Please continue to keep those impacted by the east coast and gulf hurricanes and west coast fires in your prayers.

Now, I return you to Benji as he navigates through what remains of Abbeville's football season."

SEPT 26 Week 6 Preview vs Batesburg-Leesville

Hurricane Florence is still wreaking havoc on the Pee Dee region of South Carolina and while a game against Hartsville would have been a lot of fun, that community is still far from returning to normalcy. Horry, Georgetown and Darlington Counties have taken a beating and they are still battling flood waters and all the tragedy that ensues. Some things are bigger than football and we will continually keep those communities in our thoughts and prayers.

For us though, finally, it's game week. It seems like it's been six months since the Panthers strapped on that Block A helmet and faced an opponent on the gridiron. A much-needed bye week on September 14th, followed by the Hartsville cancellation on the 21st has kept the Panthers on the practice fields and out from under the Friday night spotlight. This Friday a familiar foe will come to town. Hite Stadium will be open for business as we welcome in the Batesburg-Leesville Panthers.

B-L and Abbeville have faced each other 42 times, dating back to the 1950's. The overall record couldn't get any closer as both Panther teams have won 21 times each. The next win will obviously break the all-time tie in a series that has produced some classics. Who can forget the Upperstate Championship game in 2000? Played in a driving rain storm, Matt Hagen kicks his only field goal of the season and sends A-Town to Columbia with a 3-0 win. And God rest his soul, Layfatte Miller's last second score that sent Hite Stadium into a frenzy and gave Abbeville a huge come from behind win. Batesburg-Leesville beat Abbeville at home in the Upperstate Championship game in 2003. That was also the last game that South Carolina Football Hall of Fame head coach Dennis Botts ever coached. History, tradition and a good spirited rivalry is what makes this game that we love so special.

Let's look at this year's match-up. Unlike Abbeville, B-L has had some coaching turnover. From 1992 until 2012 B-L had two coaches. Phil Strickland (92-02) and Courtney McInnis (03-11). Since 2012, head coach Gary Adams is the third coach to lead the purple Panthers. Perry Woolbright led B-L to the State Championship game in 2016 and then left for 5A Lexington the next year. Speaking of state championships, B-L claims 7 state titles in their history (27-28-79-95-99-05-13). This season they are 2-2 with wins over Ridge Springs Monetta and Mid Carolina. Their two losses were to Gilbert, and a shootout with Newberry (41-39).

The Purple Panthers like to spread it out on offense. You'll see three and four wide receiver sets most of the night. They use an "H-Back" as a lead blocker on most running plays and they try to stretch you with long passes to open up their running game. Quarterback #1 Ke'shoun Williams can throw it around the ball field as well as anyone. B-L uses slants and quick screen passes to keep defenses moving side to side before laying it out there 30 or 40 yards. Tay Wilson, #9, is the running back that often splits out as a slot receiver, he's joined by #10 DT Jackson. Jackson is a

6'4" junior that when paired up with #11 Shauntrel Hendrix, becomes a deadly duo on the edges for the B-L Panthers. On the season B-L averages scoring 27.5 points per game while giving up 28.5 points per game on defense. Coincidentally, B-L hasn't played in two weeks either. Their bye week was also followed by a cancellation against Lexington.

The hometown Panthers are just itching to play a game. Just line somebody up and let's play. That seemed to be the mood around the locker room earlier this week. When talking to head coach Jamie Nickles, he stated that, *"The guys should be fully rested and ready to go. We're just glad to be back home and ready to get this one started."* When asked about their schedule during the layoff, he said, *"We practiced six days during the last two weeks. It's almost like when I played back in the 80's. You practiced for a month before that first jamboree. You thought that jamboree would never get here. That's where we are, just ready to get to gameday."*

The Panthers are 4-0 on the season. They are unanimously ranked #1 in AA and currently ranked 4th regardless of classification in the state of SC. The Panthers are averaging 50.2 points per game offensively, while giving up 11.2 points per game on defense, including back to back shut outs to start the season. Junior quarterback JD Moore leads the Panther offense that is averaging 322 yards rushing per game. He's also tossed 6 touchdowns this year. Moore also leads all rushers with 438 yards and 8 rushing TD's.

The Panther defense has been crazy good this year. They have twice as many turnovers as their opponents have third down conversions. Think about that for a minute. They have forced 13 turnovers this season and they've only given up 6 third down conversions. Insane. Tyreke Campbell leads the team in tackles with 35. Nate Temple leads the team in sacks with four and Carson Smith leads the team in tackles for loss with six. Add in one of the best kickers in the state in Dylan Beauford, and you've got one talented football team.

The rivalry will be renewed this Friday at 730 PM. Remember that Hite Stadium has a clear bag policy in place with no exceptions, so get there early to avoid long lines. This is the region opener, and a huge game with playoff seedings at stake. Check back next week for a full review and a look ahead to the Panthers Thursday night contest at Fox Creek. As always…

God Bless and Go Panthers!

No Yoda sporting a Panther mascot outfit miraculously appeared from the beyond to Benji this year. Bobby Leon Smith, rest his soul, sat out any making predictions for the 2018 run at another championship. Did that mean he won the bet with Jerry Winn, another Panther manager from way back when? Jerry didn't haunt Benji's dreams either. What did this mean for the chances of a fourth state title? The spiritual world remained deathly quiet while the Panther roared loudly, thus far clawing their way through the competition. Benji recaps the feline frenzy played out on the football field.

Leaving No Doubt, the Panther-Panther Recap

Earlier last week Abbeville Panther head coach Jamie Nickles was worried. That's nothing new. He always worries, but he had a cause for his concern. His team, undefeated, ranked #1 in the state in AA, had not played a game in two weeks. It had been three weeks to the day, at the time of kickoff. He was concerned with them being rusty, and not being in "game shape". One of the many details of Coach Nick's job is to cover every detail, and make sure the team is prepared for anything that can happen when they are on the field of play. How do you prepare a team for something that had never been done? No Abbeville football team in 101 years had two consecutive bye weeks in the middle of the regular season. Were they going to be focused, prepared, ready, in shape…his worries and the list goes on and on. It took a total of about four minutes to answer his questions. Yes, they were ready. More than ready, they were hungry, and it showed on the field and on the scoreboard.

Batesburg-Leesville returned the opening kickoff 50 yards and immediately was set up in Abbeville territory. A Cruz Temple interception squashed B-L's opening drive and ignited an Abbeville team that played with grit, heart and a deep desire to win. A 14-yard sprint by Courtney Jackson (2-59-1) started the Abbeville scoring onslaught that didn't end until Coach Nick called off the dogs in the 3rd quarter. Leading 7-0, three minutes after Jackson's touchdown run, Dominick Washington (6-76-1) barreled into the endzone to put the Panthers up 14-0.

Ja'Bryan Sanders (3-57-2) scored three minutes later, and then JD Moore (7-97-1) out sprinted the B-L defense for a 60-yard TD run to make the score 27-0. Moore found Quad Woods for a 20-yard TD pass on their next possession for his 7th TD toss of the year. The scoring continued as Robin Crawford (6-29-1) found pay dirt to put the Panthers up 41-0 with 2 minutes left before halftime. Ja'Bryan Sanders out raced the B-L defense for a 27-yard score in the third quarter and the Panthers led 48-7. The Panther defense got in on the scoring fun when B-L running back Tayvon Wilson was stripped of the ball. Nate Temple scooped and scored from 31 yards out. 55-7 was the final score, and honestly, it wasn't that close.

The Panthers averaged 9.9 yards per play. They rushed for 365 yards and controlled the game from the opening whistle. The Panther defense was suffocating again. B-L faced eleven third downs on Friday night and they only converted twice. For the season, the Panthers are holding their opponents to a 15.5% third down success rate. That's salty, gritty and just plain nasty.

Next will be a THURSDAY night game at Fox Creek. As always…God Bless and Go Panthers!

Benji's preseason prediction: A-Town Panthers 36 – B-L Panthers 23 – he got the win right.

Fox Creek, where in the world is Fox Creek? I had to give Benji a shout out from the beach to inquire where this team resided. And why in the world was this being set as a Thursday night match-up? A strange season indeed, a bye week, a flood cancelation and now a Thursday game, what next, a no disqualification triple threat match, teams to be determined? Now I return your reading back over to its regular scheduled programming. Take it from here, Benji.

Week 7 Preview @ Fox Creek

Are you not a fan of Thursday night varsity football? Blame Luke Bryan. The country star is holding his "Down on the Farm" tour in North Augusta on Friday night. Fox Creek Head Coach Derrick Quinn reached out to Abbeville Athletic Director Tad Dubose earlier this summer suggesting a time change for the game because of the concert. They agreed to play on Thursday. So here we are. Week seven of the regular season *(I can't believe it is already week seven)* and week two of region play. Let's take a look at how the Panthers and the Predators stack up against each other.

Fox Creek can be considered new blood. The program began in 2006 under coach Russ Schneider. They endured a rough start, winning just 5 games over their first four seasons. Since then, it's been a steady climb for the Predators. A couple of eight-win seasons saw a slight drop off last year as the Predators finished 6-5, including a first round loss to Chesterfield. This year Fox Creek is 3-2 (0-1) on the season with wins over Wagner-Salley (19-12), Johnson (33-8), and McCormick (42-6). They have since lost two straight to Crescent (35-29) and Ninety Six (41-17). This is the first ever meeting between Abbeville and Fox Creek.

Panther Head Coach Jamie Nickles had this to say about Fox Creek,

> "They are definitely a good team. This will not be a show up and win type of game. We don't have any of those types of games on the schedule. The size of Fox Creek impresses me. Their quarterback might be 250 pounds. And they like to sling it. They are heavy on RPO, this is kind of RPO region, so we'll get to see that a lot. Fast, they have some real burners. It'll be a great challenge for us."

The big QB that Coach Nickles speaks of is #3 Cam Mitchem. He's 6'2 and listed at 235 pounds. He is completing 53% of his passes this season. He's thrown eight touchdowns to just one interception. His favorite target is Junior Wide Receiver Jatonious Butler. He's a speedy slot guy who has 16 catches and 5 touchdowns on the year. The Predators are not just an aerial attack team, they are balanced and like to run the football out of four and five wide receiver sets. Leading rusher Darius Curtis averages 8.2 yards per carry and has scored five touchdowns on the ground so far this year. QB Cam Mitchem also gets his fair share of carries, he leads the team in carries, and is second on the team in yards rushing with 245 yards. If Mitchem gets into a rhythm and Fox Creek finds rushing lanes, they can be dangerous.

Defensively Fox Creek returns the majority of their team from last year, including the entire front seven. Linebacker Errius Ishmal leads the team with 62 tackles and 11 tackles for loss. Jalen Jennings has 41 tackles, and defensive line mates Terreco

Ramage and Bobby Mays have combined for 60 tackles and 21 tackles for loss this season. As a unit, Fox Creek has an amazing 56 total tackles for loss in their five games. They make teams play behind the chains and it allows them to be more aggressive with blitzes and unique coverages.

With Abbeville (5-0 – 1-0), what you see is what you get. You know what's coming offensively. Stopping it is an entirely different animal. Speed, speed and more speed. It's not coachable. It's not attainable. You either have it or you don't. Abbeville has a lot of it on both sides of the ball. So much so that the Panther running backs are as fresh as a daisy at this point in the season. Offensive Coordinator Mark Smith has done a tremendous job spreading the ball around to all his playmakers. Quarterback JD Moore leads all ball carriers (50-535-9) *the first number is carries, followed by yards and then touchdowns*. He's followed by Courtney Jackson (33-332-6), Ja'Bryan Sanders (21-274-5), and Dominick Washington (30-274-2). As you can see by the numbers, each ball carrier is averaging 10 yards per carry, or just under. That's incredible. All of that would not be possible if not for one of the best offensive lines that Abbeville has fielded, well, maybe ever? Jake Hill, Trai Jones, Conner Nickles, DaDa Bowie, DeMichael Johnson and tight end Tillman Allen have been steady as a rock all season. They are punishing opposing defensive lines and helping the Panthers rush for 330.6 yards per game while averaging 51.2 points per game. Those are PlayStation numbers that are being played out right before our very eyes each week.

The Panther defense is special this season. They've faced option teams, traditional pro/ I-formation teams, spread teams that like to throw, spread teams that like to run, and they've shut all of them down. The Panther D led by defensive coordinator Tad Dubose is allowing 10.4 points per game. I'd love to single out the defensive line, or the linebackers, or even the secondary as being the key reason for the success. The thing is, you can't just point to one position group. This defense is so good at every level. Speed is again the culprit. Abbeville's defensive lineman (*tackles -tackles for loss-sacks*) Nate Temple (25-6-4.5), Carson Smith (35-6-3.5), Ar'Darius Burton (22-4) and Ami'leon Mattison (13-2-1). When they don't make a play behind the line of scrimmage, they are making room for Linebackers Luke Evans (35-2), Cruz Temple (20-2-2int) and Tyreke Campbell (37-4-1) to roam free and wreak havoc. The secondary locks down receivers and provides great run support with David Cobb (29-2), Malik Leach (23tkls), Quadarius Guillebeaux (20-1-1), Joc Norman (23tkls) and Jhalyn Shuler (24-4). Collectively the Panther defense has caused 15 turnovers this season and only allowed their opponents to complete 9 of 58 third down conversions. With this defense, and kicker Dylan Beauford blasting every kickoff through the endzone, opposing offenses don't have a great shot at scoring. The Panthers are ranked unanimously #1 in AA and 4th overall in the state regardless of classification for a reason. They are historically good this year. How good? Come see for yourself Thursday night in Fox Creek.

As always…God Bless and Go Panthers!

These are excerpts from Greenwood's Index Journal prior to Thursday's showdown from staff writer, Greg Deal.

Silver Bluff's De'Angelo Bryant has history with Abbeville. The Bulldogs' head coach was a player on the 2000 team that defeated the Panthers for the state championship at Williams-Brice Stadium in Columbia. He also has a healthy respect for the Class 2A No. 1-ranked Panthers (6-0 overall, 2-0 in Region 2-2A).

Bryant was quoted as saying,

> "Abbeville is a very well-coached football team. It is evident in the way they compete. They are physical on both fronts and have talent at the skill positions. It is evident that the team has great cohesion with one another and the coaching staff. They remind me of the 2000 and 2001 state championship teams that I was a part of, at Sliver Bluff."

Coach Nick commented,

> "We're preparing for a very good Silver Bluff team. I'm impressed with their athleticism. I have a great respect for their program. We must concentrate on the fundamentals and technique. We must block the inside gaps. We can't wait on them to come get you."

Thursday night streaming from the beach was a change from normal but gameday is gameday, right? WZLA in my headphones I listened as always. Here you have happy Thursday thoughts from a Google search.

Happy Thursday Sayings

1. Be in love with every minute of your life – live every day like it's your last.
2. Be happy with what you have while working for what you want.
3. It's Thursday. Let's get shaken and stirred.
4. You have to value all the things that you have right now.
5. Inspire others, give thanks and live in the moment every day of the week.
6. Think positive and positive things will happen.
7. One small positive thought in the morning can change your whole day.
8. Optimism is a happiness magnet. If you stay positive, good things will happen to you.
9. Let God guide you in your path today. He will provide you the strength that you need.
10. Always think about positive thoughts so that you can move forward and be an inspiration to other people.
11. A new day also means a new beginning. Forget about the past and have a fresh start.

The envelope please, Benji, and the winner is…

The Donut Gang

Anytime a football team's regular schedule is thrown off, there is cause for some concern. We are creatures of habit. Most well coached football programs stick to a routine. Especially if that routine has produced six state championship game appearances in eight years. While a Thursday night game wasn't the end of the world, I'll be honest, a little luster was lost not playing on a Friday night. The Panthers, however, did what great teams do. They adjusted, handled their business and went home with another dominate 50-0 victory over the Fox Creek Predators.

The ending score wasn't necessarily indicative of how the game began. The Panthers offense looked flat on their first couple of drives. It wasn't until Courtney Jackson (7-58-2) powered into the endzone with 1:30 left in the first quarter that you began to see some energy on the A-Town sideline. That energy led to a Quadarius Guillebeaux interception on the next Fox Creek drive. JD Moore (11-147-2) scooted 33 yards for a touchdown just 52 seconds after Jackson's TD run and the Panthers led 15-0 after the first quarter. Jackson and Moore added TD runs of 16 and 80 yards to send the game to halftime with the Panthers leading 29-0. Robin Crawford (4-18-1), Cruz Temple (2-18-1) and Malik Leach (2-8-1) capped the 2nd half scoring and the Panthers rolled to their second straight region win. Back up QB Hunter Rogers (6-97) helped control the clock and lead the Panthers in the third and fourth quarters.

Even though the Panthers grinded out 489 yards rushing at 11.4 yards per carry, the story of the night was the defense. Interceptions by Quadarius Guillebeaux, Malik Leach and David Cobb, who swiped two picks on the night, kept the Fox Creek offense rattled. Fox Creek's highly touted QB Cam Mitchem was harassed all night by Jihad Washington and the speedy and a relentless Panther defensive line. Mitchem finished 3 of 13 passing for 34 yards and 4 interceptions. He rushed 12 times for just 26 yards. Overall, Fox Creek only managed 100 total yards on 40 plays. That's an average of 2.5 yards per play. When the clock hit zero's, the 'Donut Gang' had another shut out and a date with some Krispy Kreme's this coming Tuesday.

Benji's preseason prediction: Panthers 52 – Predators 17. Okay, he almost nailed this one, so we should be satisfied with that, so long as the Panthers remain on the winning end of the stick.

Next up is the Silver Bluff game, which is this coming Friday at Hite Stadium-Dennis Botts Field. And, be sure to grab something Pink to wear. It's Breast Cancer Awareness Month, and the Panthers are supporting the cause with it is the annual PINK OUT game. All fans wear your Pink! As always… God Bless and Go Panthers!

Week 7 in the rearview mirror, the Panthers continued their dominance. Benji also continued his noneventful spiritual and dream state, again wondering if the second shoe would drop and put a stop to the ride toward Benedict College and a December fairytale ending. It seemed unlikely but never get too over confident. One can be quickly humbled in a blink. The Panthers were clearly on a path to make history once again, but you had to reach the finish line first. It was way too early to celebrate. Benji just kept true to the course, taking one game at a time, as did the Abbeville Panthers, and he tossed out the match up based on the stats and as he envisioned it.

Week 8 Preview vs. Silver Bluff

Another familiar foe will roll into Hite Stadium Friday night. The Silver Bluff Bulldogs will make the hour and a half trek up Hwy 28 to take on the undefeated, unanimous number one ranked Abbeville Panthers in a Region 2-AA battle. The Panthers and Bulldogs have shared the spotlight on the biggest of stages before. In 2000 the Bulldogs defeated Abbeville at Williams Brice Stadium to capture the State Championship in an instant classic. The Panthers returned the favor in 2015 at Charlie W Johnson Stadium, when they beat SB 45-27 to capture their 7th State Championship. All in all, the Panthers and Bulldogs have met 10 times in their history, with the Panthers holding a 6-4 advantage in the series.

This season, head coach D'Angelo Bryant will bring his Silver Bluff squad into Hite Stadium looking for their first Region win of the season. SB is 3-3 on the year and 0-2 in Region play. The Bulldogs, after 23 very successful seasons under the direction of Al Lown, have found themselves in a rebuilding mode as of late. Lown suffered one losing season in his tenure, and since his departure in 2015, the Bulldogs have gone 3-7 and 5-6 in the last two seasons. Bryant has brought in a renewed enthusiasm to the Bulldog program that he once played for, under Lown. In fact, Bryant was on the 2000 State Championship team that beat Abbeville. In an article from the Aiken Standard newspaper, Bryant was quoted as saying, *"The great part about it is these guys, their freshman year, were under my former head coach, coach (Al) Lown. I think that they see some of the same principles that I carry on through coach Lown as well. Just really getting back to that type of standard is my No. 1 priority for these guys, but to also bring a little bit of my style and my flavor of some things that I've done."*

His style and flavor started with changing the entire offense. No more double wing for SB. They are now a spread team who run primarily a run-pass-option (RPO) style of offense. Yet they still incorporate some of the Wing-T principals. Defense has always been the calling card for the Bulldogs. On the season SB is averaging 28.3 points per game while giving up 17.3 on defense. The linebacker corps may be the strength of the Bulldog defense. The senior laden group is led by #14 Jamey Bing, #7 Jarvis Brown and #21 Jimmie Foreman. Jamal Washington, #3, is the do it all QB for SB, he's also a senior. A big arm and plenty of speed, Washington is the catalyst for the SB offense. Dameon Green, #25, another senior is a team captain and plays free safety. In all the Bulldogs have 21 seniors on their roster. Coach Bryant has this program on the upswing and mark my words, it won't be long before Silver Bluff is playing for championships again.

The Panthers (6-0 2-0) are riding a wave of momentum that few programs have ever experienced. Undefeated and three-time reigning State Champs, they'll be putting their 28-game home winning streak on the line. In fact, the Panthers are on a 14 game overall winning streak. The last loss was at Newberry College last season vs. Hartsville. Last week it seemed like a business trip to North Augusta. This week, there will be a little more juice in the tank. Back at home, under the lights, and a traditional powerhouse program to face. The Panthers players have one goal in mind. Every player interviewed says they want to win of course, but they want to be better than the 1996 edition of Panther football. That's a tall task, as the 1996 team is debated as the best to ever wear the Garnet and Gold. The 2018 Panthers are well on their way. They have beat their six opponents by an average score of 51-8. They've pitched three shutouts and seem to score at will. The Panthers are averaging 357 yards rushing per game. They are accomplishing that total at an average of 9.4 yards per rush as a team. The turnover margin is astronomical. The Panthers have only turned the ball over twice this season on offense, while getting 22 turnovers on defense. A +20 turnover rate would make any coach in the country happy. Defensively the Panthers have only allowed 11 third down conversions all season as well. Opposing teams are converting 3rd downs at a rate of only 16.4%. To compare that number, The University of Miami leads all of college football with a defensive 3rd down conversion percentage of 19.8%. Bama, 29.4%. As you can see, the Panthers are playing an incredible brand of defense this season.

Hite Stadium will be alive with enthusiasm Friday night. The weather will be perfect, and the Panthers will be trying to take one more step toward a Region Championship and moving a step closer to the playoffs. Remember a clear bag policy is still in effect at Hite Stadium. Also, the handicap section at Hite Stadium is marked with blue paint and the handicap logos. No bag chairs should be placed in this area, as it is designated for fans with disabilities. Also, photographers must have an Associated Press pass to take photos on the sidelines. October is Breast Cancer Awareness month, and all Panther fans are encouraged to wear Pink to the game. It's a PINK OUT at Hite Stadium-Dennis Botts Field. Kickoff is set for 7:30. As always… God Bless and Go Panthers!

Special things happen to special people. Wayne and Benji, well established booth buddies, had a treat in store for the Silver Bluff game at Hite Stadium. No. This isn't one of those paranormal occurrences or a premonition of a historical seasonal ending. Benji recalls just what happened in the game and then some.

Panthers Remain Undefeated

The Panthers improved to 7-0 on the season and 3-0 in region play as they rolled to a 36-7 victory Friday night over region foe Silver Bluff (3-4/0-3). The score doesn't offer a fair representation of the actual game. Meaning, it's wasn't nearly that close. The Abbeville defense smothered the Bulldogs for four quarters while the Panthers chewed up yards and the clock offensively. The game never found a rhythm though. It was like sitting in stop and go traffic on the interstate. Once you think it's about to take off, you must slam on breaks again. The culprit? Penalties. The Panthers and Bulldogs were both penalized nine times each. Eighteen total penalties for 164 total yards. Far and away the most penalties in a game for Abbeville yet this season. The Panthers average 3.6 penalties per game. Aside from the flags, the Panthers were dominate, again. The defensive performance against the Bulldogs may have been the best of the season. Silver Bluff had 73 total yards of offense. Washington, the SB quarterback was held to two pass completions on 14 attempts for 20 total yards. SB rushed for 53 total yards, with most of that coming on the final drive of the game. Abbeville's offense on the other hand, pushed, bullied and bulldozed their way to another outstanding performance. 295 yards on the ground, while averaging almost seven yards per play.

Ja'Bryan Sanders (4-45-1) got the scoring started with 8:06 to go in the 1st quarter with a 21-yard touchdown run. On the Panthers next possession, penalties stymied their drive and Dylan Beauford drilled a 43-yard field goal to give AHS a 10-0 lead with 5:18 to play in the opening stanza. Quarterback JD Moore (6-21-1) found the endzone with 1:38 left to give the Panthers an impressive 17-0 lead as the first quarter ended. Courtney Jackson (10-85-1) punched it in from 5 yards out and JD Moore found Quad Woods on a 25-yard touchdown pass just before halftime to stretch the lead to 29-0 at the break. Robin Crawford (5-33-1) scored the Panthers only touchdown in the 2nd half. The defense was staring at their 2nd consecutive shutout, and fourth shutout of the season when their donut dreams got dashed with 1:45 left in the game. A SB running back found the endzone from nine yards out. The Panthers improved their home win streak to 29 games and won their 15th consecutive game overall. The Panthers defense did not allow a 3rd down conversion (0-9). They are holding their opponents to 14.4%.

Halftime resembled more of a 'make a wish' moment for Wayne and Benji. They were joined by a special guess that humbled the two broadcasters. Pinching themselves they took turns sponging in the magical moment.

Benji,

"I can check that one off the bucket list. Got to interview one of my all-time favorite players, CJ Spiller."

Wayne,

"Nice of former Clemson great C. J. Spiller to spend some time with us at the Abbeville game."

The Panthers will take the show on the road this coming Friday. Another region game looms as the Panthers will face a tough group of Tigers from Saluda at Bettis-Herlong Stadium. A full preview of the Panthers and Tigers will be available later this week. As always…God Bless and Go Panthers!

The following is an excerpt from Greg Deal's Greenwood Index Journal article titled *No worries: Abbeville rolls over Silver Bluff in region matchup.*

Coach Jamie Nickles was worried. He didn't know how his Abbeville team would respond after not getting to practice Thursday in preparation for Friday night's home game against Silver Bluff. The Panthers didn't practice because schools in the area were closed in anticipation of inclement weather related to the remnants of Hurricane Michael. After the first quarter, Nickles stopped worrying.

Coach Nick summarized the game,

> "I was really concerned about us being ready to play. Give our seniors a lot of credit because we came out ready. I thought we had a great first quarter. I always love to practice on Thursday. It's just something about getting that last day of mental preparation. I thought we played well as a unit early. We got some three-and-outs on defense and had great field position the entire first quarter.
>
> It's getting that time of year when it cools down and you start hearing the crispness of the game. It's something about this time of year.
>
> I really don't concentrate on next week's game until tomorrow (Saturday) morning. I like to take 12 hours to decipher this and evaluate this performance. We're 3-0 in a tough region, but there's still a lot of work left to be done."

If ever we needed a little help from those dearly departed visitors from Benji's dreams, it might be now. Time to phone a spiritual friend. Coaches Hite and Botts could probably offer a boat load of advice. Oh well, the ghosts from season's past remain hush-hush so far. This continued to raise an eyebrow or two from our Mr. Greeson who had grown accustomed to apparitional intervention last season. There was little he could do about it now but press onward and into a season so far favoring our Garnet and Gold Panthers, year one of the second one hundred.

Week 9 Preview @ Saluda

So, we meet again. The 46th meeting between the Panthers (7-0) and Tigers of Saluda (5-3) will take place this Friday night at Bettis Herlong Stadium. Abbeville holds an all-time record of 30-15 against the Tigers. These two teams have played some classics over the last handful of years. The last three years the Panthers and Tigers have played in the Upperstate Championship game against each other. The Panthers won all three games in route to their current streak of three consecutive AA State Championships. This week's game may not hold a trip to Columbia as the final prize, but major region and playoff implications are at stake. A playoff atmosphere, high energy and a swell of emotion will certainly fill a packed house Friday night. Let's take a look at how both teams have fared so far this season.

Tiger Head Coach Stewart Young has led the Saluda football program to its most successful run in program history. Since taking over in 2014 Young has put together a 34-7 record over the last three years. This edition of Tiger football is quite impressive as well. All the lights shine on three-year starter, quarterback #8 Noah Bell. The 6'2" 205lb junior is the leader of the team. A big accurate arm, quick precise decision making, and the speed to escape the pocket makes Bell the most dangerous, complete quarterback that the Panthers have faced this season. On the year Bell is 94-185 for 1,571 yards and 21 touchdowns. He's not the only player on the team of course, Kendarius Graham is a senior running back that gets his share of carries, and catches. Graham at 5'8" is small in stature but runs big. He has speed to get to the edge and he can lower his pads and pick up yards between the tackles as well.

Saluda is a spread team, like many are these days. They will put four and five wide receivers on the field often. They are also not scared of a trick play or a gadget formation. It's fun to watch the creativity of the Saluda offense. The Tigers are averaging 32.8 points per game on offense, while allowing 16 points per game on defense. The common opponents with Abbeville so far this season are Southside Christian (30-17 loss), Sliver Bluff (10-0 win) and Fox Creek (41-0 win). Saluda will play Batesburg-Leesville next week to finish out their region schedule. The Tigers have lost 8 of the last 10 games versus the Panthers. Five of those contests were in the playoffs where the Panthers won all five. The Tigers only wins in the last 10 games came in 2003 (9-7) and in 2013 (10-7). So, if history is any indicator, the Tigers want to play a low scoring game.

To say the Panthers are rolling is an understatement. Offense, defense, special teams, they are clicking and hitting their stride at the right time. It's almost championship season late October and into November is when you want to hit your peak as a team, and that seems to be case at Abbeville High. A smothering defense and a big play offense have complimented each other all season. The Panthers are 7-0 on the season 3-0 in region play and have outscored their opponents 342-59. A-Town averages 48.9 points per game on offense and is allowing a measly 8.4 points per game on defense. There's a new leader in the clubhouse defensively too. Carson Smith is your new leading tackler, which is crazy considering he's a defensive lineman. Leading tacklers usually play in the linebacking corps. Smith has recorded 45 tackles, 8 tackles for loss, 3.5 sacks and has caused and recovered a fumble this season. The Panther defensive line has been disruptive and dominate so far this year recording 23 tackles for loss and 11 sacks. And that's just the starting four. This defense gets off the field as well any team ever. They have only allowed 11 of 76 3rd down conversions this season. That's a 14.4% success rate for opposing offenses. It helps when you are +19 in the turnover category as well.

The other side of the ball hasn't been too shabby either. The Panther offense is built on speed and physicality. The O-Line takes pride in bulldozing their way down field while one of six different ball carriers zip by defenders at a break-neck pace. The Panthers average 343.6 yards per game rushing. Starting QB JD Moore leads the clubhouse with 703 yards on the ground and 12 touchdowns. Moore, Courtney Jackson, Dominick Washington and Ja'Bryan Sanders, have combined for 1,891 rushing yards and 29 touchdowns. Moore has also thrown 8 touchdown passes on the season. Gabe Calhoun has emerged as a huge threat in the punt return game as well. Big plays and quick strike capability have been the offense's calling card this season. The Panthers have hit their opponents with 44 plays of 20 or more yards this season. That's over 6 plays per game of 20 or more yards, on average.

Can the Panthers continue their historic run? Can Saluda get revenge for three season's worth of heartbreak? Find out at Bettis Herlong Stadium Friday night. Kickoff is at 7:30. As always…

God Bless and Go Panthers!

I can recall streaming the Saluda game last year, the nail biter testing an old man's heart. Living at the beach is supposed to minimize the stress level from your life. Not on this night. The march to a third state title seemed a bit iffy, even to a loyal listener and AHS 71' graduate. The Panthers prevailed though. Why should I have ever doubted the outcome, right? This is the 2018 encounter so digging up the past serves no real purpose. Benji dubs this recap 'Road Warriors.'

Road Warriors of October

The Panthers improved to 8-0 overall and 4-0 in region play with a decisive 31-13 win over Saluda on Friday night, the Panthers 16th win in a row. The Panthers also concluded their regular season road schedule with a perfect 5-0 record. AHS started out their scoring with a Dylan Beauford 37-yard field goal. Ja'Bryan Sanders (11-64-1) out ran the Tiger defense for a touchdown late in the first quarter. Courtney Jackson (12-152-2) had his most productive game of the year and scored the first of his two touchdowns on the night, a 10-yard run, and then caught a two-point conversion pass from JD Moore to put the Panthers up 17-0. Saluda got on the board with seconds remaining in the half and the Panthers led 17-7 at halftime. Ja'Bryan Sanders returned the 2nd half kickoff back 68 yards and two plays later Courtney Jackson scored again on a 21-yard TD run. Dominick Washington (10-104-1) ended the scoring for the Panthers with 9:35 remaining in the game with a powerful 2-yard TD run and the Panthers walked out of Herlong Stadium with a 31-13 win and took another step closer to its 27th Region Championship.

The Panther defense was creative, physical, and disruptive. Three times Saluda got inside the Panther 20-yard line and all three times they came away with zero points. Two goal line stands highlighted the Panthers physical dominance of the line of scrimmage. The entire defense played lights out, against a very good Tiger passing attack.

Benji's preseason prediction: Panthers 24 – Tigers 21.

Congratulations are in order. Nate Temple and Courtney Jackson have been selected to play in the annual Shrine Bowl. That game will be played on December 15th, 1pm at Wofford College.

HOMECOMING game versus Region rival, the Ninety Six Wildcats is next. It's not often you get to play your rival, on homecoming, for a Region Championship. This one is going to be electric. As always…God Bless and Go Panthers!

The following excerpts of the Abbeville-Saluda game are from Greenwood's Index Journal.

No. 1-ranked Abbeville headed to the third quarter ahead by just 10 points against a feisty Saluda team. Things changed quickly in the second half. Abbeville's JaBryan Sanders returned the second-half kickoff 75 yards, and then Cortney Jackson scored on the first play of the half on a 21-yard scamper to extend the lead as the Panthers went on to secure a 31-13 Region 2-2A victory against the Tigers on Friday night at Bettis Herlong Stadium.

Coach Nick in a post interview,

> "That was a big game. It's always tough playing down here. I have a lot of respect for their program. Give our kids a lot of credit. Just a hostile environment, and I really thought we played our tails off tonight."

Coach Nick commented on Jackson's third quarter touch town that put the Panthers ahead 24-7, and Abbeville holding Saluda out of the endzone and on the goal line the next position,

> "I thought it changed the momentum. When we held them on the goal-line stand, I thought that was the turning point in the game. Then our offense was able to get the ball off the goal line. That's just gutting it out."

Saluda coach Stewart Young said going for the touchdown was the right call,

> "We could have kicked the field goal, but I don't think our kids get confidence out of that. I think we wanted a touchdown. You had to score. I didn't know if we'd ever get down to the 1-yard line again.
>
> I thought we played very, very hard all the way through. I told our team that's been our trademark this year. We haven't quit. We went toe-to-toe with what most people would say, rightfully so, is the best team in the state. Going forward, we feel like we're going to have a chance to make a run. We really do."

On October 21, 2018,

Three Lakelands players were named to the 82nd Shrine Bowl of the Carolinas. Emerald tight end Luke Deal, Abbeville running back Cortney Jackson and Abbeville defensive end Nate Temple are three of 44 seniors from South Carolina who will face the North Carolina Tar Heels at 1 p.m. Dec. 15. Deal is an Auburn commit and Temple has committed to Middle Tennessee State.

Benji sat in the catbird's seat at WZLA's Golden Palaces staring at an envelope addressed to the station but marked for him. The return address was Ninety Six, more specifically, the Wildcat's high school address. He opened it, wondering who from the school would be sending him a letter. Inside he found sketches of tombstones with key players' names scribbled on the them. At the bottom was written, *Share with your football team.* What kind of sick joke was this wondered a very frustrated and disgusted Benji Greeson? He held the letter in both hands, contemplating ripping it to pieces.

"What are you doing there,' asked Lacey, Benji's sister and radio cohost.

Benji blinked, looked over at her and then back at the paper he had been holding in his hands. Instead he saw his cell phone. He eased backwards in his chair, flustered and confused.

"You look like you've seen a ghost. What was on your phone?"

All Benji could think was, they're backkkkkkkk, but he just shook his head and tried to pull it together. What does this mean, he wondered? All season they had left him alone. Why now? And what did it mean? Bad vibes entered his mind, tombstones possibly spelling doom for his Panthers. Could this premonition be a bad omen signaling that the Wildcats would bury the Panthers in Friday's contest? Benji tried to shake it off, just that of an overactive imagination, maybe just jitters the late in the season. He wouldn't allow it to interfere with his weekly game preview.

Region Championship Preview

This season has been a blur. It seems like yesterday it was August 17th and Panther Nation was swelling with excitement about making a trip to Lincoln County for the season opener. Fast forward 10 weeks later and Panther Nation is again swelling with excitement about the possibility of a 27th Region Championship, a #1 seed, and homefield advantage in the playoffs. The Panthers have held on to their #1 pre-season ranking in AA for the entire duration of the regular season. Now the Panthers are ready to begin the third and final phase of their year. Championship Season. It all starts this Friday night, on Homecoming, as the boys from A-Town will welcome into Hite Stadium their region rival. the Ninety Six Wildcats. Dating back to 1951 the Panthers are 44-13-1 versus Ninety Six. Abbeville currently holds a five-game win streak over the Wildcats. The longest win streak in the rivalry was when the Panthers reeled off 10 straight from 1970-1981. Ninety Six's longest win streak in the series started in 2012 when they won 4 in a row (12, 13 and twice in 14). Abbeville and Ninety Six have played against each other seven times since 2014. They faced each other twice last season with Panthers taking both games (54-16 & 42-7). Two teams, in close proximity, who are very familiar with each other, usually makes for a fun spirited game.

The Wildcats are 8-1 on the season, 3-1 in region play and ranked 6th in AA. They were undefeated until last week when they dropped a headscratcher to Silver Bluff 17-0. The Wildcats have shown no mercy this season. Regularly dropping 40, 50, 60+ points on its opponents. Over the course of the season the Wildcats are scoring 36.5 points per game on average while allowing 23.4 points per game on defense. Offensively the Wildcats are led by dynamic dual threat quarterback Kentavius Williams. When he's in the game, Ninety Six is a different team. Explosive, dynamic, thrilling. Insert any adjective you'd like to insert. He does it all. Runs, throws, returns kicks, plays defense. There were two occasions this season when Williams didn't play the majority of the snaps, a 12-0 win versus Dixie (suspension) and pieces of the game versus Silver Bluff last week (injury). Word out of Ninety Six is that Williams is healthy and expected to play in Friday night's game. You wouldn't expect any less from that caliber of an athlete in a game of this magnitude.

The Panthers are sitting in the driver's seat. Undefeated on the season, and protecting a 29-game home winning streak, and a 16-game overall win streak. Wire to wire unanimously ranked #1 in AA, the Panthers are the definition of an elite program whose performances have matched their accolades. On the season the Panthers are out scoring their opponents 373-72. Which is an average score of 46.6 to 9. Abbeville has the #1 ranked scoring offense in AA and the 3rd ranked scoring defense. The Panthers are +18 in turnover margin this year, giving up just three turnovers on the season while creating 22 takeaways. The stingy Panther defense has allowed their opponents to convert 15 of 91 third downs (16.5%) and gives up just over 200 yards per game. Tyreke Campbell is your new leading tackler with 57 tackles, 4 tackles for loss and 1 sack. Carson Smith (54tk-9tfl-3.5sk) Luke Evans (52-3tfl) David Cobb (46-4-2 ints) and Nate Temple (46-8-5.5) are also key contributors on a defense that could go down as one of the best to wear the A.

On the other side of the ball, most nights it's like watching a garnet and gold blur reminiscent of a NASCAR race. Ball carriers zipping up and down the field with ease. Ask any of the numerous backs on the team and they'll immediately give credit to the Panther offensive line. The big uglies up front have dominated the line of scrimmage in every game so far this season. Trai Jones, Jake Hill, Connor Nickles, DaDa Bowie and DeMichael Johnson have paved the way for the Abbeville offense to average 346.9 rushing yards per game. That's 8.8 yards per carry. JD Moore is still the clubhouse leader with 81 carries for 741 yards and 12 touchdowns. He's complimented by a bevy of running backs. Courtney Jackson (62-627-11) Dominick Washington (55-498-3) and Ja'Bryan Sanders (36-383-7) get the honor of leading the top ranked offense in AA football.

It's been a fun season to this point. There's still a lot of football to be played and a few championships on the table, just waiting for someone to earn them. It's homecoming, it's a region championship, a top ten match-up, versus rivals. This is what football is all about. As always…God Bless and Go Panthers!

That ghostly, imaginary or whatever you'd call a letter that wasn't really there, had not appeared to point to a Panther loss apparently. So, how was Benji to interpret it then? Instead, he attempted to block it from his mind. A sane man does that. A sane man doesn't encounter apparitions from the past like he had last season. Why did they use him as some sort of contact vessel? And, why now, again? What next, the duo of Hite and Botts magically appearing and questioning his fishing skills as they hinted at something bigger? Just once Benji wished these spiritual encounters would be square shooters and stop dealing in rhymes and riddles. No, he just wished they would leave him be. No, not that either. They were important and usually signaled something special. Special, just maybe…

Recap time…

The Untouchables

The Untouchables. No, not the 1987 movie with Robert De Nero and Sean Connery. I'm talking about the 2018 Abbeville Panthers. They have proven once again to be, untouchable. Teams that run the option, teams that run a spread. Teams with great quarterbacks, teams with great linebackers, running backs, head coaches, teams with great wide receivers. None of them could touch the 2018 Abbeville Panthers. Teams with twice the student enrollment. Teams with much nicer facilities, newer uniforms, shiny buses and an array of fancy pre-game entrances. None of them could hold a candle to the boys from A-Town. The Abbeville Panthers just completed the 2018 season undefeated, untied and honestly, untested. You'll never hear a coach or player mutter those words because of the culture instilled into the program. Numbers however, don't lie. As the clock struck zero Friday night, and the Panthers collected their 27th Region Championship and #1 seed in the AA playoffs, reflections of one of the single greatest seasons in Panther Football history came to mind.

Remember the hype that preceded the opening game at Lincoln County? The "game 'cross the river" was going to be a measuring stick. Nobody walks into Larry Campbell Stadium and wins easily. The Panthers then proceeded to roll to a 57-0 victory. The worst home loss in Lincoln Co. football history. The most points ever scored by an opponent in LC football history. That was foreshadowing. That was a precursor to things still to come. Southside Christian was the only team to come within two scores of the Panthers all season. The Panthers finished the regular season 9-0 and beat their opponents by an average of 45.7 to 8.9. The powerful A-Bone offense rushed for an average of 339.8 yards per game. As a team the Panthers averaged 8.7 yards per rush. They only turned the ball over four times the entire season and scored 44 rushing, and 9 passing touchdowns on the year. The Panthers were kings of the big play this season as well with 56 plays of 20 or more yards on the year. That is an average of 8 plays of 20 or more yards per game. Offensively, it wasn't a one man show, more like a committee of stallions daring anyone to get in their path toward greatness. While many more contributed, for the sake of time and space, here are some individual numbers on the season, offensively, for the Panthers.

JD Moore – Rushing stats-87 carries – 843 yards – 9.7 yards per rush – 14 touchdowns – 93.7 yards rushing per game – Passing stats – 18 completions – 35 attempts – 388 yards – 9 touchdowns – 2 interceptions

Season Rushing Stats:

Courtney Jackson – (68-677-12) Dominick 'The Bus' Washington (63-550-3) Ja'Bryan 'Dooley' Sanders (43-434-8)

Robin Crawford (28-146-3) Hunter Rogers (27-140) Himize Rayford (9-79-1) Cruz Temple (8-68-1) Gabe Calhoun (1-45) Malik Leach (5-40-1) Q. Gullibeaux (4-34-1) Tyrell Hadden (3-12) M. Wilson (1-5)

Season Receiving Stats:

Ja'Bryan Sanders (5-155-3) Qua Woods (9-120-4) Courtney Jackson (4-96-1) Robin Crawford (1-21-1) Tillman Allen (2-4)

Gabe Calhoun led the team with 210 kick return yards, followed closely by Ja'Bryan Sanders with 199 kick return yards.

Of course, the Panther skill players would shift all their praise and eye-popping numbers toward their offensive line. The big boys up front paved the way for one of the most prolific offenses in Abbeville Football history. The combination of Jake Hill, Connor Nickles, Trai Jones, DaDa Bowie, DeMichael Johnson and Tillman Allen at Tight End, battered, bruised and bullied opposing defenses into submission all season long. The O-Line looked like they were in mid-season form from the opening kickoff in August and they only improved as the season progressed. Everything starts up front, and this group of Hogmollies deserves all the praise and spot light as any position group on the team.

I'm not sure there are enough adjectives, adverbs and praise that can be typed to accurately describe the Abbeville defense this season. They willed their way to three shutouts, and three other games where only one score was surrendered. They routinely stymied the toughest of offenses in a variety of ways. There were goal-line stands, huge hits, tackles for loss and a truck load of turnovers created by one of the most prolific defenses in Panther football history.

This may seem like a 'mission accomplished' article. When in reality, it's not. I'm merely closing one chapter as we get ready for the real season. *Championship*

Season. This team's record is now 0-0. The playoffs are a completely different beast. It's do or die, every week. Win or go home. The boys in Garnet and Gold know what's at stake, and they are primed and ready to make a run at a fourth consecutive AA State Championship. The mission is clear, and the first test toward greatness is going to be played on Friday, November 9th at 7:30 PM as the Panthers welcome to Hite Stadium the Andrew Jackson Volunteers in Round 1 of the AA State Playoffs.

We'll be taking a break with the team this week and be back next week with a full preview of the Panthers round one game. As always…God Bless and Go Panthers!

Letter number 2 from Andrew Jackson Highschool this time and inside were those tombstones with key players names from the offense and defense scribed on them. Again, it encouraged that Benji share this with the Panther football players. He woke to the sounds of his alarm, signaling the beginning of another workday. Still, these letters, there was something familiar about them.

November 7 -Round One Preview vs Andrew Jackson

It's about this time of year, a little rain moves in and the sweltering summer temperatures finally break. There's a crispness in the air, the leaves begin to change, and darkness comes earlier and earlier. When Autumn rolls around each year, you can rest assured that the Abbeville Panthers are still hard at work preparing for the final third of their season. It's playoff time again and this year's Panther squad has their eyes set on history. However, you can't win a fourth consecutive State Championship unless you win round one first. Hite Stadium will be alive and rockin' as the Panthers welcome in the Andrew Jackson Volunteers this Thursday at 6pm.

Andrew Jackson finished the season with a 6-4 record and grabbed the final #5 seed by finishing 5th in Region 5-AA. The Vols won their first four contests of the season before dropping 4 of their next 6 games. Their losses, North Central (28-17), Buford (28-7), Chesterfield (17-14) and Pageland Central (45-14) were all region games. As you can see most were tightly contested games and that gives a big nod to the AJ defense.

Abbeville head coach Jamie Nickles said, *"These guys are huge up front. They have the biggest defensive line we've played this season. Big and strong. It'll be a game won in the trenches, and they have some big ones."*

Andrew Jackson had five players earn first-team all-region honors, including #99 Ben Hinson, the region co-defensive player of the year, as an offensive and defensive lineman.
Senior #22 Luke Faulkenberry was selected as a running back, while sophomore receiver #3 OJ White was named to the all-region team. AJ senior kicker #5 Avery Funderburk was selected as the all-region kicker and #7 Jamie Hinson, a Vols senior, was chosen as an athlete. Hinson is a player that wears many hats for AJ. They use him a kick returner, slot receiver, running back, he's even taken snaps at QB. It'll be interesting to see how Vols head coach Todd Shigley uses him against the Panthers. Shigley, in his 2nd season at the helm of the Vols, missed the playoffs last season with a 3-7 record, but doubled last year's win total already this season. AJ averages 27.3 points per game on offense, while giving up 16.7 points per game. Their wide open, tempo based spread offense hinges on #8, junior QB Chas DeBrul. He has a big arm and can scramble as well. DeBrul's numbers are off this year, as he broke his collar bone earlier this season, but returned to play the last game of the

year. In DeBruls first game back, he tossed two touchdown passes and clinched a playoff spot for the Vols.

The Panthers are poised, focused, rested and healthy. The team is aware of the historic run they are on. They are salivating at the chance to begin the playoffs and stake their claim as one of the best to ever wear the A. This year's senior class has never lost a playoff game. They are 15-0 in playoff games. They have never lost a home game. Should the Panthers win this week it will be the 30th consecutive home win and the 17th consecutive win overall. No Senior class has ever played in as many games, won as many rings or dominated in the way that this year's Senior class has dominated. Blame it on whatever you choose; Talent, consistency, continuity, coaching, conditioning or maybe there *IS* something in the water. Whatever the reason, the boys from A-Town are ready to get after it.

The Panthers have outscored their opponents 411-80 this season. That's an average of 45.6 – 8.8. Abbeville's scoring defense is ranked 3rd in AA while its offense ranks #1. The offense averages 8.7 yards per rush attempt this season. They've found the endzone 44 times on the ground and have only given up 4 rushing touchdowns on defense this year. The Panthers are +21 in the turnover margin and holds the opposing offenses to 16% on 3rd down conversions. The offense has been a big play, quick strike offense all season long, posting 56 runs of 20 or more yards. Coach Nickles won his 10th Region Championship as head coach with the 38-8 win over Ninety Six and finishes the regular season with an all-time record of 156-39-1. Come out and see the Panthers as they try to extend their historic streak and continue on the playoff road to Columbia. As Always…God Bless and Go Panthers!

By the way, Benji had predicted a Panthers 48-0 win over the Wildcats to close out the season.

November 12 Back in Black

The Panthers rolled through the first round of the AA State Playoffs this past Thursday night with a convincing 54-13 win over the Andrew Jackson Volunteers. Hundreds of fans braved temps in the 40's and an off and on rain storm. The win moved A-Town to 10-0 on the season. The Panthers extended a hand full of different streaks as well. Abbeville has now won 17 games in a row, dating back to the Hartsville loss last season. Abbeville has now won 30 consecutive games inside of Hite Stadium dating back to October of 2014. This year's seniors also extended their personal/all-time leading playoff record as they now sit at 16-0 in the playoffs. All of that is well and good, but the real story…Those uniforms.

The players have begged to wear the all black combination all season long. Courtney Jackson was quoted in the Index Journal, *"I saw them my freshman year in the closet, and I was asking everybody if they want to wear them,"* Jackson said. *"And they were like 'Yeah, yeah, that would be a good thing.' And then Coach Nick finally let us bring them out."*

Panther Seniors – 36 Tyreke Campbell, 72 Jake Hill, 2 Courtney Jackson

Coach Nickles also told the Index Journal, *"Cortney and those seniors have been begging and begging to wear them,"* Nickles said. *"As you can tell, they're outdated. They're not modern jerseys, they're rec jerseys. I told them they can if they won the region and we are retiring them."*

The Panthers are undefeated in the all black uniforms, dating to a handful of games from 2006-2009.

As far as the game itself, the Panthers jumped out to a 27-0 first quarter lead thanks to two JD Moore touchdown runs (65 and 27 yards), a Ja'Bryan Sanders 11-yard scamper and a 14-yard pass from Moore to Panther tight end Tillman Allen. The second quarter belonged to Andrew Jackson, for the most part. A couple Panther miscues led to a touchdown and two AJ field goals. Moore broke an 80-yard run before getting tackled at the AJ one-yard line, and then scored on a QB keeper on the very next play. The Panthers led 33-13 at the half. The 2nd half was all A-Town. I'd like to know what was said in the locker room because the Panthers opened up the second half focused and full of fury. Ja'Bryan Sanders found pay-dirt from 9 yards out, followed by a physical 29-yard touchdown run by Courtney Jackson where he bulled his way through the AJ defense. Robin Crawford sailed in from 34 yards out with 10 minutes to play in the 4th quarter and that was final score of the night as the Panthers enjoyed a round one win, 54-13. The Panthers rushed for 359 yards on 38 attempts.

The defense played lights out, especially in the 2nd half. Cruz Temple picked off Andrew Jackson QB Chas DeBrul twice, Gabe Calhoun got one pick, and the Panther defense recorded five total sacks in the second half. Andrew Jackson was forced to become one dimensional and it fell right into defensive coordinator Tad DuBose's masterplan. DeBrul finished 21 of 50 passing for 166 yards, no touchdowns and three interceptions. Andrew Jackson finished with negative 15 yards rushing.

The Panthers will face the North Central Knights this coming Friday, November 16th at Hite Stadium. As always…God Bless and Go Panthers!

You got it. Letter number three showed up in another Benji dream leading to the showdown with North Central. If it had been real, he might have shared it with Coach Nick, his coaching staff and the team. It wasn't though and explaining it might land him in a straitjacket and leave Wayne alone in the broadcast booth. Wayne, maybe he should tell Wayne? Then it clicked. Benji remembered. He knew the significance and origin of the tombstones and their taunts.

November 14 2nd Round Preview vs. North Central

The Panthers advanced to the 2nd round of the South Carolina AA Playoffs last Thursday with a 54-13 win over the Andrew Jackson Volunteers. The win put the Panthers in the 2nd round for the 23rd consecutive season. You read that right. Abbeville has advanced to at least the 2nd round of the playoffs every year since 1995. This year's 2nd round opponent will have basically the same drive as Andrew Jackson had. The North Central Knights also hail from Kershaw, SC and they will make the trek to Hite Stadium this Friday night to try their bid at upsetting the top ranked, undefeated Panthers. Here's a preview of Friday night's contest.

North Central (8-3) will get their very first ever shot at A-Town Friday night. The teams have never met on the gridiron. The one common opponent the two teams share this year was Andrew Jackson. North Central beat AJ 28-17 on September 12th. The Knights finished 5-1 and in 2nd place in Region 4-AA. Their only conference loss came to the hands of region winner, Buford, who shut them out 21-0. A Week Zero loss to Camden (38-0) and a week 3 loss to 1-A powerhouse Lamar (33-7) are the only blemishes on an otherwise impressive resume.

Coach Tyrone Drakeford has brought North Central to new heights this season. A playoff win and an 8-3 record is the best season the Knights have enjoyed since a 6-5 record and a playoff berth in 2012. The Knights will try to spread out the Panthers defense with four and five wide receivers most of the night. They will maintain a balanced attack by running and throwing out of their wide-open formations. This team uses everybody. Multiple quarterbacks, multiple running backs and a slew of receivers as well. QB #6 Austin Bowers a 5'10" 160lb junior (*56-95 852 yards 13 TD 8int-34 rushes 155 yards 1 TD*) will see the majority of the snaps and lead an offense that averages 29.4 points per game this season.

North Central will also use #1 Avante Reynolds in a variety of ways, QB, RB and WR (29-54 488 yards 7 TD–19 rushes 87 yards–5 rec 76 yards). Reynolds could be the best athlete on the North Central roster. Team captain and senior #8 Jamel Jones (*53 carries 459 yards 6 TD–13 receptions 158 yards 1 TD*) is the workhorse at RB for the Knights. The big receiving threat that the Panther defenders will have to blanket is #13, 6'1" 170lb Markell Portee (*30 receptions 634 yards 11 TD*). He's big, fast and very good in open space. The Knights defense is giving up 18.3 points per game this season and #15 Kaleb Haven and Jamel Jones are huge contributors at linebacker for the Knights.

As for the Panthers, they just continue to do Panther things. All season we've chronicled the dominance they've displayed on the football field. As records fall and streaks lengthen, the boys in Garnet and Gold seem to keep their head down and just go to work. During a conversation with Head Coach Jamie Nickles earlier this week he mentioned, *"These guys just love each other. They want to win for each other. They want to block for each other. They are just a big ole' family and they want it for their brother as badly as they want it for themselves."*

Wants and desires are futile if you're not willing to work to see those things to fruition. And work is exactly what they've done this season. The Panthers offense is averaging 46.5 points per game. The four 'headed monster' in the offensive backfield is running behind what some are calling the best offensive line in Abbeville football history. Jake Hill, Trai Jones, DeMichael Johnson, DaDa Bowie, Conner Nickles and Tillman Allen at tight end, have bulldozed their way through their first ten adversaries. Depth has been a big key for this team this season. The additions of youngsters Davis Sutherland, Ean Laughlin, Demetris Harris, Jake Adams and Pierce Royster on the O-Line has built quality depth and allowed the first five guys to have fresh legs this deep into the season. Offensive line coach Wayne Botts has got to be giddy when thinking about his future Hogmollies.

The guys that get a lot of the headlines and spotlight are the A-Town running backs. And they deserve every bit of praise that can be bestowed upon them. The ground game has produced 3,417 yards this year on 388 carries. That's an average of 8.8 yards per carry over the course of 10 games. Impressive. The Panthers have reached the endzone 51 times via the run game this season. They've held on to the ball extremely well too. The Abbeville offense has lost 6 turnovers all season. Junior QB JD Moore leads all rushers (*100-1,027-17*) in attempts, yards and TD runs. He averages 102.7 yards per game on the ground at a clip of 10.3 yards per carry. Senior Shine Bowl participant Courtney Jackson (*74-732-13*) is an averaging 9.9 yards per carry. A first down every carry, again, impressive. The Bus, Dominick Washington (*71-619-3*) and super speedster Ja'Bryan Sanders (*47-442-10*) round out the four 'headed monster'. Throw in sure handed Quad Woods (*9 receptions- 120 yards- 4 Tds*) and you've got a very talented, very fast, very physical offense. The recipe for success.

As much love as the offense gets, the Panther defense might be the best group on the field. Depth again plays a huge part. No Panther starters play on both sides of the ball, which is a rare feat for an AA school with less than 500 students. There seems to be a new star each week and that's part of the reason the Panthers are only allowing 8.9 points per game this season. Sophomore Cruz Temple (*61 tackles-1 sack-4 ints*) seems to be hitting his stride at linebacker. He had 17 tackles versus

Ninety Six and he swiped two interceptions versus Andrew Jackson. Big brother and Shrine Bowl selection Nate Temple (*62 tackles – 9.5 sacks*) couldn't let little brother have all the spotlight. So, he added three more sacks last week to his already team leading total.

The Panther linebackers enjoy space to roam and find the football because of the success of the Panther defensive line. Carson Smith (*72 tkls – 10 TFL – 3.5 sacks*) Ar'Darius "Bone" Burton (*37 tkls – 5 TFL*) and Jihad Washington (*41 tkls – 2 TFL – 2 sacks*) have allowed the Panther linebackers to make 208 total tackles on the year. Led by team tackle leader Tyreke Campbell (*74 tkls-5 TFL-1 sack*) and sophomore Luke Evans (*63 tkls-3 TFL*), not much gets by these guys. The defensive backs have played as well as you could have hoped this year as well. David Cobb (*57 tkls – 6 TFL – 2 Int*), Joc Norman (*41 tkls*), Gabe Calhoun (*35 tkls – 2 TFL – 1 int*), Malik Leach (*55 tkls – 1 int*) and Jhalyn Shuler (*57 tkls – 6 TFL – 1 int*) lead the charge against team after team that runs four and five wideouts on the field. Don't forget about Junior kicker Dylan Beauford who is 3 of 4 on field goals, 47 of 54 on extra points and has boomed 44 of 80 kickoffs out of the endzone. He's helped pin opposing offenses deep in their own territory most of the season.

North Central represents an unfamiliar foe. They are a worthy playoff caliber team with talent in multiple places. This could be the biggest test of the season for the Panthers. North Central has also issued a challenge to their fan base. They want to turn Hite Stadium green. Weather has been an excuse for many Panther fans as of late, but surely on a clear, dry and cool November night, Panther Nation won't let an opponent even out their home field advantage. Come early, let's pack The Hite, be loud and show these Panthers how proud you are of them. Kickoff is set for 7:30 and the gates will open at 6. As Always…God Bless and Go Panthers!

Excerpts from the Greenwood Index Journal 11/18/2018: Abbeville leads the way with 6 players on annual All-Lakelands team

The reigning Class 2A state champion Abbeville Panthers account for six players on a list of 28 players who will be honored during Monday night's All-Lakelands banquet. The 23rd annual banquet, which recognizes the top football players in the Lakelands, starts at 7 p.m. Monday at St. Mark United Methodist Church in Greenwood.

Abbeville's two Shrine Bowlers, seniors Cortney Jackson and Nate Temple, lead the way for the Panthers. Jackson finished the regular season with 677 yards and 12 touchdowns on 68 carries, adding four receptions for 96 yards and a touchdown. Jackson also returned one kickoff for a touchdown. Temple led the team in sacks with seven. He logged 57 tackles during the regular season, including nine tackles for loss.

Temple is joined by fellow defensive lineman Carson Smith, a junior who had 65 tackles, including 10 tackles for loss and four sacks. Senior Gabe Calhoun represents the Panthers in the defensive backfield after tallying 29 tackles and six pass break-ups. Senior Jake Hill is a three-year starter along an offensive line that allowed Abbeville to rush for more than 3,000 yards in nine games. Abbeville placed at least one player on offense, defense and special teams, with junior Dylan Beauford rounding out the Panthers' selection after recording 41 touchbacks and an average of 39 yards per punt.

Benji opened up to Wayne Stevenson.

"I've received the letters the last few weeks beginning with the Ninety Six game. Well, I haven't actually received any letters."

"Which is it," asked Wayne, "You did, or you didn't receive letters?"

"I didn't actually receive real letters."

"You received 'unreal' letters then?"

"Yeah, exactly."

"Benji, why do I feel I'm in the middle of an Abbot and Costello skit? And please don't tell me Why is on second base or something like that."

"I knew this was going to be difficult. Let me try this instead. What would come to mind if I said envelops were received from high schools and inside were drawings of tombstones with Abbeville players' names on them?"

"I would say don't blame me this time."

"Exactly."

"So, you received these then?"

"Not exactly."

"So, what exactly did you receive then?"

"I've had these visions, dreams of the post marked mail, taunting Abbeville, me, of the upcoming game. You did this when you were in school, didn't you? We wrote about it in the book."

"I did, or we did, John Benjamin and me, but I swear I had nothing to do with this. John passed away earlier this year, so he couldn't have done it either. What am I saying? You said it didn't really happen."

"That's just it, Wayne. You're right. It didn't really happen. I get that. It's a sign though."

"A sign that you are going wacky, my friend."

"This kind of stuff happened to me all last season. I just never told anybody."

"Smart move. For your sake, I won't tell anyone either."

November 19 The Pilgrims

What does the Abbeville football team and the pilgrims have in common?

They are always mentioned on Thanksgiving. (feel free to use that over your turkey and dressing this week)

A hard fought 24-7 victory versus North Central guaranteed a Turkey-Day practice for the boys from A-Town. In most years a Thanksgiving practice means an Upperstate Championship game appearance, but this year because of Hurricane Florence's regular season interruption, things got pushed back a week. It was no walk in the park for the Panthers however. North Central was a tough, scrappy bunch that stood toe to toe with Abbeville. At least defensively. The Knights crowded the line of scrimmage, blitzed nearly every play and left little room for the Panthers offense to operate. Abbeville scored quickly as they only needed four plays to find pay dirt after they received the opening kickoff. Courtney Jackson (13-42-1) scored first from five yards out and a Dylan Beauford PAT put the Panthers up 7-0 just a minute and thirty-one seconds into the game. A North Central punt gave the Panthers the ball back and Ja'Bryan Sanders (10-71-1) scored with 6:11 to play in the first quarter. Abbeville jumped out to a 14-0 lead before the home crowd could get settled in their seats. But that's when the game changed.

The barrage of rushing yards and scoring ended. Both defenses began playing at a very high level and yards were at a premium. The Panthers defense harassed the North Central quarterback all night. The defensive line, Carson Smith, Nate Temple, Ar'Darius Burton and Jihad Washington were virtually 'unblockable'. Cruz Temple collected another interception as North Central completely gave up on even trying to run the football. The Panthers limited the Knights to negative 41 yards rushing for the game. The third quarter was quiet, but the Panthers put together a nice scoring drive at the end of the third. JD Moore (10-68-1) bulled his way into the endzone with 11:54 to play in the 4th quarter to put the Panthers up 21-0. A Dylan Beauford 31-yard field goal stretched the lead to 24-0 on the next Panther possession. North Central scored with 17 seconds left in the game to erase the shutout. The Panther defense held North Central to 133 total yards. Although, the Panther offense was held to its season low, 285 total yards including 270 on the ground, which is 65 yards less than their season average.

The Panthers moved to 11-0 on the season. Winners of 19 straight games, they will get to protect their home field at least once more this season. They may have dropped Pageland from their name, but to Abbeville fans and former players, Pageland-Central represents some of the toughest played games in Panther football history. We'll have a full preview of the Panthers versus the Central Eagles posted later this week.

As always…God Bless and Go Panthers!

Benji received no haunting mail this week, convincing him that confessions are good for the soul. Wayne would probably keep a close eye on him again though, hoping he didn't go psycho in the booth and on the air. No mail, Benji became panic stricken. Could this mean that the streak had come to an end. Did it spell doom for the Panthers against Central? Had he cursed the outcome by sharing what had happened with Wayne? Second guessing and back peddling served no purpose now. It was time for him to post his preview and just hope for the best. Benji was a believer in destiny and this team was destined for more greatness yet.

November 21 Quarterfinals Playoff Preview vs Central

For those of us that lived through the 90's Central High School doesn't ring a bell, but throw the word Pageland in front of or behind it, and memories begin to flood in. Some of those memories are great, some are heart wrenching. The 1971 Panther football team defeated Pageland-Central 14-7 to claim Abbeville High's very first State Championship. The Panthers would not defeat the Eagles again for another 29 years. Granted, they only played a handful of times during the playoffs, but the drought was painstakingly brutal for many very talented, State Championship caliber Panther teams. The Eagles hold an all-time record of 7-2 versus the Panthers. The 1971 win, and a 2nd round playoff win in 2000 are the only two victories in the series for the Panthers. The win in 2000, a 28-25 slobberknocker, came in the waning moments as Layfette Miller (RIP) scored with only seconds remaining. In the 3rd round of the 1994 season, the Panthers were poised for a State title run behind Troy Gamble, Theo McCouller and many other Panther greats, only to lose on a controversial call late in 4th quarter by a score of 7-2. The 1997 Panthers, fresh off an undefeated State Championship in 1996 lost in the Upperstate Championship game 14-7. And the following year, in 1998, a last second touchdown propelled the Eagles to a 29-28 win. As you can see, these two teams bring out the best in each other. Games are tightly contested and as physical as a bunkhouse stampede. The odds makers have the Panthers as a heavy favorite, but if history is any indicator, this will be one of those bloody nose, bruised knuckles knock down drag out, type of games. A game not for the faint of heart, a game that will test your manhood. Let's look at how the Eagles and Panthers stack up on paper.

The Central Eagles are 8-4 on the season. They lost their first two region games of the year to Buford (14-12), and North Central (41-21) and finished 3rd in Region 4, but they haven't lost since. Each of the Panthers first two playoff opponents have come from Region 4. Don't let the North Central game score fool you. There were multiple Eagle players that were unavailable to play in that game. The Eagles and the Panthers are very similar in styles of play. Central is an option, run first, pass *maybe*, team. This team is very different from the pass happy teams the Panthers have played the last several weeks. To make the option offense work you must have a great offensive line, a savvy athletic quarterback, and a combo of speed and power from your running backs. Sound familiar? Central has all of that and then some. Led by quarterback #17 Curt Chapman, the Eagles have a stable full of running backs to carry the load. Senior #2 JR Reid (133-1,103-11) is the work horse who chews up yards at a nice 8.3 yards per carry. Jamiah Smith, #5 (92-623-7) is another big running back that they use as a battering ram. When they throw, #1 Ron Benjamin (11-250-4) is the main target. The Eagles have used eleven running backs this season. They also employ a very big, fast defense. #7 Daylan Robinson is the unquestioned leader. He's a four-year starter at middle linebacker. He's 6'2" 230lbs, runs a 4.8 forty, and averages over 10 tackles a game. Robinson is a North/South All-Star selection with over 110 tackles on the season. He's a grown man that plays fast and as physical as any linebacker in the state.

The Panthers are going to basically be looking in the mirror Friday night. Abbeville's run heavy offense is a little more spread out and sideline to sideline oriented than that of their counterparts, but the similarities are scary. The Panthers are led by junior quarterback JD Moore (117-1,095-18). A gifted runner who has vision and speed. The combo of Courtney Jackson (87-774-14), a Shrine Bowl and All-Lakelands selection, Ja'Bryan Sanders (57-513-11) and Dominick Washington (81-681-3) have ran their way to an 11-0 record this season. The Abbeville offensive line, who will be the first to tell you that they want to improve on last week's performance, will be greatly tested again with constant blitzes, and a stacked line of scrimmage. All-Lakelands selection Jake Hill will lead the Panther hogmollies in what may be their most physical game to date.

If the old cliché holds true, then the Panthers should be just fine. The cliché? Offense sells tickets, defense wins championships. Four Panther defenders were selected to the All-Lakelands team. Carson Smith, Nate Temple (also a Shrine Bowl selection), Gabe Calhoun, and Dylan Beauford were all inducted into the all-star team this past week. Beauford was selected as a punter. They harassed quarterbacks all season long collecting 28.5 sacks on the season. They play in the opponent's backfield with 62 tackles for loss, and they make their opponents turn the ball over, a lot. The Panthers have caused 28 turnovers on the season. Third downs are especially tough for the Panthers opponents. They have allowed just 19 third down conversions on the season, out of 133 attempts. That's 14.2% and that number is insane. The Panther defensive backs like to hit, and they'll get their chance this week as they'll be counted on for run support in this game.

If you enjoy old school, smashmouth football. This is the game for you. If you like big hits, and a game that will be played by two very good football teams. You don't want to miss what I'm sure will turn into an old fashion donnybrook. The winner of course will move on to the Upperstate Championship game, and the loser's season will end. Can the Panthers exorcise the demons of the 90's? Will Central derail Abbeville's historic run? The answer to those questions will be played out in front of your very eyes this Friday night inside Hite Stadium. Gates open at 6:30 and kickoff is at 7:30.

I hope you all have a happy and safe Thanksgiving with family and friends.

As always…God Bless and Go Panthers!

November 26 Hello Upper State

The Panther defense harassed, bullied, and overwhelmed the Central Eagles offense for 48 minutes this past Friday night. With temps in the low 40's and sporadic rain showers, the Panthers stayed hot on the field. The Abbeville defense controlled the game from the opening kick, never allowed a point and collected six Central turnovers in a 39-0 rout. The Panthers punched their ticket to their 4th consecutive Upper State Championship game with the win.

The Panthers forced a 3 and out early and got their offense rolling. Dylan Beauford hit a 38-yard field goal to get the scoring started in the first quarter. The defenses seemed to be getting a feel for each offense until the 2nd quarter when the Panthers opened the flood gates. After a Central punt, the Panther offense marched right down the field and Courtney Jackson (12-79-2) punched in his first of two touchdowns to put the Panthers up 10-0. JD Moore (15-69-1) broke loose on a 34-yard TD scamper with 3:39 to play before the half. A Central turnover gave the Panthers the ball right back and a crazy string of events then took place. The Panthers were content to kick a field goal and take a 20-0 lead into halftime. The wet ball was bobbled a little on the snap, Hunter Rogers collected the ball, scrambled to his right and found Joc Norman in the endzone for a touchdown. The Panthers line up for the extra point, and the exact same thing happened again. This time Rogers rolls to his left and finds Courtney Jackson in the endzone for a two-point conversion. The Panthers led 25-0 at the half. Ja'Bryan Sanders flashed speed, power and vision with his 71-yard kickoff return for a TD to open the 2nd half. Later in the 3rd quarter, Courtney Jackson punched in his 2nd touchdown of the game from four yards out and that ended the scoring on the night. The Panthers ended the Eagles season with a 39-0 shutout.

Panther defenders collected four interceptions, one each by Quadarius Gullibeaux, Jahlyn Schuler, David Cobb and Titus Paul. Central's leading rusher, 1,300-yard back JR Reid was limited to one yard on seven carries. Reid was injured late in the game and helped off the field and carried to medical help by a couple Panther players. A true sign of respect and sportsmanship. Central mustered 86 yards rushing, most of which came late in the 4th quarter against reserves. Chapman, Central's QB finished 4 of 15 passing for 27 yards, no touchdowns and four interceptions. The Panthers defended their home turf for the 33rd consecutive time and moved their win streak to 20 in a row.

The Panthers will now get to face Southside Christian at Sabre Stadium, this coming Friday November 30th at 730pm. The winner plays for a State Championship the following week at Benedict College. A full Upperstate Championship preview will be available later in the week. As always…God Bless and Go Panthers!

T. Allen Winn Recap, my first game this year:

We just so happened to have been in Abbeville on Friday, having traveled earlier in the day from Myrtle Beach. We would be attending our brother-in-law's funeral on Saturday. Friday night in A-Town was supposed to be cold and rainy. I had been straddling the fence on whether I should go or listen to the game from the comforts of the Solomon's home on Wardlaw Street. I could hear the pre-game activity just a stone's toss away inside of Hite Stadium. I always stream the games from the beach, but my gut told me that Benji and Wayne would never let me live it down if I didn't attend. Settled, I layered up and headed over, solo, after Jerry Solomon chickened out on accompanying me. The forecast of rain weighed heavy on his decision.

Listening to the play by play and color commentary from Wayne and Benji on the radio makes one visualize the antics on the field. They do a wonderful job from the booth for those of us unable to attend. There's something to be said though, watching the crowd, seeing old friends and meeting new ones while standing along the fence behind the granite bleachers. It gets the old juices flowing, the band playing the national anthem while watching those Panthers make their grand entrance down the center aisle of the bleachers. While I missed the play by play commentary streaming in my ears, it put things in perspective watching this team live, taking care of business with an arsenal of offensive and defensive weapons.

The rain held off for the most part, light to heavy drizzle. I was prepared and weather resistant for the most part. I appeared for a quick cameo on the air with Benji and Wayne at half time, my first ever time in the confines of the stadium's cramped booth. Just after I entered and climbed the steep wood steps (my ladder, their steps), the skies unleashed with a downpour. A few minutes later as I prepared to exit the shelter, preparing for deluge outside, it abruptly stopped. I took my position behind the fence and readied for the second half. Abbeville continued doing what Abbeville does, score quickly and often.

The one play or incident that spoke volumes for the Abbeville Football program happened when two Central Eagle players were injured on the same play from scrimmage, Abbeville with the ball and hustling down the Abbeville sidelines. It took quite some time for them to upright the fallen players. One finally made it back across the field. The second was not faring so well though. Out of nowhere, two Abbeville players assisted two Eagle's coaches in hoisting up the player and carrying him the distance of the Abbeville bench to a golf cart. That's something you don't see every day. It speaks volumes for the Panther program and the morals instilled in the players by the coaching staff. Attending the game had been the best decision I had made. I planned next to be in Columbia when the Panthers would go for their next championship, fourth in row, after they win the upper state that is.

Excerpts from Greenwood Index Journal titled 'Inspirational night: Panthers rout Central for berth in Upper State finals' as reported by Greg K. Deal, November 24th.

Coach Jamie Nickles said earlier this week that winning the turnover battle usually decides who wins playoff games. Abbeville (12-0) had no problem with that Friday night in its third-round Class 2A state playoff matchup against Central (8-5). The No. 1-ranked Panthers came up with six turnovers - two fumble recoveries and four interceptions — and didn't have any of their own in an impressive 39-0 victory on a chilly and wet night at Hite Stadium.

Coach Nick was quoted as saying,

> "We had a great week of preparation. We were impressive all the way around – in all three phases of the game. We created a few turnovers tonight. That was really important. If you turn the ball over, it's hard to beat a good football team. I thought we controlled the line of scrimmage. And that's saying something when you control the line against Central. I thought we were explosive at times, and then we had some good drives"

The Panthers also got an inspirational speech before the game from a former player, Dureal Elmore, who tore his ACL before facing Central in 2009.

Coach Nick,

> "I had to keep them (the players) locked up in the building until 6:30 to come out and warm up. They were ready to play about 4:30, thanks to him. The credit for this one goes to him and these kids."

Uneventful events were a welcome sight. Things that go bump in the night had deserted Benji's night time slumber. Again, good sign or bad sign? While there was no doubt in Benji's mind of the Panthers' capabilities and determination, he had leaned too much on the premonitions from people of the past. No mail, no bass boats, no ringing cow bells gave any hint to the Upper State outcome. Ask A-Town. Little doubt existed that these Panthers were destined to make history and set a bar of epic heights. Flying solo, Benji tossed out his game preview.

Upper State Championship Game Preview

The 2018 season kicked off Week Zero on August 17th. Rain, hurricanes, flooding. It's been a tumultuous season, schedule-wise. Bye weeks, Thursday night games, cancelled games, extra weeks added. Weeks where practices were limited, or non-existent altogether. Through all the ups and downs, the extreme heat, the relentless rain, and now the cold November nights. Here we are. The Upper State Championship game. Forty-three teams in AA began this season with hopes of playing this coming Friday night, yet only two remain in the Upstate. One, the grizzled veteran who has seen it all, withstood it all and overcame all obstacles time and time again. The other, a well-oiled machine, filled with talent, desire and dreams of upending the defending champs. Who will prevail? Will it be the vets with experience, savvy and tenaciousness on their side? Or will it be the newcomers, who want to stake their claim as the perennial powerhouse program in the Upstate?

The Southside Christian Sabres (11-2) are no stranger to big games. They won the Class A-Division 1 State Championship in 2015. The next season they were moved into the AA classification. This season is the deepest playoff run they've made since joining AA. Their first three playoff opponents all came from Region 2, the Region that Abbeville plays in, and won in the regular season. The Sabres defeated Silver Bluff (35-7) in round one, Ninety Six (33-15) in round two, and last week SSC beat Saluda (34-21) to punch their ticket to the Upper State title game. The Panthers and Sabres have already met once this season. A 43-28 Abbeville win in Week 3 of the season was a back and forth contest until late in the game. SSC outgained Abbeville in that contest 482-480. Mostly behind the arm of stud QB JW Hertzberg. In the previous contest Hertzberg threw for 376 yards and four touchdowns. The junior signal caller has tossed the ball for 2,153 yards and 23 touchdowns on the season. The balanced offensive attack of SSC is one of the big reasons they have been so successful this season. Running back #44 Mallory Pickney (6'0" 215lb) could start on 95% of the teams in the state. He runs behind a massive offensive line that opens run-lanes and protects Hertzberg very well. This will sound like a broken record, but defensively, the Sabres are big, fast and physical. They are everything they're advertised to be. The leader is still four-year starter #42 JR Schroeder (6'1" 215lbs). This team will hit you all night and try to dictate the tempo of the game. Their defensive line is big and fast, their defensive backfield is solid and plays aggressively. This is a team that is really good at every level on both sides of the ball. You don't make it this far on luck. If you are playing football this week, you deserve to be there because you are a very good football team. And SSC is all of that and then some.

The Abbeville Panthers (12-0) have hammered their way through the playoffs thus far. Physicality has been the name of the game and they've flexed their muscle all season. The numbers are staggering. The win streaks are well documented. The rushing numbers, the sacks, the wins, it all paints a nice picture of how they've reached this point in the season. But, how have they *really* got this far. Ask any senior on the team and they'll tell you. Brotherhood. Community. Love. That's what it all boils down to. This senior class is 52-3-1 since they stepped foot on Abbeville High campus. The three-year starters are 40-1-1 over their career and they have three big shiny rings to applaud their efforts. A big majority of the guys on this team have played together for nearly 10 years already. While playing in the rec league playoffs, or the Rotary Bowl, these guys dreamed of one day wearing the A, suiting up in Garnet and Gold and walking down the aisle at The Hite. This Senior class *never lost a game* at Hite Stadium. They've never lost a playoff game either. This is a team of brothers with one goal, one mission and one destination in mind. From day one, minute one of this season, these Seniors have had one mindset, and winning wasn't enough for them. They want to be remembered as the best…ever. This Senior class has history, and a legacy that they want to leave behind. Some laughed at the notion, saying it was just another lofty, unattainable goal. But within the walls of AHS athletic building, they believe it. They want it, and they know what they'll have to do to achieve it. They also know that ten plus years of playing together is almost over. There are only eight quarters left in this season and the 2018 Abbeville Panthers want to finish it out like they started. Playing for their brothers.

And to the last folks leaving town Friday night, cut off the lights.

As always…God Bless and Go Panthers!

Benedict Bound

When you're faced with adversity there are two ways to approach the situation. You can back down and accept your fate, or you stare it in the eyes and do whatever it takes to succeed. The latter happened Friday night as the Abbeville Panthers punched their ticket to the AA State Championship game with a 28-21 win over Southside Christian. In a back and fourth game the Panthers found themselves trailing 21-20 with 2:35 remaining in the 4th quarter. Charlie Paciocco, whose kicks had sailed eight yards deep into the endzone all night, kicked off from his own 40-yard line. The kick was a low line drive that bounced at the 5 yard line and landed in Cortney Jackson's hands at the one. Jackson leans to the left, pacing himself as a wall of blockers formed in front of him. A lane opened near the Abbeville bench. Jackson hit the afterburners, dodged an SSC defender near mid field and the rest is history. A 99-yard kickoff return for a touchdown to send the Panthers to Benedict for the fourth consecutive year, will without a doubt be a play that will be talked about for generations.

With a TV camera in his face Coach Jamie Nickles said after the game, *"Big time players make big time plays in big time games. The kick return team, the blockers, they did a great job. The rest was up to Cortney and God."*

The Panther faithful that made the trip to Simpsonville were elated. They just witnessed history. A deafening silence fell over the SSC sidelines and home stands as their season ended abruptly. There's no consolation prize for a game well played, but SSC deserves some credit. They were tough as nails and pushed the Panthers harder than any opponent since last year's State Title game versus Bamberg-Erhardt.

The stories of Jackson's kickoff return will be retold for years, but there are a ton of unsung heroes that deserve plenty of recognition in this game as well. The offensive line played very well and had to move massive defenders all night. The running backs blocked hard for each other. The defense played as well as you could hope for. Especially with 2:18 left on the clock and a high-powered offense trying to put together a game winning drive. Dylan Beauford played as big of a role in the win as anyone. Every single kickoff that boomed off his right foot went at least eight yards deep into the endzone. He hit every PAT and he also connected on a 20-yard field goal from a very tough angle. He hit a 47 yarder in the 4th quarter to put the Panthers up 20-13 with six minutes left in the game. Beauford's eight total points scored in the game proved to be the winning margin and without his powerful, accurate leg, who knows what the outcome would have been. A total team effort led to one of the most memorable victory's in Panther football history.

The Panthers will make their 13th all-time trip to the State Championship game this coming Friday. A full preview of the title game versus the Barnwell War Horses will be posted later this week. As Always…

God Bless and Go Panthers!

Greg K. Deal of the Index Journal titled his piece, '**Back to state: Abbeville to face Barnwell next week in Columbia**'

Here are a few excerpts from his article.

Abbeville's Cortney Jackson was watching and waiting. He was waiting on his opportunity to do something big to help the Panthers reach the Class 2A state championship game for the fourth straight year. With Southside Christian taking a one-point lead with 2:34 to go in the fourth quarter, the Shrine Bowl selection stood all alone on his team's goal line for the ensuing kickoff. He caught the ball, and then the opportunity presented itself.

Cortney Jackson explained,

> "I was waiting for a hole to open and I hit it."

Jackson who took the kickoff back 99 yards on an electrifying touchdown run. Quarterback J.D. Moore ran in the conversion, and the No. 1-ranked Panthers (13-0) held on for a 28-21 victory against Southside Christian (11-3) on Friday night. Abbeville will play Barnwell, a 57-26 winner over Carvers Bay, in the state championship game 8 p.m. next Friday at Benedict College in Columbia.

Coach Nick,

> "When you get to this point, you always tell your players that a big-time player has to make a big-time play in a big-time game. That's him and God — him and the talents the good Lord gave him. When he caught it, I thought one guy was going to get him, and then I saw it part, and I was like, "Oh my goodness, here he goes.' He just took over from there, and it was a heckuva play.

Game week, Benji arrived at the radio station Monday morning and came to a screeching halt at the front entrance to the Golden Palaces. Hanging there on the door, a black wreath, one that resembled the one described by those who had found the notorious wreath hanging on the Panther locker room door. Wayne Stevenson and John Benjamin had been responsible for the original wreath of black flowers, intended to fire up the Panthers for a critical matchup, thinking it had been sent by the opposing team. That incident had occurred during the Coach Hite era. Benji reached for the card attached, waking up suddenly and gasping for air. Poof, no wreath, just another one of those timely dreams.

Benji later shared the experience with Wayne Stevenson. Wayne realized the significance and quickly pointed out that his coconspirator must have been responsible. John Benjamin, rest his soul, had passed earlier in the year. He had reached out and laid the groundwork, presenting the wreath as a calling card. This was meant to fire up the 2018 panthers, if only they could have seen it. Neither Wayne or Benji was going to confess what had happened and how it had been interpreted. Wayne told Benji, we got this. Four in a row, could it really be possible? Stay tuned. One more obstacle to hurtle.

December 6, 2018 AA State Championship Game Preview

The late, great Vince Lombardi once said, 'I firmly believe that any man's finest hours – his greatest fulfillment of all that he holds dear – is that moment when he has worked his heart out in good cause and lies exhausted on the field of battle – victorious.'

Have truer words ever been spoken? You take pride in things that you've worked for. You take care of and appreciate those things a little more when you've given your all to achieve that certain prized possession. The culmination of this 2018 football season is just hours away. The work, the sacrifice, the determination started in January. Work-outs, weight lifting, spring practice, 7 on 7 camps, summer camp, fall practice and thirteen grueling games have led us here. The 2018 AA State Championship Game. There are 60'ish young men, that will wear the Garnet and Gold Friday night, that have worked their hearts out to get to this point. A great opponent awaits with the same hopes and dreams, but only one team can hoist the trophy after forty-eight minutes of battle. Let's look at these two worthy adversaries.

The Barnwell War Horses (13-0) are making their first State Championship game appearance in 21 years. They've been close in years past but couldn't quite find the right formula to make it out of the Lower State Championship game. On eight different occasions since 1960, the War Horses season ended in the Lower State Championship game. On seven different occasions, they made the State Championship game. They are 2-5 in State Title games. The wins were back to back in 1987 and 1988. Both wins came against Pageland-Central. To say this team is hungry to snap a 30-year title drought would be an understatement. So hungry, they scrapped their traditional wish-bone offense last season for a wide-open spread attack.

Barnwell head coach Dwayne Garrick said in the State Championship press conference,

> "Well, we played in the Lower State championship the last two years, and the defense was just so tough in the last two football games that we just figured we had to do a little something over the offseason to get us over the hump. That's kind of been the phrase we've used all year is 'over the hump. We were heavy on 7 on 7s this summer, we've just made that switch and made that transition, and a lot of it has to do with Craig. I mean, Craig throws the ball very well, gets it out of his hands quick. So, really thought that was something we'd have to do to get to this point."

The Craig he mentions is junior quarterback #11 Craig Pender. Pender has had a very nice season passing the ball. He's thrown for nearly 2,300 yards with 35 touchdowns against just seven interceptions. His 70% completion rate is as impressive as the rest of his stats. He also has 43 carries for 216 yards rushing. Of course, he needs help, and he has plenty of it. Dallyon Creech, #5, a 5'11" 170lbs junior is the War Horses leading receiver (33-533) and leads the them on the ground as well (95-680). In fact, Barnwell has produced the #1 offense in AA football this season, scoring 571 points. They average 43.9 points per game while surrendering 12.2 points per game. The 12.2ppg is good enough for the 5th best defense in AA. The offensive line is huge. Bookended by tackles #67 Briggs Kearse (6'4" 315) and #75 Isiah Williams (6'4" 300). The wide receivers are tall and fast, and there's a hundred of them.

Abbeville head coach Jamie Nickles said,

> "Their size and speed are impressive. They look like Clemson when they step off the bus."

Coach Nickles is no stranger to games at Benedict College. Friday night when the whistle blows, he will have coached in his 7th game at Benedict. He has been a part of ten State Championship games as a coach and one as a player as well. The spotlight this season hasn't necessarily been on any one specific player. Instead, the whole senior class, who will strap on the A one last time, has been the focal point. The numbers they have put up are astronomical. 53-3-1 is their record since stepping foot on campus. The three-year starters are 41-1-1. They've claimed four straight Region Championships, four straight Upper State Championships, and have won three consecutive State Championships. The most in school history for any Senior class. Win, lose or draw this Class of 2019 will be remembered for generations.

This team has dominated opponents since day one. The 57-0 shut out a Lincoln Co. was an eye opener and set the tone for much of the season. The Panthers (13-0) rarely played starters in the 2nd half of any game this year until deep in the playoffs. The A-Bone offense has produced points (42.8 ppg) and yards (4,759) by the boat loads. They've been quick strike, with 78 plays of 20 or more yards, and they've been methodical sustaining drives of 10 or more plays on numerous occasions. They've scored by land, (58 rushing touchdowns) and by air (12 TDs). The leading rusher is junior quarterback JD Moore (157-1291-20). Moore is the point guard that distributes the ball and maintains a cool, level headed approach to games. Moore is also the fourth QB to lead the Panthers to a State Championship game in as many years.

Cortney Jackson (111-916-16) leads all running backs in yardage and touchdowns, but also leads the team in all-purpose yards with 1,297 rushing, receiving and kick returns. Ja'Bryan Sanders (71-624-11) has also eclipsed the thousand-yard mark in all-purpose yards with 1,196 total yards. Dominick Washington (96-780-3) has been the steady hand at fullback, used as a battering ram run blocker and short yardage specialist. None of those rushing and passing yards would be possible without the consistent, road grading blocking of the Abbeville O-line. Trai Jones, DaDa Bowie, Conner Nickles, Jake Hill, DeMichael Johnson, along with Tillman Allen at tight end have played very well this year. They have graded out at 90% for the season. Quad Woods (10-135-4) stretches the field at wide receiver and is an outstanding down field blocker. Put all those key ingredients together and you've got a record setting, speedy, powerful offense that's looking to make history.

Defense wins championships and the Panther defense has been championship caliber since Week Zero. Recording four shut-outs and four other games where only one score was recorded, points are at a premium for opposing offenses. Leading tackler, Tyreke Campbell (91 TK – 5 TFL – 1 SK) has set the tone all season with smart, physical play at his linebacker position. Campbell will be the first to tell you that the defensive line helps give him space to roam and find the football. Nate Temple, Carson Smith, Ar'Darius Burton, and Jihad Washington have willed their way into the opposing backfields all season. Temple, a University of Pittsburg commit, leads the team with 12.5 sacks and 11 more tackles for loss. Smith leads the team with 16 tackles for loss.

All in all, the defensive line starting four have collected 261 tackles, and 36 tackles for loss. Jahlyn Shuler has roamed the entire field all year long. He may cover a wide receiver one play, he may be in the backfield stuffing the run the next. Shuler has 84 tackles, 10 for loss and a sack on the season. Malik Leach, David Cobb, Quadarius Guillebeaux, Joc Norman and Gabe Calhoun have gelled into a force in the defensive backfield. Along with Luke Evans, and Cruz Temple the Panthers have swiped 16 interceptions and recovered 18 fumbles on the season. A +28 turnover margin has propelled this defense into rarified air. They have also only allowed their opponents to convert 26 of 153 third downs over 13 games.

Maybe the biggest weapon on the team is the right leg of kicker Dylan Beauford. He's been consistently accurate on PAT's putting 56 of 63 through the uprights, and he's connected on 7 of 9 field goals. His long of 47 yards in last week's Upper State Championship game was a thing of beauty. The points are important, but his kickoffs are equally as important. Most every kickoff sails into the endzone and pins the opponent 80 yards away from their endzone. An 80-yard drive against the aforementioned defense, has been a huge key to the success of this team.

The Panthers went wire to wire ranked #1 in AA this season. They've won 21 games in a row, including three consecutive State Titles. Unfortunately. that means nothing Friday night. The wins, the rankings, the blow-outs. None of that matters. I guarantee that Barnwell does not care about the accolades and awards this team has gathered over the last four years. This group of Panthers will have to play their best game yet. They get one more shot to play with their brothers. Some of these guys have played together for 10 years and this is the last time they'll get to take the field as a team, as a band of brothers. They will get one last chance to prove to the world who we know they are. Champions.

See ya at Benedict. As always…God Bless and Go Panthers!!!

T. Allen Winn,

> "I've tossed in a heaping helping of good ole fashion tongue and cheek fictional humor in this two-year tribute to our Panthers as Benji laid it on the line with his insight, previews and outcomes of the past two seasons. Now for a serious tone though. I'm an AHS Class of '71 graduate and have been a loyal fan and follower of Panther football. But one could not ignore the unfolding events a week prior to the state championship game. In a week for preparation and celebration leading to the Barnwell-Abbeville showdown at Benedict College, the headlines were filled with negative tones after an unfortunate occurrence at the hands of three Abbeville football players. I do not mention this to take away from what this team has accomplished but in fairness, it can't just be swept under the rug and hidden. It is news and will be part of history for those wishing to look back on it, whether you want to or not.

Living at the beach, I got my first whiff of what had happened many days after it happened, seeing a post on Face Book referencing an article in Greenwood's Index Journal. The local paper had always favored the Panthers positively, so you can imagine how this one struck me as odd. It had been written by Adam Benson. I do not know Benson, but the article was titled, *Panthers on championship hunt: Deer carcass dump doesn't sideline players.* Staff writer Greg Deal contributed to this report. Perplexed by the title, I read the article online. I must admit, it was quiet disturbing, especially the timing of it, leading into the state championship, a game we planned to attend. This would be our second state championship trip to Columbia from Myrtle Beach in the past three years. We had witnessed them win their second in a row.

I'll not go into the content of the article because anyone from Abbeville and especially those who are loyal fans and supporters, are aware of it and have opinions one way or the other. To understand the ramifications of the incident I contacted Benji via a text and his return text simply stated, 'too much to cover in a text, I'll call you." And he did, while we were in route gameday to Columbia. He caught me up to speed, tossing in his opinion on the incident. It saddened me to see the integrity of the football program, the coaches, the players, the school and the town negatively portrayed by one inappropriate and reckless event. I can only imagine the reaction of the parents of those involved. Kids will be kids was repeated often. Not one to cast stones, kids can often make bad decisions. With that, you must face the consequences of your actions.

I have no idea what the outcome will be for what happened or how the coaches, school and town will move past it. My only concern is that appropriate actions are taken to address what happened, something that promotes the integrity of the team, the school and the town. Faith, family and football have been a mantra professed by Abbeville Panther football teams for decades. I only hope that the foundation that the program was built on will be rectified in a manner that supports these beliefs. Poor judgement comes with consequences and lessons learned. I leave this in the hands of the parents, the coaches, the school and Abbeville to decide what is appropriate to ensure that lessons have indeed been learned and measures have been taken to restore any blemishes incurred. Hopefully those involved will be mentored by those seeking to mold character and instill the values expected by those wearing the garnet and gold. And as Benji always says, *God Bless the Panthers."*

FOUR-Ever to Thee

What a night it was. When the final whistle echoed through Charlie W. Johnson Stadium the Abbeville Panthers (14-0) accomplished a feat that few teams have ever accomplished. Four consecutive State Championships. The Panthers dominated the game from the opening kickoff and the Class of 2019 cemented themselves as the winningest class in AHS history.

To recap the game, it was never in doubt. Barnwell (13-1) received the opening kickoff and immediately met a fast and ferocious defense. The Abbeville defensive line refused to be blocked. They pressured, hurried and harassed Barnwell QB Craig Pender all night. The Panther linebackers flew to the football and defensive backs blanketed the Barnwell receivers. JD Moore capped a 6 play 64-yard drive on the Panthers opening possession with a 22-yard touchdown run. Moore's 21st TD run of the season. Barnwell found the endzone on a 71-yard punt return to tie the game, and that was the last time the War Horses would see the endzone for the next 40+ minutes of game time.

Cortney Jackson raced to his first of two touchdowns on the night with a 37-yard run, stiff arming and spinning his way to a Panther lead late in the first quarter. After yet another Barnwell three and out, Jackson sprinted 16 yards to the endzone to put the Panthers up 21-7 early in the 2nd quarter. Barnwell mounted a drive as the first half was nearing conclusion. Then, Panther senior defensive back David Cobb stepped in front of a Pender pass and took it to the house 94 yards. The Panthers led 28-7 at that point and the game was basically a formality. Abbeville received the 2nd half kickoff and it took them less than three minutes, and six plays for JD Moore to find Ja'Bryan Sanders running wide open down the middle of the field. The 35-yard touchdown toss was Sanders' 5th TD reception of the season.

More defensive dominance lead to a punishing 11 play 64-yard drive that took nearly 5 minutes of game clock away. Dominick "The Bus" Washington bulled in from a yard out to extend the Panther lead to 41-7. With a minute left in the 3rd quarter, JD Moore found Ja'Bryan Sanders wide open yet again, and watched as the speedster out ran everyone for a 68-yard touchdown run. That touchdown ended the Panthers scoring on the night. It also sent a large majority of Barnwell fans to the exits. Barnwell entered the game with the #1 scoring offense in AA. They finished with 254 total yards (68 of which came on the final drive), three turnovers and was shut out by the Panther's first team. The starters were pulled, and the celebrations began. A late Barnwell touchdown closed out the scoring and the Panthers won their fourth consecutive State Championship, the 10th in school history by a final score of 48-14.

The Seniors on this team deserve to be celebrated as the greatest Senior class to ever walk the halls. Here are some of the numbers from their career.

Overall record since stepping foot on campus: 54-3-1

Record since sophomore year (most didn't play as freshman): 42-1-1

3 consecutive Region Championships

4 consecutive Upper State Championships

4 consecutive State Championships

The Class of 19' lost to one AA team. (Strom Thurmond 20-7 in 2015)

They never lost a home game 32-0

The never lost a playoff game 20-0

The average score in all four State Championship games: 39 vs. 17

This season the Panthers averaged 43 points per game on offense while giving up just 9 points per game on Defense.

The Panther offense averaged 328.4 rushing yards per game, finishing the season with 4,598 rushing yards and 62 rushing touchdowns.

The Panther offense only turned the ball over 9 times all season. 3 interceptions, 6 fumbles. The Panther Defense intercepted their opponents 18 times and recovered 21 fumbles. That is a +30-turnover margin on the season.

The Panthers finished with 85 plays of 20 or more yards on the season.

The Panther Defense only allowed 16 touchdowns all season. 8 rushing, and 8 passing.

Opposing offenses finished 31/165 in third down conversions on the year. An 18.8% success rate.

Abbeville is now tied for 2nd in All-Time State Championships, in South Carolina, won on the field with 10. Only Byrnes (11) and Lake View (10) have double digit championship wins.

Head Coach Jamie Nickles is now tied for 2nd in ALL-TIME State Championship wins (6) as a head coach in South Carolina. Only legends Willie Varner, and John McKissick have more, and they are tied with (8)

Congrats to the 2018 Abbeville Panthers. You rewrote history and did it in dominate fashion. It's been a pleasure covering you all for this season and I can't wait until next year. Get ready A-Town fans only 249 days til kickoff!

As Always…God Bless and Go Panthers!

T. Allen Winn,

> "Judy and I proudly sat in the stands watching the Abbeville Panthers carve their piece of A-Town history, no streaming from the beach for this one. Memories are for the making and we thoroughly enjoyed making ours along with the bleachers filled with loyal fan faithful. Many proud parents smiled and cheered as their sons made their mark on the gridiron or their daughters yelled well practiced cheers from the sidelines. Grandparents, uncles, aunts and town folk stood united as the young men from AHS finished with an unblemished 2018 record and their fourth state title. Faith, Family, Football, and Forever to Thee."

2018 Post Season Accolades, Awards and New Beginnings

How can you top winning a fourth consecutive state championship? Really. Four state championships make an incredible statement alone. Dynasties are built by teams, but teams require team play and individual talents. When combined this becomes the perfect combination. Abbeville secured a place in the history books doing something almost beyond the imagination. The seniors had indeed accomplished what no other band of seniors had ever come close to doing. The following is a tribute to those achievements by this bunch of seniors and the supporting cast ensuring that the panthers were and would be a team to be reckoned with for many seasons ahead.

May 20th, 2019, I happened to be in Abbeville sitting in with Benji on his morning radio program. Off the air we reminisced about Abbeville's accomplishments and the outstanding run they had experienced. Benji was preparing to emcee the Athletic Banquet at Lander to commemorate those who had made the impossible possible. Benji told me that he had watched some practices, his gut telling him that a fifth consecutive championship is possible with the talent oozing Panther pride. The defense could be a force to reckon with and the speed in the backfield looked extremely promising. Buckle up as we share the amazing talent of the young men who etched their names in the record books.

Juniors receiving Post Season Awards

Jhalyn Shuler: Outside linebacker – All Region/Sports Report All State

Carson Smith: Defensive Line – All Region/All Lakelands

Ar'Darius Burton: Defensive Line – All Region

Dylan Beauford: Specialist – All Region/All Lakelands/Sports Report All State

JD Moore: Quarterback – All Region/Sports Report All State

Trai Jones: Offensive Line – All Region/Sports Report All State

Connor Nickles: Offensive Line – Sports Report All State

DeMichael Johnson: Offensive Line – All Lakelands

Seniors receiving Post Season Awards

Gade Calhoun: Defensive Back – All Lakelands

David Cobb: Defensive Back – Sports Region All State

Malik Leach: Defensive Back – All Region

JaBryan Sanders: Running Back – All Region * JaBryan will be playing football at Coffeyville next season.

Lion's Club Players of the Month

September: Senior Tyreke Campbell * He will be playing football at Newberry next season

October: Senior Tillman Allen * Tillman will be playing football at Erskine next season

November/December: Senior Dominick Washington

Special Awards

Team Above Self Award: Jake Hill started for three years in the Panther's offensive line. He was chosen All Region/All Lakelands/Sports Report All State. Jake will be playing football at Coastal Carolina next season.

Defensive Player of the Year: Nate Temple started for three years in the Panther's defensive line. He was also chosen Region Defensive Player of the Year/All Lakelands/Sports Report AA defensive player of the year/AA lineman of the year and was chosen to play in the 2018 Shrine Bowl. Nate will be playing football at Pittsburg next year.

Offensive Player of the Year: Courtney Jackson for three years in the Panther backfield. He was chosen Region Player of the Year/All Lakelands/Sports Report AA Player of the year/AA back of the year and was chosen to play in the 2018 Shrine Bowl. Courtney will be playing football for Coffeyville next year.

Now let's talk the junior varsity, the farm club for Abbeville Panthers. This group of young men with a record of 7-0 were Region Champions. They completed their third consecutive undefeated season. The coaching staff is responsible for grooming the next generation of A-Town players ready to step in without missing a beat. They faced their toughest challenge against Southside Christian in a real nail biter. The outcome was eventually decided by a two-point conversion in overtime. The coaches and staff live by the mantra: *Although we strive to win games, our biggest challenge is winning the game of life.* They'd like to thank everyone for trusting them to help train and mentor these young men.

Junior Varsity Player of the Year: Thomas Beauford

Junior Defensive Player of the Year: Malachi Wilson

Perspective from the Booth 2019

Benji Greeson and Wayne Stevenson, the voices of 'Atown' on the radio, are gearing up for the 2019 season, calling them like they see them. These are their thoughts going into the 2019 Panther's football season.

Benji Greeson,

"So, what's a team to do when they are coming off an unprecedented fourth consecutive state championship? What are the expectations? Surely a small rural school, with a smaller player pool to choose from, with less funding than nearly everyone around them and facilities that have been crumbling for a quarter century couldn't possibly keep up this firestorm of dominance, right?

WRONG.

The names may have changed some, but the 'A' will be well represented again this season. Yes, gone are the Jake Hill's (Coastal Carolina) and the Nate Temple's (Univ of Pittsburgh) and the Cortney Jackson's (Coffeyville), but don't discredit this team simply because you don't know their names…yet. The sneak peaks and glances that the Garnet and Gold Spring game have given us, and some of the spring and summer conditioning practices that us die-hards stand around and watch tell us one thing tell us that these boys are going to be good, really good, again.

Returning at the quarterback position is JD Moore, a senior with serious speed and a year of experience under his belt. He has a big, physical offensive line in front of him, led by Conner Nickels and Trai Jones, who just recently committed to play college football for the University of South Carolina. Navi Marshall and Tyrell Hadden will add more speed in the backfield as will a host of other potential ball carriers. The defense is what has had everyone buzzing here in the pre-season. Carson Smith, Ar'Darius "Bone" Burton, Gus Hill and Trai Jones are very large, very fast and very physical young men. They, with the help of others could produce the most dominate defensive line in the state of South Carolina this season. The sky is the limit for this group of Panthers.

Can they protect a 33-game home winning streak? Hartsville and Southside Christian, two very good teams, will be welcomed into Hite Stadium this season. Can this group extend their 20-game playoff win streak? Can this team, this program, become the first team ever in the history of South Carolina High School Football to win five consecutive State Championships? Only time will tell, but I do like their chances. If were a betting man, I'd feel secure putting the farm up, backing the boys from the 'A'."

This is Benji's first 2019 entry in Atownpanthers.com titled The Catalyst:

Catalyst (cat-a-lyst) *noun:* A person or thing that precipitates an event.

When you think of a football team, what is the person or thing that precipitates an event? Who is the group, or unit that makes everything happen? Where does the success or failure of each offensive play come from? The answer is simple, and most football guys will tell you. Offensive success always starts up front, in the trenches with the big boys, *The Hawg Mollies*, the *Big Uglies.* Abbeville will be putting a big, tough, gritty, experienced group of Hawgs on the offensive line this year. The Panthers lost two college caliber O-Lineman to graduation. Jake Hill is suiting up for Coastal Carolina this season, and Tillman Allen is red shirting at Erskine. The rest of the Panther O-Line returns much to the dismay of opposing defenses. Speaking with Abbeville offensive line coach, (and former Abbeville Hawg Mollie) Coach Wayne Botts, he said *"Yeah we're pretty much set on the line this season. Got some good size, there ain't a lot of Joneses out there. Glad he's on our team. We'll roll with pretty much the same group as last year, Jake's spot, we'll move Davis (Sutherland) in there and that's pretty much it. We have a few guys who can play different positions. We do some cross training for them, but the starting five is pretty much set."*

He the "Jones" that he mentioned is Trai Jones. Most of you read about the 6'4" 275lb senior earlier this summer when he wowed college coaches at scouting combines. Jones picked up a scholarship offer, and subsequently committed to the University of South Carolina. His combination of power, speed and God given size make him a unique high school lineman. While Jones is a physical specimen, he's not out there by himself. Connor Nickles has cemented himself as a leader on the team and the captain of the Hawg Mollies. A three-year starter at center, and an absolute bull in the weight room, Nickles has the brains and brawn to lead this year's group of Panthers. DaDa Bowie returns for his senior season at left guard. Bowie brings a physicality to the position that you love to see out of your guards. He'll be 'climbing to the next level' often (meaning, he must block linebackers) so his quick first step, and contact seeking nature is going to suit him well this season. Davis Sutherland is the new kid on the block. He got some good playing time last season in games that got out of hand, and instantly proved he had what it takes to stand his ground in the trenches. His size, and tenacity will wear down opponents and open running lanes for Panther running backs. DeMichael Johnson returns at right tackle this season. Johnson graded out near 90% last season, which is exceptional for any lineman. Another year in the weight room and a solid couple years experience has Johnson primed to have his best season yet. He's thick, sturdy and can move and bend very well. He also can turn on the mean streak like a light switch. Jim Porter will be in the rotation this season, he's training at guard and center and will provide quality depth. Jake Adams, Dawson Hughes and Addison Nickles will also get to put their hand in the dirt this season.

From the snap of the ball to protecting the quarterback, to opening up rushing lanes, everything begins up front. The Panthers have a great group of Hawg Mollies this year and it's going to be fun watching them eat on Friday nights. Get ready Panther fans! You'll get your first peak of the champs on August 9th at the WCTEL Kickoff Classic as they will take on BHP. Until then…

God Bless and Go Panthers!

And now a few words from the radio voice of the Panthers,

Wayne Stevenson,

"I watch with much anticipation as I look down on the 2019 Abbeville Panthers. My view is from the broadcast booth high above Hite stadium. The Panthers are preparing to take the field. Tonight, they begin the defense of their four consecutive state championships.

The traditionally strong Lincoln County Red Devils have taken the field. The Panthers are on the near sideline getting their last-minute instructions from Coach Jamie Nickles and his staff.

As my mind wonders back, it is hard for me to believe that I am beginning my 28th season in this historic press box. I have been blessed to be a small part of a great football program. When I began this journey in the fall of 1992, I was a young single man. Now, I am married to the greatest woman in the world and playing the last part of the back nine. As my thoughts jump back to the field below, I am thinking. Get ready Benedict College. The Panthers are coming for number five."

As for me, ole T. Allen Winn, I hug the sidelines, from the comfy couch in our home at Myrtle Beach. I anticipate another thrill ride streaming the games on my PC, listening in as Wayne and Benji paint the gridiron canvas for the audience unable to be part of the Hite Stadium frenzy. I have missed only a couple of games over the past three seasons and have witnessed the championship wins in 2016 and 2018 from the bleachers at Benedict College. As Wayne and Benji, I am proud of our hometown Panthers, those wearing the 'A' uniforms on the field and their coaches who not only post winning season after winning season, but teach these young men the value of life, the importance of God and family and forever small town football with all goals achievable. Is number five in a row in the cards? Ask the players, ask the coaches, ask the town and I think you know the answer. I think I speak for Benji, as well as me, we are proud to be part of this magnificent journey and the preservers of history of a town we call home. As Benji always ends his post, **'God Bless and Go Panthers!'**

Here are some excerpts from two articles posted in Greenwood's Index Journal by sportswriter Skylar Rolstad, the first on May 21, 2019 titled 'Abbeville Readying New Running Backs, Staying Steady Defensively.'

Contact sportswriter Skylar Rolstad at 223-1813 or follow him on Twitter @SkyRolSports.

In the article it refers to 6-foot-2 offensive lineman Trai Jones potentially challenging the defensive challengers to get past him. Coach Nick has named him 'Mons' short for 'Monster.' Rolstad quotes Monster as saying, "It's fun being out here with my brothers. It's hot, but that's just part of ball. It's my last year here, so it's kind of sad." Rolstad states that the senior has already received offers from numerous colleges, including Georgia State, The Citadel, Furman, Army and Appalachian State. Monster is considered to be key to the Panther's run-centered offense this season.

The article states that running backs Cruz Temple and Quadarious Guillebeaux will be the go too running backs led by J.D. Moore in the quarterback spot. Rolstad quotes Coach Nick as saying, "You can't replace those guys from last year, I'm real pleased with the young guys we have there. You can't replace them; you just move on to the next group and I think our coaches take a lot of pride in being good coaches in those positions." The Panthers have won four straight championships, each led by a different quarterback.

The article praises the kicking of senior Dylan Beauford, an intricate part of the team. Coach Nick states how Dylan is one of the top kickers in the state, tried and proven last year, a viable weapon on the team. The defense receives accolades for its rising senior class mentioning Jhalyn Shuler, Carson Smith and how Coach Nick may give Jones an opportunity to play both offense and defense.

Skylar Rolstad posted the second article May 19 titled 'Abbeville Spring Game Shows off New Players, Same System.' In his article Rolstad posted that the Panthers got a taste of Texas during the spring game due to temperatures in the 90s. Coach Nick had to wait out the thermometer before starting practice because as he paints it, the South Carolina High School League requires a wet-bulb thermometer reading of less than 92.1 degrees before teams can practice. Rolstad quotes Coach Nick as saying, "You call this the spring game, but it felt more like the Sun Bowl to me." Rolstad stated in his article that despite the heat, the Panthers' defense showed plenty of intensity and size up front. On offense, new running backs stepped in the hole left by last year's quartet of speedy seniors.

The article goes onto to state how Coach Nick remains impressed by J.D. Moore at quarterback. Thomas Beauford will be the back up at the helm. Shuler is another player that can be depended on to play his linebacker position or maybe even on offense stated Coach Nick. In the article it was stated that Shuler received his sixth college offer, this one from Connecticut. Previous offers have come from Coastal Carolina, East Carolina, Wofford, Campbell and Southern Mississippi. For now, the senior looks forward to finishing it out with a group of teammates he's been with most of his life. Rolstad quotes Shuler as saying, "It works really well because we have chemistry. We've been playing with each other, the exact same people, since rec league and we got that bond. We know that the man in front of us or beside us or in front of us is going to do their job, so we have confidence."

God Bless and Go Panthers.

About Benji Greeson

Benji Greeson lives with his wife Tara and two daughters, Maci and Campbell in the hometown of the Abbeville Panthers. Benji is a 1998 graduate of Abbeville High School where he too played football. Benji is the radio station manager of WZLA 92.9fm and the host of the Southern Fried Morning Show, along with his sister and cohost, Lacey Yates. It airs weekdays 6 to 10 AM. Benji joins the voice of the Panthers, Wayne Stevenson, in the radio booth for all Panther games. Listeners can stream the games worldwide by clicking on the radio stations link. Benji is the writer/editor for the atownpanthers.com. He's a diehard Clemson Tiger football fan.

This is Benji's second coauthored book with T. Allen Winn about the hometown favorites; the first, 'All About the A, Faith, Family, Football and Forever to Thee.'

About T. Allen Winn

Ole T. Allen, like his coauthor Benji, graduated from Abbeville High School. T. Allen graduated in the spring of 1971 just before the Panthers won their first championship.

T Allen Winn began writing in 2003 while being cooped up in hotels during business travel. Completing a 650 page so called novel he became hooked. The homegrown Abbeville, S.C. boy embraced the experience completing one novel and then leaping into the next one, fun and therapy at the time. That changed in 2011 when a chance encounter brought stranger and new neighbor Bob O'Brien to his Pawley's Island doorsteps. Bob didn't realize the neighborhood home had been sold and apologized when Tom greeted him instead of the man he had expected to see. Book in hand, Bob had just published his first novel, The Toppled Pawn and explained the previous neighbor had shown interest in writing. Tom remarked he dabbled in writing to which Bob asked, do you have a manuscript? Tom replied ten. Bob had just started Prose Press, a publishing company and suggested publishing one. You can't make this stuff up.

T. Allen Winn's first novel, Road Rage joined the ranks of the published a few months later, and he owes a special thanks to Bob O'Brien for making this possible. His first seven books were published by Prose Press. In 2016, T. Allen Winn established Buttermilk Books, his publishing company. Twelve books have now been published under Buttermilk Books. He and his wife reside in Myrtle Beach, South Carolina.

Ole T doesn't write under any specific genre. He writes what strikes his fancy. If you don't see something that fits your reading wheelhouse, just tell him what you like, and he might just write it for you.

Books are available on Amazon or online where books are sold. Select books are available in Abbeville. South Carolina at Southern Succotash on Washington Street, and in Tabor City, North Carolina at Grapefull Sisters Vineyard. Or *Message* T. Allen Winn on Facebook to arrange delivery of signed copies.

Fiction from T. Allen Winn

The Detective Trudy Wagner series

Road Rage

North of the Border

Tithes and Offerings

Foot Series

Foot, Tree Knockers and Rock Throwers (1st in the trilogy)

More Fiction from T. Allen Winn

The Perfect Spook House

Dark Thirty

Lou Who

Raw Ride, a Wild West Zombie Apocalyptic Shoot'um Up

The Man Who Met the Mouse

Mister Twix Mystery, a Cat Scene Investigation

Non-Fiction from T. Allen Winn

Being Bentley, A Dog Like No Other

It's All About the 'A', Faith, Family, Football and Forever to Thee with coauthor, Benji Greeson

It's All About the Angels in the Backfield, Dawn of a Dynasty with coauthor, Benji Greeson

December's Darkest Day, While I Breathe, I Hope

The Hardwood Walker of Port Harrelson Road (based on true events in Bucksport, S.C.)

Cuz, My Brother, Life is Good, God is Good

The Endless Mulligan, Short Shots from the Golf Whomper

Memoirs

The Caregiver's Son, Outside the Window Looking In

Cornbread and Buttermilk, Good Ole Fashion Home Cooked Nostalgic Nonsense

Short Stories

For Your Amusement featured in Beach Author Network's book titled 'Shorts'

Cited Me a Bar featured in friend and author, Danny Kuhn's Headline Book's *Mountain Mysts*, Honorable Mention in Fiction at the 2015 London Book Festival and the book is endorsed by Joyce Dewitt of the sitcom *Three's Company*

Short story about Granny Bowie in friend and author Robert Sharpe's book, *The Heart and Soul of Caring*, about caregivers and their challenges

www.ingramcontent.com/pod-product-compliance
Lightning Source LLC
Chambersburg PA
CBHW080322170426
43193CB00017B/2879